KEYS TO
Thinking
and
Learning

CREATING OPTIONS AND OPPORTUNITIES

Carol Carter ▣ Joyce Bishop ▣ Sarah Lyman Kravits

Prentice Hall

Upper Saddle River, New Jersey 07458

Library of Congress Cataloging-in-Publication Data

Carter, Carol.
    Keys to thinking and learning : creating options and opportunities / Carol
Carter, Joyce Bishop, Sarah Lyman Kravits.
        p.   cm.
    Includes index.
    ISBN 0-13-086910-4
        1. Critical thinking—Studying and teaching (Higher)   2. Study skills.
    3. Learning.   I. Title: Thinking and learning.   II. Bishop, Joyce
    (Joyce L.), 1950–   III. Kravits, Sarah Lyman.   IV. Title.

LB2395.35.C27 2000
378.1'7'0281—dc21   99-048078

Acquisitions Editor: *Sande Johnson*
Managing Editor: *Mary Carnis*
Production: *Holcomb Hathaway, Inc.*
Director of Manufacturing and Production: *Bruce Johnson*
Manufacturing Manager: *Ed O'Dougherty*
Assistant Editor: *Michelle Williams*
Cover Designer: *Maria Guglielmo*
Cover Illustration: *Markku Lahdesmaki*
Marketing Manager: *Jeff McIlroy*
Marketing Assistant: *Barbara Rosenberg*

Printed in the United States of America

10 9 8 7 6 5 4 3 2 1

ISBN 0-13-086910-4

Prentice-Hall International (UK) Limited, *London*
Prentice-Hall of Australia Pty. Limited, *Sydney*
Prentice-Hall Canada Inc., *Toronto*
Prentice-Hall Hispanoamericana, S.A., *Mexico*
Prentice-Hall of India Private Limited, *New Delhi*
Prentice-Hall of Japan, Inc., *Tokyo*
Pearson Education Asia Pte. Ltd., *Singapore*
Editora Prentice-Hall do Brasil, Ltda., *Rio de Janeiro*

Contents

3 THINKING LOGICALLY
Evaluating Fact and Opinion, Assumption, and Argument   53

4 THINKING ABOUT YOUR WORLD
Recognizing Perspectives   79

5 THINKING STRATEGICALLY
Setting Goals and Planning Your Time   105

6 THINKING ABOUT HOW YOU LEARN
Learning Styles   135

7 THINKING IN THE CLASSROOM
Reading, Note Taking, Memory, and Test Taking   163

THINKING ABOUT EXPRESSION
Listening, Communication, and Writing   197

THINKING QUANTITATIVELY
Math, Science, and Computers   227

Foreword

We cannot learn without thinking, nor think without some prior learning. The two processes are inextricable and at the heart of all efforts to be educated. Without effective thinking and learning capacities, we can become slaves, rather than masters, of constant societal change and the related daily problems of our lives.

The importance of *Keys to Thinking and Learning* is that it clarifies for us how to use our minds to solve problems and make decisions. Strategic use of the mind's capacities, in school, at work, and in life, is essential for realizing our potential as human beings.

Though few people seem to have a firm grasp of strategic thinking, it is within the realm of possibility for all. Asking questions is the key to making strategic thinking possible. The central question is: What are the capacities of our minds, and when and how do we use them?

Keys to Thinking and Learning responds to this question by reducing critical thinking to its basic components and clarifying the relationship of these to more complex thinking processes. The defining of these basic mind actions and critical thinking processes is interwoven with examples and practical applications. The application of critical thinking processes to learning and to the solution of college, career, and life problems helps us to build confidence that we do have some control over our destiny. In its essence, the book is about freedom—that freedom which results from the awareness of how to use our minds.

Frank J. Lyman, Jr.

Dr. Frank T. Lyman, Jr.
Consultant in Education and Teacher Education
Former Professional Development School Center
Coordinator for the University of Maryland

Preface

The ability to think critically is one of the most important tools anyone can ever possess. It can make a difference in any situation and can be the key to success in every arena of life. In today's workplace especially, your career success and promotability will most likely depend on your ability to think critically and creatively about the decisions and problems that arise.

As with any tool, the ability to benefit from critical thinking requires a solid knowledge of how to use it. That's where *Keys to Thinking and Learning* comes in. This book is designed to help you understand how your mind works so that you can empower your critical thinking and apply it to whatever situations come your way. Through your experience of *Keys to Thinking and Learning*, you will learn about the seven primary actions of your mind—*recall, similarity, difference, cause and effect, example to idea, idea to example,* and *evaluation*—and the critical thinking processes of which these mind actions are the building blocks. Following are the thinking processes discussed in this book, and the chapters where you will find them introduced:

- Solving Problems (Chapter 2)
- Making Decisions (Chapter 2)
- Planning Strategically (Chapter 5)
- Thinking Logically (Chapter 3)
- Constructing and Evaluating Arguments (Chapter 3)
- Recognizing Perspectives (Chapter 4)

Although the first chapters of *Keys to Thinking and Learning* focus primarily on the workings of these processes of critical thinking, the rest of the chapters—on topics ranging from note taking to career exploration—involve critical thinking just as extensively. Critical thinking is not an end in and of itself. It is a means by which you can increase your understanding of the world, yourself, and your choices, a means by which you can effectively solve problems and make good decisions. Through understanding how critical thinking applies to your own life and goals, you can gain a deeper understanding of each thinking process. Knowledge is useless unless it is actively applied toward desired outcomes.

Asking questions is at the heart of critical thinking. When you can ask questions about any topic—how to read effectively, how to choose a major, what your values are, how to evaluate the media—you are thinking critically.

When the drive to know more through questioning helps you to resist making quick assumptions, you will be able to gather knowledge intelligently and comprehensively. Then you will be ready to take action—because knowledge is useless unless it is actively applied toward your goals. Knowledge and action in combination will enable you to make well-considered, responsible choices that bring you the most positive effects possible.

Keys to Thinking and Learning is designed to help you activate what you learn. The exercise set at the end of each chapter, *Building Thinking Skills*, will give you the opportunity to put your knowledge into action, applying it to your own life and situations. Each set of exercises will include the following categories:

Life Thinking: Applying What You Learn. Here you will apply critical thinking skills to your real life situations and needs.

Team Thinking: Working Together. This exercise, based on one or more chapter topics, will engage you in critical thinking with other members of a group.

Work Thinking: Career Portfolio. Here you will apply critical thinking skills toward a career-related task or goal of yours.

Questioning Your World: Information Literacy Journal. This exercise will expand your information literacy by asking you to respond to an information literacy issue in a journal entry.

Finally, *Keys to Thinking and Learning* shows you how critical thinking can foster continual improvement, growth, and learning in all aspects of work and life. In this increasingly knowledge-based society, citizens need to be informed consumers of complex information, prepared to sift through data and input carefully and then select and use it wisely. Critical thinking makes that possible. Once you master the basic thinking skills presented in this book, you will be ready to be an effective "knowledge worker," meeting and exceeding the demands of employers in the twenty-first century economy and more importantly meeting your enormous potential as a human being. We as your authors are happy to provide you with an important tool—take advantage of it and make the best of your mind and your life.

Supplements for Teachers

Instructor's Manual

This extensive kit contains materials to help you successfully teach student orientation and student success courses. Organized according to the objectives and lessons of each chapter, the kit includes transparency masters, Test Item File questions, pre- and post-class evaluations, lecture guides, and innovative tips to motivate all kinds of students. Free to instructors using the textbook. (0-13-899998-8)

Student Key Advice Video

Contains a selection of motivational tips and advice by entering college students, college students in their third and fourth years, and professionals in varying career areas. These tapes are in manageable segments designed so that they can be shown individually or all at once. Free to adopters of the textbook. (0-13-233206-X)

ABC News/Prentice Hall Video Library

This two-video set contains segments that appeared on such award-winning shows as *World News Tonight*, *Nightline*, *20/20*, and *Primetime Live*. These segments are on topics relevant to student success and have been collected into a video library. Free to adopters of the textbook. (0-13-746306-5)

Faculty Development/School In-Service Programs

Prentice Hall sponsors a variety of faculty workshops on campuses and in specific cities throughout the year. Workshops can be cross-disciplinary or discipline-specific. Many of our books qualify for special in-services with your faculty on topics that impact effective teaching and learning. Ask your local Prentice Hall representative for details.

Teacher Training Video

This library of teaching tips on student success and career development, for first-time instructors as well as those who have taught for years, provides information on how to teach multiple intelligences, critical thinking, and school-to-work transition tips. Free to adopters of the textbook. (0-13-917205-X)

Study Skills Video

This video features professional instruction on study skills and note taking, critical thinking, reading, writing, math and science, and test taking. It encourages students to utilize study skills to enhance their educational experience. Free to adopters of the textbook. (0-13-096095-0)

Student Success Supersite

www.prenhall.com/success In addition to the resources it provides for students, this Prentice Hall site includes special features for faculty, including sample syllabi, conference schedules, and presentation software downloads.

Supplements for Students

Prentice Hall's Student Success Supersite

www.prenhall.com/success This website provides an online connection to cutting-edge student success information and resources. Each main topic area for students has goal-setting guidelines, interactive quizzes, and insightful articles. Electronic journals, opinion polls, and links to related sites are also included. Topic areas featured are:

- **Majors Exploration**—contains information about various majors as well as college choice and study abroad programs
- **Study Skills**—presents ideas for skill areas such as test taking, note taking, reading, writing, and library research.
- **Career Path**—helps students explore career issues such as career choice, interviews and resumes, networking, internships, and part-time jobs
- **Money Matters**—gives tips on college financing as well as personal finances and investing
- **Fitness and Well-being**—goes into detail about personal wellness issues such as stress, drugs and alcohol, exercise, physical and mental health, and relationships
- **Student Union**—provides a chat room, news, information on campus life and student travel, games and trivia, and more

NCS Career Assessment Inventory

This inventory helps students explore personal interest patterns as they relate to the world of work. Students complete the questionnaire and mail the scoring form to the service center for assessment. Personal results are returned within 10 working days, with rating explanations. Available at a discount when packaged with the text. (0-13-264490-8)

Lassi—Learning and Study Skills Strategies Inventory

This self-scoreable inventory helps assess expectations of college in academic, social, and personal realms. Ideal for use in student orientation courses. Administration guide will be included for faculty packaging this inventory with a Prentice Hall adoption. (0-13-010376-4) (Also available on Mac or IBM disk)

Majoring in the Rest of Your Life,

by Carol Carter

Provides a practical strategy to take students from first-semester freshman year to their first job after graduation. This book offers valuable insights and advice on how to organize, think analytically, set and achieve goals, be innovative and persuasive, improve interpersonal and communication skills, and cope with stress. Available at a discount when packaged with the text. (0-13-098351-9)

Seven Habits of Highly Effective People,

Audiocassette, by Stephen R. Covey

Audiotape program teaches listeners how to achieve success in both business and personal relationships. This approach broadens their way of thinking and leads to greater opportunities and effective problem solving. Available at a discount when packaged with the text. (0-13-098377-2)

Themes of the Times,
Prentice Hall New York Times *Supplement*

Recent articles that enhance classroom discussions with real world stories that are of interest to today's students have been collected into this supplement. It maintains the *New York Times* newspaper format and is free when using the textbook. (0-13-022218-6)

Student Planner

Comprised of daily and monthly planners, calendars through the year 2001, an address book, course and class planners, and other organizing materials, the Student Planner is designed to help students organize and manage their time more effectively. Available free when packaged with the textbook. (0-13-649120-0)

Student Reflection Journal

A book that helps students get the most out of the course by encouraging them to keep track of their progress over time. Available free when packaged with the textbook. (0-13-672826-X)

CD-ROM Shrink-wrap Options

Each of these CD-ROMs is available for $5 or less when packaged with a copy of this text.

Student Organizer

Designed exclusively for students by Centaur Academic Media, this ultimate organizational tool includes scheduler, timeline, major/minor planner, address book, personal finance planner, internet site, grade calculator, and tutorial. Available in a cardboard sleeve for $5 net.

Prentice Hall Self-Assessment Library

Easy to use, this library provides 45 assessments, each with instant feedback. Assessments help students learn more about themselves and how they relate to others. The three categories—"What about me," "Working with others," and "Life in organizations"—will provide students with insights they will need to be successful in the business world. Available in a cardboard sleeve for $5 net.

Simon & Schuster Handbook For Writers with Merriam-Webster's Collegiate Dictionary and Thesaurus

A comprehensive multimedia handbook for writers. Compatible with the most popular work processing software, this CD will enable students to seamlessly access grammar tips, punctuation, guidelines for writing reports, and advice on the writing process as well as other dictionary and thesaurus resources. Available in a cardboard sleeve for $4 net.

Problem Solver

Interactive computer simulations in educational psychology. This is a cross-platform CD-ROM containing simulations that help students experience and explore Piaget's developmental stages, misconceptions about the role of prior knowledge in learning, and more. Available in a blister pack for $3 net.

Career Opportunity Locator

This employment opportunity database contains data from several prominent statistical resources that will enable students to make career decisions based on their own preferences for interest areas, geography, income expectations, and educational or training requirements. Available in a cardboard sleeve for $5 net.

Acknowledgments

This book has come about through a heroic group effort. We would like to take this opportunity to acknowledge the people who have made it happen. Many thanks to:

- Dr. Frank T. Lyman, Jr. for the use and adaptation of his Thinktrix critical thinking system, his thoroughgoing review of the material, and his continuing support and insight.
- Instructors at DeVry around the country who emphasize critical thinking in their student success courses and encouraged us to develop this book.
- Jackie Fitzgerald, who emphasized the importance of a book like this for helping students understand how critical thinking and problem solving can improve their lives.
- Doug Clark, math specialist from the University of Missouri-Columbia Learning Center, for his material on math, science, and computers.
- Barbara Soloman for her Learning Styles Inventory.
- Marjorie Den, librarian at Connecticut Public Library in Westport, CT, for her assistance with the revised material on library research.
- Michelle M. Williams and Kelley Forrester for their invaluable assistance.
- Author Cynthia Leshin for the appendix on Internet research.
- Our terrific editor, Sande Johnson.
- Sue Bierman, currently in faculty development for Prentice Hall, for her innumerable contributions and editorial advice.
- Everyone in production who went out of their way to get the job done in a very short time frame, especially Gay Pauley, Mary Carnis, Marianne Frasco, Maria Guglielmo, Adele Kupchik, Marc Bove, Steve Hartner, and Patrick Walsh.
- Our marketing gurus, especially Jeff McIlroy, Kateri Drexler, and Barbara Rosenberg.
- Frank Mortimer for his work on the website and technology.
- The Prentice Hall representatives and the management team led by Jerome Grant, who have shown tremendous support for the success of students of all ages.

- Our families and friends, who have encouraged us and put up with our work schedules.
- We extend a very special thanks to Judy Block, whose research and work on the study skills material, revision of the library material, and editing suggestions on the text as a whole were essential and invaluable.

Finally, for their ideas, opinions, and stories, we would like to thank all of the students and professors with whom we work. Joyce in particular would like to thank the thousands of students who have allowed her, as their professor, the privilege of sharing part of their journey through college. We appreciate that, through reading this book, you give us the opportunity to learn and discover with you—in your classroom, in your home, on the bus, and wherever else learning takes place.

About the Authors

Carol Carter is Vice President and Director of Student Programs and Faculty Development at Prentice Hall. She has written *Majoring in the Rest of Your Life: Career Secrets for College Students* and *Majoring in High School*. She has also co-authored *Graduating Into the Nineties, The Career Tool Kit, Keys to Career Success, Keys to Study Skills, Keys to Effective Learning*, and *Keys to Success*. In 1992 Carol and other business people co-founded a nonprofit organization called LifeSkills, Inc., to help high school students explore their goals, their career options, and the real world through part-time employment and internships. LifeSkills is now part of the Tucson Unified School District and is featured in seventeen high schools in Tucson, Arizona.

Joyce Bishop holds a Ph.D. in psychology and has taught for more than twenty years, receiving a number of honors, including Teacher of the Year. For the past four years she has been voted "favorite teacher" by the student body and Honor Society at Golden West College, Huntington Beach, CA, where she has taught since 1986 and is a tenured professor. She is currently working with a federal grant to establish Learning Communities and Workplace Learning in her district, and has developed workshops and trained faculty in cooperative learning, active learning, multiple intelligences, workplace relevancy, learning styles, authentic assessment, team building, and the development of learning communities. She also co-authored *Keys to Success, Keys to Effective Learning*, and *Keys to Study Skills*.

Sarah Lyman Kravits comes from a family of educators and has long cultivated an interest in educational development. She co-authored *The Career Tool Kit, Keys to Success, Keys to Effective Learning*, and *Keys to Study Skills* and has served as Program Director for LifeSkills, Inc., a nonprofit organization that aims to further the career and personal development of high school students. In that capacity she helped to formulate both curricular and organizational elements of the program, working closely with instructors as well as members of the business community. She has also given faculty workshops in critical thinking, based on the Thinktrix critical thinking system. Sarah holds a B.A. in English and drama from the University of Virginia, where she was a Jefferson Scholar, and an M.F.A. from Catholic University.

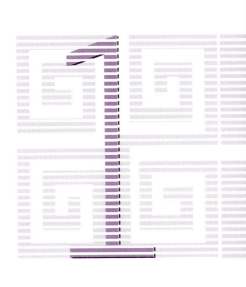

Critical Thinking

Thinking Critically

Interacting with Information

Y ou are a thinker. Your mind has extraordinary power that shows in everything you do, from small chores (comparing prices on gasoline or planning your day) to complex situations (writing a new computer program or sorting out a long-standing family argument). Your mind is able to process, store, and create with the facts and ideas it encounters. Critical thinking means making the best use of these and other capacities of your mind.

Understanding how your mind works is the first step toward critical thinking. When you have that understanding, you can perform the essential critical-thinking task: asking important questions about ideas and information. This chapter will show you the mind's basic actions, reintroducing you to the way your mind works. You will explore what it means to be an open-minded critical thinker, able to ask and understand questions that promote your success in college, career, and life.

In this chapter, you will explore answers to the following questions:

- What is critical thinking?
- Who is a critical thinker?
- How does your mind work?
- What are inductive and deductive thinking?
- What are the types of knowledge?

WHAT IS CRITICAL THINKING?

If you read ten books on critical thinking, you probably will encounter ten different descriptions of what "critical thinking" means. You might see it referred to as "higher order" thinking or "metacognition" (thinking about thinking). You may wonder whether it is the same as any other kind of thinking, or whether it involves criticism. You might react negatively to it, figuring that the word "critical" implies something difficult and negative.

Actually, critical thinking is "critical" mainly in the sense of one particular dictionary definition of *critical:* "indispensable" and "important." It is not a secret, tricky process that you have never encountered or used before. It is not something that only "smart" people can accomplish. You think critically every day, even though you may not realize it.

A Definition of Critical Thinking

The following is one way to define critical thinking, taking its many varied aspects into consideration.

> Critical thinking is thinking that *goes beyond the basic recall of information* but depends on the information recalled. It focuses on the *important, or critical,* aspects of the information. Critical thinking means *asking questions.* Critical thinking means that you *take in information, question it, and then use it* to create new ideas, solve problems, make decisions, construct arguments, make plans, and refine your view of the world.

The focus on critical thinking has increased as the world has become more saturated with information. You may hear the current time referred to as the "information age," in which each of us is bombarded every day with more information than anyone can possibly absorb. Information flows into your consciousness through television, newspapers, magazines, radio, the Internet, and the people with whom you interact. The more that comes your way, the more effort is necessary to sort through what's useful and not useful, what you believe and don't believe, and what is important in regard to what you already know and what is not. The more you improve your critical thinking, the better you will be able to swim in the ever-increasing sea of information—a skill that will help you both at school and on the job.

One way to clarify a concept is to take a look at its opposite. For example, if you were examining a gum condition in a dental hygiene class, you could begin to figure out what it is by ruling out other conditions with which you are familiar—"It's not gingivitis because . . . ." Similarly, you can clarify what critical thinking is by looking at what happens when people *don't* think critically. Not thinking critically means not examining critical or important aspects through questioning. A person who does not think critically tends to accept or reject information or ideas without examining them. Table 1.1 compares how a critical thinker and a non–critical thinker might respond to particular situations.

Think about responses you or others have had to various situations in your life. Consider when you have seen critical thinking take place and

"We do not live to think, but, on the contrary, we think in order that we may succeed in surviving."

JOSÉ ORTEGA Y GASSET

TABLE 1.1   Not thinking critically vs. thinking critically.

YOUR ROLE	SITUATION	NONQUESTIONING (UNCRITICAL) RESPONSE	QUESTIONING (CRITICAL) RESPONSE
Student	Instructor is lecturing on the causes of the Vietnam war.	You assume everything your instructor says is true.	You consider what the instructor says, write questions about issues you want to clarify, discuss them with the instructor or classmates.
Spouse/partner	Your partner thinks he/she does not have enough quality time with you.	You think he/she is wrong and defend yourself.	You ask your partner why he/she thinks this is happening, and together you see how you can improve the situation.
Employee	Your supervisor is angry with you about something that happened.	You avoid your supervisor or deny responsibility for the incident.	You determine what caused your supervisor to place the blame on you; you talk with your supervisor about what happened and why.
Neighbor	People who differ from you move in next door.	You ignore or avoid them; you think their way of living is weird.	You introduce yourself and offer help if they need it; eventually, you respectfully explore your differences.
Consumer	You want to buy a car.	You decide on a brand new car and don't think through how you can pay for it.	You evaluate the effects of buying a new car versus a used car; you decide what kind of payment you can handle each month.

when you haven't, and what resulted from each way of responding. This will help you begin to see what kind of an effect critical thinking can have on the way you live.

The Path of Critical Thinking

Look at Figure 1.1 to see a visual representation of critical thinking. Asking questions—the central part of the process—is the key to what makes you a critical thinker. Without asking questions about the information you take in, you would have no way to evaluate or change the information. Your output would mirror your input—unexamined and unchanged. For example, when you type a letter into a computer and print it, the computer does not think critically about your material. It spits out your letter exactly as you entered it (save, perhaps, a few changes made by the spell checker). The computer does not question you. Your mind, however, is far more discriminating than a computer. You have the power to question, use, and transform the information you encounter in your life.

Taking In Information

Most of the material in this book focuses on the second and third stages of critical thinking—questioning and using information. The first step of the process, however, is just as crucial. Your senses, especially your ability to hear and observe, allow you to take in information.

The information you receive is your raw material, the clay you will examine with questioning and mold into something new. The most crucial part of taking in information is to do so accurately and without judgment, because you want the material you work with to be as close to its natural state as possible. Just as the purest, finest ingredients allow a chef to make a rich cake, or the highest quality parts allow a car manufacturer to create a smooth-running automobile, the clearest, most complete information gives

FIGURE 1.1 Critical thinking path.

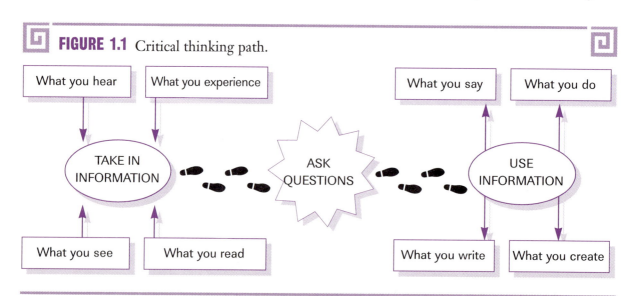

you the best material with which to work as you think. It gives you the most assurance that your final thought output will be as accurate and comprehensive as it can be.

For example, you are drowsy one day in your Biology course and you copy a biological principle inaccurately from the board. During a test later in the semester, you write a response to an essay question on this principle and feel confident about your work. You then are shocked when you get your test back and receive no points for what you thought was a well-constructed, thoughtful essay. You had no idea that your original idea—the "material" with which you worked—was inaccurate.

In another scenario, say that you overhear part of a negative comment your spouse makes on the phone, and it sounds like it is about you. You spend the rest of the day fuming about it and decide not to come home for dinner after class and not to call to check in. By the time you return late in the evening, your spouse is worried sick about you. Only after an argument do you figure out that the comment had nothing to do with you at all. You made decisions based on inaccurate intake of information.

The first step of being a critical thinker is to take in information completely, accurately, and without judgment. Then, when you have collected your raw material, you can begin to sift through it—to discover its important or critical aspects through questioning.

Questioning Information

A critical thinker asks many kinds of questions about a given piece of information, such as: *Where did it come from? What idea or principle explains it? In what ways is it true or false? How do I feel about it, and why? How is this information similar to or different from what I already know? Is it useful or not? What caused it, and what effects does it have?* The center of the process is the questioning of what you have taken in.

Asking questions of information takes effort. Crucial to the questioning process are

- Knowing what questions to ask
- Knowing when to ask
- Wanting to ask

You need all three of these to make the most of your ability to question. It may not matter how much opportunity you have to question the information that comes your way if you don't know what to ask, have no idea when to ask it, and don't have any real desire to ask. What to ask and when to ask are covered in detail throughout this book. Whether to ask—the desire to ask—is up to you. Your desire to ask is often stimulated by the information and your perception of its usefulness.

As an example of the questioning process, consider the following as your "information in": You encounter a number of situations—financial strain, parenting on your own, and being an older student—that seem to be getting in the way of your success at school. Whereas nonquestioning thinkers may assume defeat is on its way, critical thinkers will put their minds into action by examining the situation with questions. Here are some examples of questions you might ask:

> *"What exactly are my obstacles?* Examples of my obstacles are a heavy work schedule, single parenting, being in debt, and returning to school after ten years out." **(recall)**

> *"Are there other cases different from mine?* I do have one friend who is going through problems worse than mine, and she's getting by. I also know another guy who doesn't have too much to deal with that I can tell, and he's struggling just like I am." **(difference)**

> *"Who has problems similar to mine?* Well, if I consider my obstacles specifically, my statement might mean that single parents and returning adult students will all have trouble in school. That's not necessarily true. People who have trouble in school may still become successful." **(similarity)**

> *"What is an example of someone who has had success despite obstacles?* What about Oseola McCarty, the cleaning woman who saved money all her life and raised $150,000 to create a scholarship at the University of Southern Mississippi? She didn't have what anyone would call advantages, such as a high-paying job or a college education." **(idea to example)**

> *"What conclusion can I draw from my questions?* From thinking about my friend and about Oseola McCarty, I conclude that people can overcome their obstacles by working hard, focusing on their abilities, and concentrating on their goals." **(example to idea)**

> *"Why am I worried about this?* Maybe I'm scared of returning to school and adjusting to a new environment. Maybe I'm afraid to challenge myself, which I haven't done in a long time. Whatever the cause, the effect is that I feel bad about myself and don't work to the best of my abilities, and that can hurt me and maybe even my family, who depends on me." **(cause and effect)**

> *"How do I evaluate the effects of my worries?* I think it's harmful. When we say that obstacles equal defeat, we can damage our desire to try to overcome them. When we say that successful people don't have obstacles, we might overlook that some very successful people have to deal with hidden disadvantages such as learning disabilities or abusive families." **(evaluation)**

Remember these types of questions. Most of this chapter will focus on how to use them to **analyze** the information that comes your way. When you explore the seven mind actions later in the chapter, refer to these questions to see how they illustrate the different actions your mind performs.

Using Information

After taking in and examining information, critical thinkers try to transform it into something they can use. They use information to help them solve a problem, make a decision, learn or create something new, or anticipate what will happen in the future. In this stage of the process, you can **synthesize** what you know and have learned and present something completely new, such as an idea, a product, a process, or an approach.

Analyze
To determine the nature of a complex whole by dividing it into its parts or elements and studying them.

Synthesize
To combine diverse parts or elements into a coherent whole.

This part of the critical thinking path is where you benefit from the hard work of asking questions, building new ideas through the creative action of your mind. This is where inventions happen, new processes are born, theories are created, and information interacts with your own thoughts to create something new. It is the most productive of the stages of critical thinking.

 ## WHO IS A CRITICAL THINKER?

Before current times, critical thinking was found primarily in logic and reasoning courses that were not available to all students. Some educators assumed that people are born with a certain level of thinking ability that would basically stay with them for life. Therefore, it seemed normal if some students "got it" and some didn't. Schools often focused on teaching knowledge and processes rather than teaching thinking skills.

Many educators now believe that critical thinking can be taught in much the same way as any other skill—for example, shooting a basketball or using a word-processing program on the computer. Even though factors such as genetics, education, and experience may contribute to the development of a unique thinking ability in each person, that level is not set in stone. Anyone can develop the ability to think critically, no matter the "starting point." The educational world is helping students learn to think in a way that takes them beyond regurgitating on a test what they have heard in class or read in a book.

Characteristics of Critical Thinkers

The first answer to the question "Who is a critical thinker?" is, "Anyone who wants to make the effort to think critically." Another answer lies in what the book *Dimensions of Learning* calls "habits of mind." According to authors Robert J. Marzano and Debra J. Pickering, a person who thinks critically

- Tries to be accurate.
- Attempts to be clear.
- Keeps an open mind.
- Restrains impulsivity.
- Takes a thoughtful position.
- Responds to the feelings and knowledge of others.[1]

The word "habit" is important here. A habit is something that you do regularly and often without being conscious of it. You develop it by doing it again and again over time. If you can practice these habits often enough for them to become second nature to you, you will think critically with less effort and consciousness.

Other characteristics of a critical thinker are shown in Table 1.2. You will learn what actions underlie these qualities as you read through the rest of this chapter and Chapters 2, 3, and 4.

TABLE 1.2 Characteristics of a critical thinker.	A CRITICAL THINKER IS	A CRITICAL THINKER
	• Observant	• Works to avoid assumptions
	• Curious	• Resists manipulation
	• Empathic	• Takes time
	• Attentive	• Looks for connections
	• Honest with self	• Judges based on evidence
	• Willing to reason and reflect	• Asks questions

The Value of Being a Critical Thinker

It's easier to put effort into doing something when you understand how the effort will benefit you. Critical thinking has many important advantages. Following are some of the positive effects, or benefits, of critical thinking.

You will increase your ability to perform thinking processes. Critical thinking is a learned skill. As with any other skill, the more you use it, the better you become at it. The more you ask important questions, the better you think. The better you think, the more effective you will be when completing coursework, managing your personal life, and performing on the job.

You can produce knowledge rather than just reproduce it. The interaction of newly learned information with what you already know creates new knowledge. Its usefulness can be judged by your ability to apply it. For instance, it won't mean much for an education student to quote the stages of child development on an exam unless he or she can evaluate children's needs on the job.

You can be a valuable employee. You won't be a failure in the workplace if you follow directions. You will be even more valuable, however, if you ask strategic questions—ranging from "Is there a better way to deliver phone messages?" to "How can we increase business?"—about how to make improvements. Employees who think critically will be more likely to make progress in their careers because they tend to help move the company ahead rather than just maintain the **status quo.**

TERMS

Status quo
Existing state of
affairs.

You can increase your problem-solving creativity. Critical thinking means devising new and different questions to ask, possibilities to explore, and solutions to try. Creativity is essential in producing new ways to solve problems. Being creative broadens your perspective as you cope.

So how do you start to develop your critical thinking abilities? Rather than jump right into solving your biggest life problems and planning your activities over the next ten years, begin with the most basic building blocks of thinking. Your mind performs some basic moves, or actions, to understand relationships among ideas and concepts. Sometimes it uses one action by itself, but most often it uses two or more in combination. These actions are the blocks you use to build critical thinking processes.

HOW DOES YOUR MIND WORK?

The workings of human thought can be mysterious. Scientists still are not exactly sure how the mass of cells in your brain produces everything the mind can create. Nevertheless, the different moves, or actions, the mind makes during thought processes are more apparent.

Mind Actions

Educators Frank Lyman, Arlene Mindus, and Charlene Lopez[2] studied the mind's actions with numerous other instructors. Based on their observations of how students think, they identified seven primary actions—seven building blocks of thought—and named them. These actions are not new to you even if you have never before thought much about how you think (most people have not). They represent the ways in which you think all the time. Their names refer to concepts already familiar to you.

Through exploring these actions, you can go beyond just thinking and learn *how* you think. This will help you take charge of your own thinking. The more you know about how your mind works, the more control you will have over what you do with it, just as having a solid understanding of how a machine works or a formula is applied will help you use it more effectively. You can begin your development of skill in critical thinking by exploring these mind actions so that you can consciously use them as critical thinking "tools."

Following are detailed explanations of each of the mind actions, including examples. For each action you will see some additional terms that refer to that mind action. This is to help you associate the mind actions with ideas that are familiar to you already or with other thinking terms you may encounter at school and in life. There are many different ways of naming what your mind does when it performs these actions. The names here are chosen for their straightforwardness and clarity.

As you read, write your own examples in the blank spaces. *Icons* or pictures—one representing each mind action—will help you visualize and remember them.

Recall

This is the simplest action. When you **recall,** you name or describe facts, objects, or events, or put them into sequence. Although critical thinking goes beyond recall, remembering (or recollecting) is the essential first step in any thinking process. Without being able to recall information, you would have nothing with which to process new information.

EXAMPLES:

- Naming the steps of a geometry proof, in order
- Remembering your best friends' phone numbers
- Listing the main points of a business memo

Also called: facts, sequence, description, detail
Your example: Recall two important school-related events this month.

_____

_____

The icon: A capital R stands for recall or remembering.

Similarity

This action examines what is **similar** about two or more situations, ideas, people, stories, events, or objects, comparing them to one another. There is a range of similarity, from exactly the same to almost completely different and everywhere in between. For example, identical twins probably are far more similar than a man and a woman who are not genetically related. The man and woman may still have similarities, though (number of fingers, high energy, dark brown hair).

EXAMPLES:

- Comparing notes with another student to see what facts and ideas you have both considered important
- Analyzing the arguments you've had with your partner this month and seeing how they all seem to be about the same problem
- Looking at how two of your employees seem to clash in a similar way each time you hold a staff meeting

Also called: analogy, likeness, comparison, comparing
Your example: Tell what is similar about two of your best friends

_____

_____

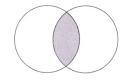

TERMS

Venn diagram
A graph that uses
circles to repre-
sent logical
relations between
sets of informa-
tion.

The icon: The **Venn diagram** illustrates the idea of similarity. The two circles represent the things being compared, and the shaded area of intersection indicates that they have some degree or element of similarity.

Difference

This action examines what is **different** about one or more situations, ideas, people, stories, events, or objects, contrasting them with one another. As with the concept of similarity, there is a range of difference. The two things being contrasted can be different in any way and to any degree. Even as the identical twins are highly similar, they may prefer different courses of study, for example.

EXAMPLES:

- Seeing how you react differently to two different styles of instruction (one of your instructors divides the class into small groups for discussions, and another keeps desks in place and delivers lectures)

- Contrasting your energy level on a day when you combine work and school with how you feel on a day when you attend class only
- Noticing how your state of mind changes as your income fluctuates

Also called: distinction, contrast, contrasting, differentiating

Your example: Explain how your response to a course you like differs from how you respond to a course you don't like as much.

_____

_____

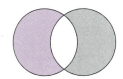

The icon: Here the Venn diagram is used again, to show difference. The non-intersecting parts of the circles are shaded, indicating that the focus is on what is not in common.

Cause and Effect

Using this action, you look at what has **caused** a fact, situation, or event and/or what **effects,** or consequences, come from it. You examine what led to something and/or what will follow because of it. Cause and effect may be simple to analyze, as in what caused a glass to break, or complex, as in determining the causes of prejudice.

EXAMPLES:

- Staying up late at night causes you to oversleep, which has the effect of your being late to class. This causes you to miss some of the material, which has the further effect of your having problems on the test.
- Eating a big lunch at work leads to your feeling drowsy around 3 p.m.
- When you pay your phone and utility bills on time, you create effects such as a better credit rating, uninterrupted service, and a better relationship with your service providers.

Also called: reasons, consequences, prediction

Your example: Name what causes you to like your favorite class, and the effects that liking the class has on you.

_____

_____

The icon: The arrows, pointing toward one another in a circular pattern, show how a cause leads to an effect.

Example to Idea

From one or more **examples** (facts or events), you develop a general **idea** or ideas. One way of coming up with an idea is to group similar facts or events together, which may show you a pattern that allows you to make a general classification or statement about the group. Classifying a fact or event in this way helps you build knowledge (for example, you know what the Boston Tea

Party was, but grouping it with other events of the Revolutionary War may help you learn the role it played in the larger concept of how the colonies became the United States). This mind action moves from the specific to the general, from the concrete to the abstract.

EXAMPLES:

- You have had trouble finding a baby-sitter. A classmate even brought her child to class once. Your brother drops his daughter at day care and doesn't like not seeing her all day. From these examples, you derive the idea that your school needs an on-campus day-care program.
- You examine what dogs, whales, and tigers have in common (classification as mammals).
- You see a movie and you decide it is mostly about pride.

   Also called: generalization, classification, conceptualization, induction, inductive reasoning, abstracting, hypothesis

   Your example: Name activities you enjoy; from them, come up with an idea of a class you would like to take.

_____

_____

The icon: The arrow and "Ex" pointing to a light bulb on their right indicate how an example or examples (the known) lead to the idea (the light bulb, representing the unknown or new idea).

Idea to Example

In a reverse of the previous action, you take an **idea** or ideas and think of **examples** (events or facts) that support or prove that idea. This mind action moves from the general to the specific, from the abstract to the concrete. Idea-to-example thinking builds knowledge as well. For example, for a presentation on the Revolutionary War, you want to illustrate the idea of rebellion against authority. You investigate facts and events and see that the Boston Tea Party is an example that supports your initial idea. Examining the important details within your examples will help you justify your idea.

EXAMPLES:

- For a paper, you start with this thesis statement: "Men still have an advantage over women in many areas of the modern workplace." To support that idea, you gather examples: Men make more money on average than women in the same jobs, there are more men in upper management positions than there are women, and so on.
- You tell your child that she should do her homework before going outside to play. You explain that she will be able to focus on concepts better right after she learns them in school that day, and that she will enjoy her evening more if she doesn't have the homework hanging over her head.

- You talk to your instructor about changing your major, giving examples that support your idea, such as the fact that you have worked in the field to which you want to change and you have fulfilled some of the requirements for that major already.

Also called: categorization, substantiation, proof, deduction, deductive reasoning, constructing support

Your example: Name an admirable person. Give examples that show how that person is admirable.

_____

_____

The icon: In a reverse of the previous icon, this one starts with the light bulb and has an arrow pointing to "Ex." This indicates that you start with the idea (the lit bulb, representing the known), and then move to the examples that support it (the unknown).

Evaluation

Here you **judge** whether something is useful or not useful, important or unimportant, good or bad, or right or wrong by identifying and weighing its positive and negative effects (pros and cons). Be sure to consider the **context,** because the same choices might receive very different evaluations in different situations. For example, a cold drink might be good on the beach in August but not so good in the snowdrifts in January; and pizza for dinner might be great for one person but not fun for someone who can't digest cheese. With the facts you have gathered, you determine the value of something for you in terms of both predicted effects and your own needs. Cause-and-effect analysis always accompanies evaluation (in evaluating, you ask, "What is, or would be, the effect if . . . ").

TERMS

Context
Written or spoken knowledge that can help illuminate the meaning of a word or passage.

EXAMPLES:

- For one semester, you schedule classes in the afternoons, spend nights working, and plan to study in the mornings. You find that you tend to sleep late and lose your only study time. From this harmful effect, you evaluate that it doesn't work for you. You decide to schedule earlier classes next time.

- Your mother is not well and needs help with her day-to-day activities. You consider the possible effects of bringing in a home health aide, moving her to an assisted living facility, and setting up a schedule for her children to help her at her home. Together you decide that a home health aide would be the best choice right now.

- Someone offers you a chance to cheat on a test. You evaluate the potential effects if you are caught. You also evaluate the long-term effects of not actually learning the material and of doing something ethically wrong. You decide that it isn't right or worthwhile to cheat.

Also called: value, judgment, rating

Your example: Evaluate your mode of transportation to school

_____

_____

The icon: A set of scales out of balance indicates how you weigh positive and negative effects to arrive at an evaluation.

The best way to remember the mind actions is to visualize the icons. You also may want to use a *mnemonic device*—a memory tool, as explained in Chapter 7—to remember them. You could make a sentence of words that each start with the first letter of a mind action, such as "Really Smart Dogs Cook Eggs In Enchiladas" (the first letter of each word stands for a mind action).

How Mind Actions Build Thinking Processes

The seven mind actions are the fundamental building blocks that are the foundation of the more complex thinking processes. Using these actions consciously as tools allows you to solve problems, make decisions, create, and learn. You rarely will use one at a time in a step-by-step process as they are presented here. You usually will combine them, overlap them, and repeat them, using different actions for different situations. For example:

- When a test question asks you to define or explain prejudice, you might give examples, similar to one another, that show your idea of prejudice (combining *similarity* with *example to idea*).
- When deciding whether to take a course that has been recommended to you, you find similarities and differences in what your friends have said about the course, think about what positive effects taking the course may have on your major or career choice, and evaluate whether it is a good decision (combining *similarity, difference, cause-and-effect,* and *evaluation*).
- When asked to defend your position on gun control, you discuss the causes of recent violent events, the effects of the latest Congressional votes, and statistics about gun purchases and manufacturing (combining *idea to example, cause-and-effect,* and *similarity*).

"He knows enough who knows how to learn."
HENRY ADAMS

When you combine mind actions in working toward a specific goal, you are performing a thinking process. In the next few chapters you will find explorations of important critical-thinking processes: solving problems, making decisions, constructing and evaluating arguments, thinking logically, recognizing perspectives, and planning strategically. Each thinking process gives you the chance to put your thinking into action, directing your energy toward broadening your knowledge and achieving your goals. Figure 1.2 shows all of the mind actions and thinking processes together and reminds you that the mind actions form the core of the thinking processes.

FIGURE 1.2 The wheel of thinking.

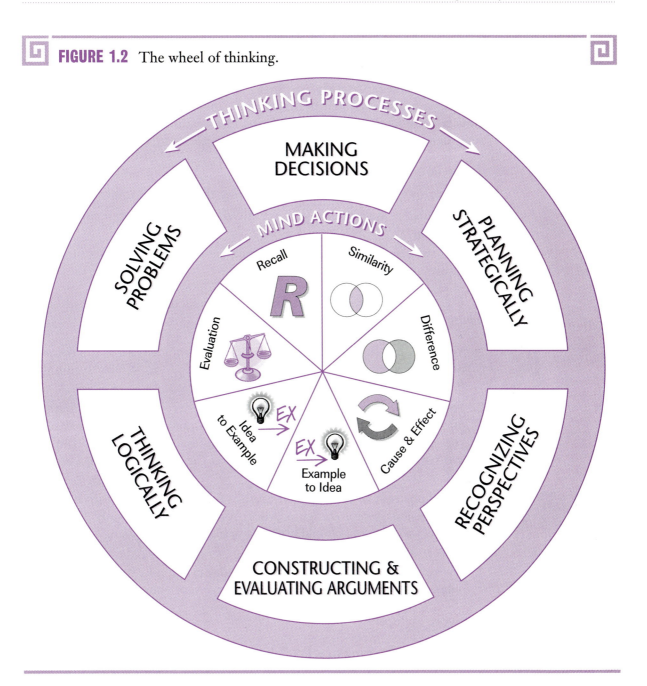

WHAT ARE INDUCTIVE AND DEDUCTIVE THINKING?

Among the thinking terms you are most likely to encounter in your school and work are *inductive* thinking and *deductive* thinking. You already know how to think inductively and deductively; you have done so many times before. In fact, although you may not realize it, you have studied them in the previous section of this chapter. They merit their own separate section here because they are such widely used thinking patterns, and because the terms *induction* and *deduction* are commonly used in other material about thinking.

Inductive Thinking

Inductive thinking is the process of working from the known example(s) toward the previously unknown idea. You learned the basics of inductive thinking when you studied the example-to-idea mind action in this chapter. Inductive thinking helps you use existing information to come up with something new. The process, broken down into more detail, looks like this:

1. Focus on available information
2. Look for a pattern or connection among the pieces of information
3. Formulate a classification of the pattern, or a general statement about its meaning
4. Test the classification or general statement to see how it applies to other information[3]

Following is a step-by-step example of inductive thinking, also called *induction*.

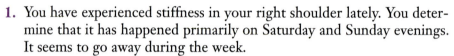

1. You have experienced stiffness in your right shoulder lately. You determine that it has happened primarily on Saturday and Sunday evenings. It seems to go away during the week.
2. You examine what you could be doing on the weekend that you don't do during the week to irritate your right shoulder muscle. You note that you spend your weekdays in class taking notes and at work as a courier, and you spend your weekends primarily at the computer doing assignments and papers.
3. You compare how you use your muscles for class and work with how you use your muscles for computer work. You decide that the only difference in how you use your shoulder on the weekend involves using your computer mouse with your right hand.
4. To test your idea, you spend a free weekday evening working on the computer, take a weekend night off, and observe how your shoulder reacts.

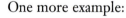

One more example:

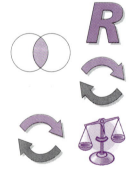

1. You are late arriving to school almost every day.
2. You examine your mode of travel and see that you hit traffic at very nearly the same spot on any day that you leave the house after 8:00 A.M.
3. You decide that hitting that particular traffic at that particular time is preventing you from arriving on time to class.
4. To test your idea, you try two tactics. One morning you take a different route to school, and another morning you take your regular route but leave a half-hour earlier.

Deductive Thinking

Deductive thinking is the process of supporting a given idea based on examples and evidence. You learned the basics of deductive thinking when you studied the idea-to-example mind action in this chapter. When you think deductively, you rely on what you know to support a **hypothesis** or general-ization. In greater detail, the process looks like this:

TERMS

Hypothesis
A tentative
assumption made
in order to exam-
ine and test its
effects

1. Identify a situation or case.
2. Name a principle or generalization that you believe applies to the situa-tion.
3. See if the situations or cases fit the principle.
4. If they fit, see what you can conclude about the specific situation or what you can predict about similar situations in the future.[4]

Following is a step-by-step example of deductive thinking, also called *deduction*.

1. The situation: You have trouble focusing during two of your classes (a Monday-Wednesday literature seminar and a Tuesday-Thursday sociol-ogy class in lecture format).
2. The generalization: Hunger distracts a student's attention in class.
3. You note that both classes meet in late morning and run over into the time when you normally would eat lunch. Because these classes are so different otherwise, you can't find any other reason why you would be distracted in both.
4. You conclude that your hunger is preventing you from concentrating in class and that you need to take classes at different times or eat some-thing in the late morning before the classes meet.

One more example:

1. The generalization: People who like each other work well together.
2. The situations: Different ways in which you and your coworkers have been teamed up on projects.
3. You note that the teams that are accomplishing more have at least one pair of close friends in them and that they have fewer pairs of people who are known to dislike each other.
4. You conclude that in the future the teams should be chosen with an eye toward who enjoys working with one another.

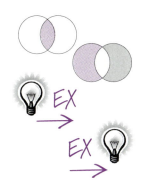

Often, you probably perform inductive and deductive reasoning without thinking about it. The more you think about it, though, the more adept you will become at using it consciously and deliberately to make sense of the information you encounter. Being aware of the two main types of knowledge will help you take in the information with which you reason.

WHAT ARE THE TYPES OF KNOWLEDGE?

Your ability to acquire knowledge can benefit from an awareness of exactly what you are acquiring. Knowledge can be divided into two basic categories, *declarative* and *procedural*.[5]

Declarative knowledge refers to what the learner *knows* or *understands*—concepts or principles, facts, descriptions, episodes or events, cause-and-effect relationships, and sequences. Declarative knowledge focuses on the *who, what, where, when,* and *why.* Examples of declarative knowledge include the following:

- Types of numbers
- French verbs
- Leaders of Asian countries
- The events of the industrial revolution
- The causes of AIDS

"Minds are like parachutes. They only function when they are open."

SIR JAMES DEWAR

Procedural knowledge refers to what the learner is able to *do*—follow processes, perform actions, and demonstrate skills. Procedural knowledge focuses on the *how.* Examples of procedural knowledge include the following:

- How to balance a spreadsheet
- How to use mind actions to think critically
- How to make an omelet
- How to organize a date book

Methods of education change with the times. Educators often have prioritized memorization of information, which led to the dominance of drilling and the "three R's" approach ("reading, 'riting, and 'rithmetic"). Declarative knowledge was the emphasis. Recently, perhaps in response to the world's ever-increasing pace and ever-growing bank of information, education has shifted focus to teaching students procedural knowledge—how to use and perform with information. Likewise, the modern workplace focuses on action. Employers look for people who have specific procedural skills rather than just extensive declarative knowledge.

No matter what the current emphasis, both kinds of knowledge are important to your success. You need declarative knowledge to be able to develop procedural knowledge, and procedural knowledge reinforces declarative knowledge. Successful performance of skills and actions depends on your understanding of those skills and actions. For example, it would be awfully hard to know how to repair a car unless you know what each part does, how the parts connect to and work with one another, and where they are located in the engine. In addition, working on the car reinforces your knowledge of the parts.

Furthermore, a large part of critical thinking involves comparing new information with what you already know. Your prior knowledge provides a framework within which to evaluate new information. For example, thinking critically about the statement "Shakespeare's character King Richard III is like an early version of Adolf Hitler" is impossible without basic knowledge of World War II and Shakespeare's play *Richard III.*

The bottom line is that you cannot interact critically with knowledge until you acquire it. As you think critically, you reinforce your knowledge and acquire more. In making your way through your coursework, try to balance your efforts so you build both types of knowledge. Together they will give you the best foundation on which to build new ideas.

Κρινειν

The word "critical" is derived from the Greek word *krinein*, which means to separate in order to choose or select. To be a mindful, aware critical thinker, you need to be able to separate, evaluate, and select ideas, facts, and thoughts.

Think of this concept as you apply critical thinking to your education, workplace, and personal life. Be aware of the information you take in, and be selective as you process and evaluate it. Critical thinking gives you the power to make sense of life by deliberately selecting how to respond to the information, people, and events that you encounter.

Chapter 1   Building Thinking Skills

Name _____   Date _____

LIFE THINKING: Applying What You Learn

1.1 *The Mind Actions*

Reinforce your knowledge of the mind actions—and of how your mind works—by applying them to a situation in your own life. In this case, think about one class meeting you attended this week.

Recall. What did you cover in the class? What was the class format? Recall everything you can about the class.

_____

_____

_____

_____

Similarity. How was this class—in topic, format, or experience—similar to a class meeting in any of your other courses?

_____

_____

_____

_____

Difference. How was this class—in topic, format, or experience—different from a class meeting in any of your other courses?

_____

_____

_____

_____

Cause and effect. What were the effects of the class on you—your knowledge, your state of mind, or your feelings? In other words, what was your reaction to the class?

_____

_____

_____

_____

Example to idea. From looking at the examples of your reactions to the class (topic, format, other aspects of your experience), what idea comes to mind? (For example, you might have an idea about your future studies in this area, about what kind of classroom format suits you best, or about how you need to approach this course in order to succeed.)

EX

_____

_____

_____

_____

Idea to example. Taking the idea you just came up with, name some examples of how you could put that idea to work.

EX

_____

_____

_____

_____

Evaluation. Evaluate your experience in the class. Useful or not so useful? Positive or negative effects?

_____

_____

_____

_____

1.2 *Being a Questioning Thinker*

As in Table 1.1, explore critical and noncritical approaches. For each category, describe a recent occurrence in your life and write a possible critical and a noncritical response (these do not necessarily have to be the response you had).

College occurrence:

_____

_____

Noncritical response:

_____

_____

_____

Critical response:

_____

_____

_____

Work occurrence:

Noncritical response:

Critical response:

Personal life occurrence:

Noncritical response:

Critical response:

1.3 *Declarative and Procedural Knowledge*

To solidify your understanding of the difference between these two types of knowledge, list five examples of each that you have used in the last week.

DECLARATIVE KNOWLEDGE

1.
2.
3.
4.
5.

PROCEDURAL KNOWLEDGE

1. _____

2. _____

3. _____

4. _____

5. _____

At this point in your life, which type of knowledge seems more important to you, and why?

_____

_____

_____

_____

_____

_____

_____

_____

  TEAM THINKING: Working Together

1.4 *Inductive and Deductive Thinking*

Gather in groups of five or six students (or if your class has ten or fewer people, gather as a class). If you have time, do both the inductive and deductive exercises below. If you are short on time, choose one.

Induction: Twenty Questions

One person secretly chooses an object in the room. The other members of the group ask yes-or-no questions to determine what the object is. In this way, the group is working from example (answers to the questions, indicating the characteristics of the object) to idea (the object, when they finally guess it).

Deduction: Supporting a Statement

As a group, members think about changes they think should happen at their school—in the academic system, support for students, schedule, or any other aspect that concerns them. They choose one change and come up with a statement that expresses the group's position. Independently, each group member then writes down examples or evidence that he or she believes supports the statement. After a few minutes of writing, the group comes together again and compares the examples and evidence. The group compiles them into one paper, with the statement at the top and the examples and evidence listed below it.

WORK THINKING: Career Portfolio

 1.5 *Investigate a Career*

Choose one career that interests you. Use your mind actions to ask important questions about all aspects of this career. Be an investigator. Find out as many facts as you can, and evaluate all opinions based on what you already know.

- What are the different kinds of jobs available in this career area?
- What examples can help you assess the condition of the career area (growing, lagging, or holding steady)?
- What are the pros and cons (positive and negative effects) of this career?
- What is similar about the kinds of people who tend to succeed in this career? How about the kinds of people who tend not to do well?
- To whom can you talk to find out more information about this career?
- What are the opinions of those around you about this career?
- What preparation—in school and/or on the job—does this career require?

Then write up your findings in a report. Use each question as a separate heading. Keep your research in your portfolio. Write a conclusion about your prospects in this career area, based on what you learned in your investigation.

 **QUESTIONING YOUR WORLD:
Information Literacy Journal**

To record your thoughts, use the lined pages at the end of the chapter or a separate journal.

 1.6 *You as a Critical Thinker*

Evaluate yourself as a consumer of information. Do you believe what you read? If you question information, what kinds of questions do you use to investigate it? If you trust some sources of information (magazines, newspapers, Internet, radio, television) more than others, which are those sources and why do you trust them?

Name _____ Date _____   **Journal**

Journal

Name _____ Date _____

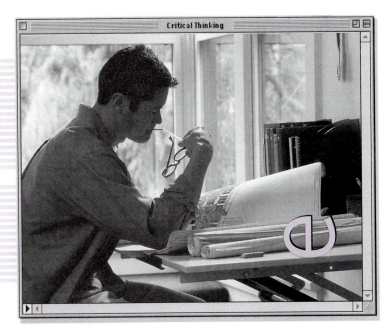

2

Thinking Skills in Real Life

Problem Solving and Decision Making

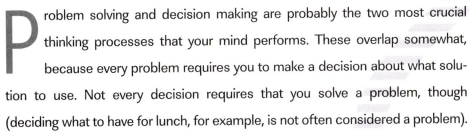

P roblem solving and decision making are probably the two most crucial thinking processes that your mind performs. These overlap somewhat, because every problem requires you to make a decision about what solution to use. Not every decision requires that you solve a problem, though (deciding what to have for lunch, for example, is not often considered a problem).

In this chapter, you will explore the problem-solving process in detail, learning the importance of defining a problem accurately even before you begin to work through it. You will examine systems for analyzing the problems and decisions that come your way. You will see how the actions of the mind form the building blocks of both processes. Furthermore, this chapter's discussion on creativity will illustrate the role that creative thinking plays in successful problem solving and decision making.

In this chapter, you will explore answers to the following questions:

- Why is critical thinking essential to problem solving and decision making?
- How can you define a problem?
- How can you analyze a problem effectively?
- How does critical thinking help you make decisions?
- How can you become a more creative thinker?

WHY IS CRITICAL THINKING ESSENTIAL TO PROBLEM SOLVING AND DECISION MAKING?

You solve problems and make decisions every day, often without consciously thinking about it. Suppose, for instance, you are moving to a new apartment. In the course of one day, you might investigate which moving company to use, figure out how to pay for packing materials, decide whom to ask to help you pack, and come up with a way to clean a stain off the carpet so you can get your security deposit back. Both processes require combinations of mind actions. To get the stain off the rug, for example, you might recall similar situations in which you used club soda and hairspray to remove a stain (a combination of recall, similarity, and cause and effect).

Although both of these processes have multiple steps, you will not always have to work through each step. As with any kind of procedural knowledge, your ability to perform the procedure will become more natural the more you do it. When you are fairly comfortable with solving problems and making decisions, your mind will click through the steps with less conscious thought. Also, you will become more adept at evaluating which problems and decisions require serious consideration and which can be taken care of more quickly and simply.

The Effects of Not Thinking Critically

Making a decision or solving a problem without thinking critically can have negative effects. Think about a decision you have made in the past that you now consider unwise. What do you wish you had done? Perhaps you have said things to yourself such as, "I should have taken more time" or, "I should have asked someone for help" or, "I should have considered other options."

It's human to act impulsively, and people often short-circuit their problem solving and decision making success by doing so. Non–critical-thinking tendencies include the following:[1]

Acting on a problem or decision before thinking it through. Sometimes people don't believe they have time to think about the problem or decision, or just plain don't. For example, you may have said something that you regretted later, or you may have dated someone whom you later wished you hadn't. You may not even have an answer to the question, "Why did I do that?"

Doing what someone else says to do without thinking it over. At times it seems easier just to follow someone else's advice, especially if the advice comes from someone you like and trust. Even so, it isn't always the smartest choice for you and your particular circumstances. Another person may not understand your needs and may not ask the questions you need to ask. For example, a friend who liked a certain class recommends that class to you, and it turns out that you like it least of all your classes. You took the advice without thinking about it and did not ask questions stemming from your own needs.

Doing nothing and waiting for the problem or decision to sort itself out. Some problems and decisions are difficult or frightening. Sometimes it seems easier just to ignore them, hoping they will resolve on their own. Unfortunately, this often results in worsened conditions. If you have a mole that seems irregularly shaped or enlarged, for example, letting it go could lead to more serious medical problems, perhaps even skin cancer.

You won't always have the ideal amount of time, energy, and available resources to solve a problem or make a decision in the way that would benefit you most. Making your best effort to think critically before acting, however, will almost always make for a better solution or decision than you would have found had you not thought at all. Give yourself the best chance to succeed by thinking critically, using whatever time and energy you have.

HOW CAN YOU DEFINE A PROBLEM?

You constantly encounter problems to be solved, ranging from typical daily problems (how to manage study time or learn not to misplace your keys) to life-altering situations (how to adjust to a severe injury or design a custody plan during a divorce). Problems pop up in every aspect of your life. You will encounter school problems (how to get into courses required for your major), work problems (how to get along with a difficult supervisor), and personal problems (how to increase your income). Being a skilled and thoughtful problem solver can help you succeed at whatever you do.

"A little knowledge that acts is worth infinitely more than much knowledge that is idle."
KAHLIL GIBRAN

Ask What Has to Be Solved

The first step is to state and define the problem clearly and accurately. Although this step may seem obvious and easy, it can be difficult and often demands a great deal of energy. If you define the problem incorrectly at the start, the most flawless problem-solving technique won't help you fix what's really wrong.

The key to defining a problem correctly is to focus on the causes of the problem rather than the effects. Take, for example, the student from the previous chapter who developed shoulder soreness from using a computer mouse. If he states the problem as, "My shoulder is sore" and stops there, he may design solutions such as "use a salve that helps muscle aches" or "get regular massages." He then may be surprised to find that the soreness keeps coming back. If, however, he defines the problem cause as, "The way I use the mouse is not comfortable for my body," he may come up with a solution such as raising his chair seat so his arm is lower when using the mouse. This solution, based on the true cause, is the one that will solve the problem.

As another example, you may have heard the Chinese saying, "Give a man a fish, and he will eat for a day. Teach a man to fish, and he will eat for a lifetime." If you state the initial problem as "The man is hungry," giving him a fish seems like a perfectly good solution. Unfortunately, the problem returns the next day, and the day after that. You could assume that this is a recurring problem—or you could think in more depth about causes and redefine the problem, focusing on this cause: "The man does not know how to find food." Given that his lack of knowledge is the true cause, teaching him to fish will truly solve the problem.

This scenario can apply to how governments deal with homeless people. Although it's important to provide food and shelter for them, simply giving them something to eat day after day is not necessarily going to improve their situation. The real problem is that most homeless people do not have jobs, or the skills necessary for jobs, that could help them provide for themselves. Therefore, a better solution would involve therapy and training programs that could help people get off the streets and into the workplace. How to do that effectively, and find the funding for it, would be the next problem to solve.

There are four steps to defining a problem.[2] Figure 2.1 is a visual representation of these steps.

1. *Collect information about the problem.* The more you know about the problem, the more likely you will be to identify its causes accurately and solve it effectively. This step has steps within it:[3]

   - *Look at different perspectives.* The more views you can gather about the problem, the more you will be able to clearly define it. Talk with anyone involved with the problem (or anyone who has observed the problem) to get their direct input and observations.

   - *Break the problem into parts, if it has them.* Sometimes one problem is actually a combination of smaller problems. Analyze the problem to make sure you have gotten as specific as possible about its parts. If it consists of smaller problems, for example, you may want to solve each separately.

   - *Be specific and clear.* As with any critical thinking process, the better information (facts and evidence) you work with, the better your final product will be.

2. *If possible, observe the problem first-hand.* If this is your own problem, you are already "in the know." If, however, you are helping to solve a problem with which you are not directly involved, a first-hand view of it will help you better understand what's at stake. For example, if you are a supervisor at work and an employee comes to you with a problem,

FIGURE 2.1 Defining a problem.

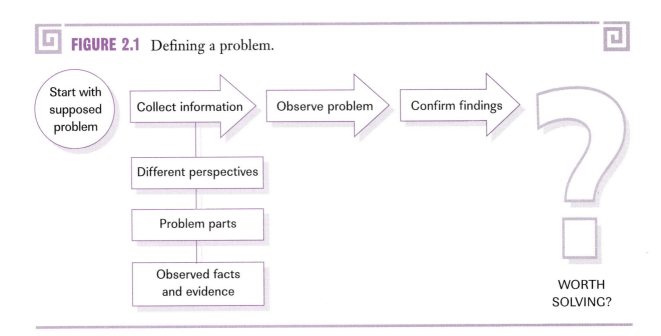

observing it rather than coming up with a solution on the spot probably will lead you to a more effective solution.

3. *Confirm your findings about the problem.* Once you have gathered all the information you can about the problem, check it for accuracy. Did you observe well and completely? Did people with whom you spoke give you the whole story? Chapter 4 will go into detail about what can get in the way of the truth.

Figure 2.2 provides a Problem Investigation Worksheet. Once you have gathered information about the problem, you have one more decision to make before you begin to solve it.

Ask If It's Worth Solving

In today's world, people are often overwhelmed with work, responsibilities, and relationships that seem to take up far more time than they should have. There are only 24 hours in a day, and it is impossible to sit down and give every problem in your life a complete, thoughtful, time-taking, problem-solving treatment. You will have to perform "problem triage"—make a quick evaluation of any problem or decision to see if it is worth your time.

For example, on a given day you begin to realize that you might not have time to grab some lunch. Is it worth troubling yourself over? Well, that's your call. Evaluate the situation by weighing the effects. If you know that you will have a chance to get a bite to eat in mid-afternoon, for example, you might want to let this problem pass by. Conversely, if you are diabetic and need to eat regularly to keep your body functioning normally, you may evaluate that this problem is worth solving.

You can use the question "So what?" to help you look at any potential problem and decide if it is worth your energy. When a problem comes up, ask yourself, "So what?" If you don't have an answer, you may be better off just

FIGURE 2.2 One problem investigated.

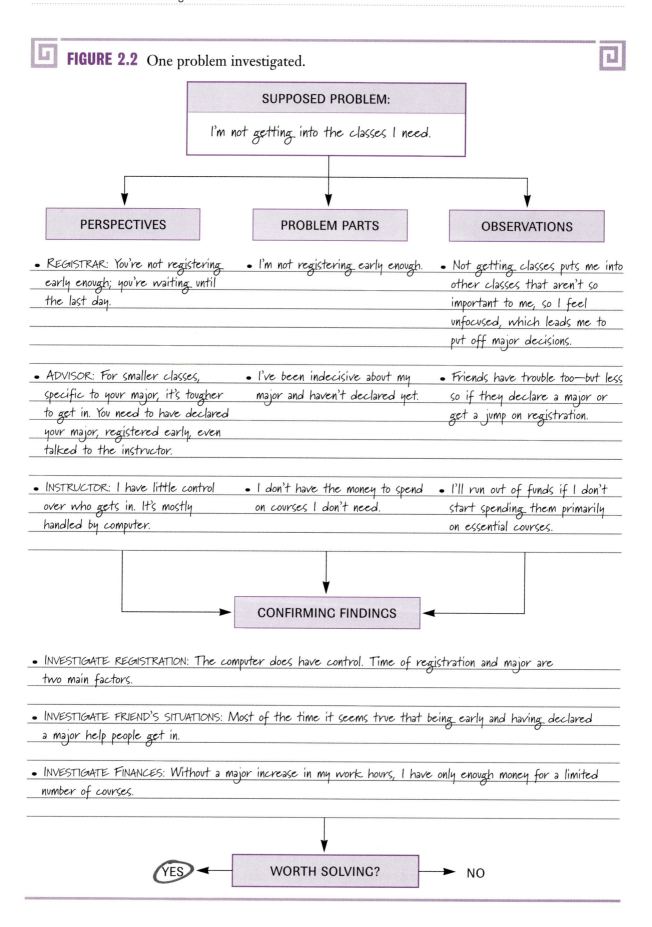

letting it be. If you do have an answer, explore what makes the problem important for you to solve. Then move on and apply the problem-solving process.

 ## HOW CAN YOU ANALYZE A PROBLEM EFFECTIVELY?

Once you have defined a problem and established that you want to solve it, walking yourself through a critical-thinking–based problem-solving plan will give you the best chance of coming up with a favorable solution. One way of getting a big-picture overview of where you want to go with a problem is to consider "present state" and "desired state."[4]

Present state. This refers to where the situation currently stands. For example, you are having a conflict with your instructor. More specifically, you need to speak with her one-on-one. You have another class during her office hours, and you don't think she is trying to accommodate your needs.

Desired state. This refers to where you or anyone else involved in the problem would like the situation to be. Continuing the example, your desired state may be to have access to your instructor for a private meeting.

Getting from the present state to the desired state is where the problem-solving process comes in. The process, however, might not always bring you to exactly where you thought you wanted to be. It may lead you to the conclusion that the desired state is not possible (or not *yet* possible). It may introduce new possibilities of desired states to you. It may raise ideas about how you can put a twist on the present state and improve the situation that way. You won't find out, however, until you try. That's what the process is for.

The Problem-Solving Plan

You can apply the following problem-solving plan to any problem. The steps below will maximize the number of possible solutions you generate and will allow you to explore each one as fully as possible. Notice the various combinations of mind actions you will use as you move through each stage of the plan. One of them—evaluation—should be ongoing throughout the course of solving any problem. As you complete each stage, evaluate whether you have sufficiently fulfilled the requirements of that stage. Details of a sample problem accompany the description of each step.

Step 1: State the Problem Clearly

What are the facts? *Recall*, from your efforts at defining the problem, the details of the situation. Be sure to name the problem specifically. For example, a student might state as a problem: "I'm getting bad grades on my quizzes." That statement, however, may actually be an *effect* of the real underlying problem: "I'm not understanding the material."

Evaluating this step: Ask: Have I been clear enough? Specific enough?

The sample problem, stated: A student is not understanding the material presented in class.

Step 2: Analyze the Causes and Effects of the Problem

Analyze, or break down into understandable pieces, what surrounds the problem. Ask yourself: What *effects* of the situation concern me? What *causes* these effects? Are there hidden causes?

Be cautious about evaluating the causes of any problem. There may be more than one cause involved, and some may have more weight or make more sense than others. Some apparent causes may be false, or "rival," causes that aren't directly linked to the problem. For example, a parent may blame boring instruction or poor cafeteria food for a child's sluggishness in school. These causes may exist, but it also may turn out that a previously unknown food allergy is keeping the child from performing at top capacity.

Evaluating this step: Ask: Have I separated out and weighed the causes effectively? Have I found them all?

The sample problem, defined: If some effects of not understanding include poor grades and disinterest, some causes may include poor study habits, not listening in class, or lack of sleep.

Step 3: Generate Possible Solutions

Remember that to get to the heart of a problem, you must base possible solutions on the most significant causes instead of putting a bandage on the effects. Use this stage to examine the causes and generate possible solutions based on them. Asking questions based on the mind actions will help:

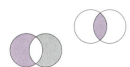

- How have you solved, or seen other people solve, *similar* problems?

- What is different about this problem that could inspire a *different* solution idea?

- Does this problem seem to be an *example* of a general *idea* or principle that you can apply?

- How can the causes be changed to create a new effect?

TERMS

Brainstorming
Spontaneous, rapid generation of ideas or solutions, undertaken by a group or an individual, often as part of a problem-solving process.

Brainstorming (discussed later) will help you come up with possible solutions. During this stage it is also helpful to consult other people for ideas. Different perspectives often lead to a wider range of possibilities.

Evaluate this step: Ask: What is the quality of the solutions I have generated? Have I come up with enough solutions?

The sample problem, with possible solution: If the student were to aim for better assignment grades to offset the low quiz grades, that might raise his GPA but probably wouldn't address the lack of understanding. Looking at his study habits, though, might lead him to seek help from his instructor or a study group.

Step 4: Explore Each Solution

Why might your solution work or not work? Might a solution work partially, or in a certain situation? *Evaluate* ahead of time the pros and cons (positive and negative effects) of each plan. Create a chain of *causes* and *effects* in your head, as far into the future as you can, to see where this solution might lead.

Ask these important questions as you evaluate:

- What resources are available to help solve the problem? Do the solutions take advantage of these resources? Does any solution require resources we cannot access?

- When does the problem have to be solved? Does each solution fit the timeline? Can the timeline be changed?

- Whom does each solution benefit? Is there a solution that is truly best for everyone involved? If not, which solution benefits the most people? Is there a workable compromise?

- Does each solution adequately address the cause(s)?

- Does each solution help reach the desired state—or improve/change the present state?

Evaluate this step: Ask: Have I thought through each solution completely?

Considered solutions for the sample problem: The student might consider the effects of improved study habits. Other possible solutions include more sleep, tutoring, or dropping the class.

Step 5: Choose and Execute the Solution You Decide Is Best

This is the action step. First decide how you will put your solution to work. Then execute your solution.

Evaluate this step: Ask: Did I execute the solution completely and effectively?

Chosen solution for the sample problem: The student could decide on a combination of improved study habits and tutoring.

Step 6: Evaluate the Solution

Look at the effects of the solution that you acted upon. What are the positive and negative *effects* of what you did? In terms of your needs, was it a useful solution or not? Could the solution benefit from any adjustments? Would you do the same again or not? In evaluating, you are collecting data. You are doing a form of research.

Evaluating this step: Ask: Did I acknowledge all of the effects, on every aspect of the situation, and weigh them all thoughtfully?

The sample problem, evaluated: Evaluating his choice, the student may decide that the effects are good but that his fatigue still causes a problem.

Step 7: Continue to Evaluate and Refine the Solution

Problem solving is a continual process. You may have opportunities to apply the same solution, or similar solutions, again and again. Evaluate repeatedly, making changes that you decide make the solution better (that is, more reflective of the causes of the problem).

Evaluate this step: Ask: Am I continuing to learn from what happened with this problem? Have I retained important knowledge that will help me with similar problems in the future? Is there an important idea (principle) of which this problem is an example?

The sample problem, refined: The student may decide to continue to study more regularly but, after a few weeks of tutoring, could opt to trade in the tutoring time for some extra sleep. He may decide to take what he has learned from the tutor so far and apply it to his increased study efforts.

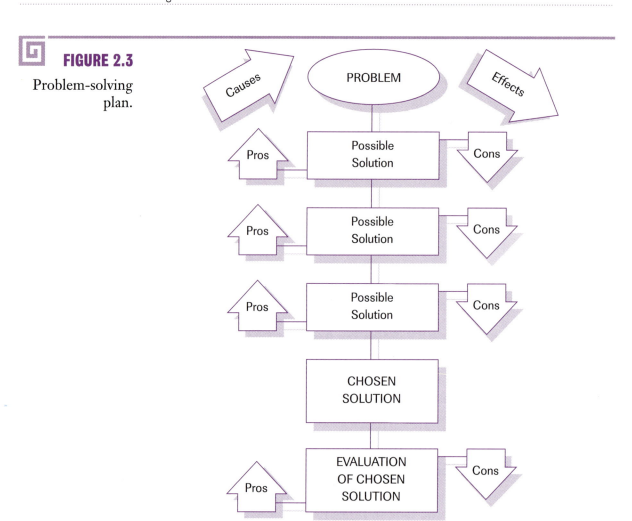

FIGURE 2.3

Problem-solving plan.

Using this process will enable you to solve school, work, and personal problems in a thoughtful, comprehensive way. The think link in Figure 2.3 demonstrates a way to visualize the flow of problem solving. Figure 2.4 shows how one person used this plan to solve a problem. It represents the same plan as Figure 2.3 but gives room to write so that it can be used as a tool in the problem-solving process.

Obstacles to Problem Solving

Problem solving is often complicated, requiring a lot of effort. Along the way, problem solvers may make mistakes that prevent them from successfully solving their problems. You already have examined one common mistake—addressing effects or false causes in the first problem statement. Some other common obstacles follow.[5]

The perfect solution. Believing that every problem has one perfect solution can intimidate you. If you come up with fifty ideas but none seems exactly right, you may think you just aren't good enough to find the right one, and you might give up. Even if you continue to try, looking for the perfect solu-

FIGURE 2.4 How one student solved a problem.

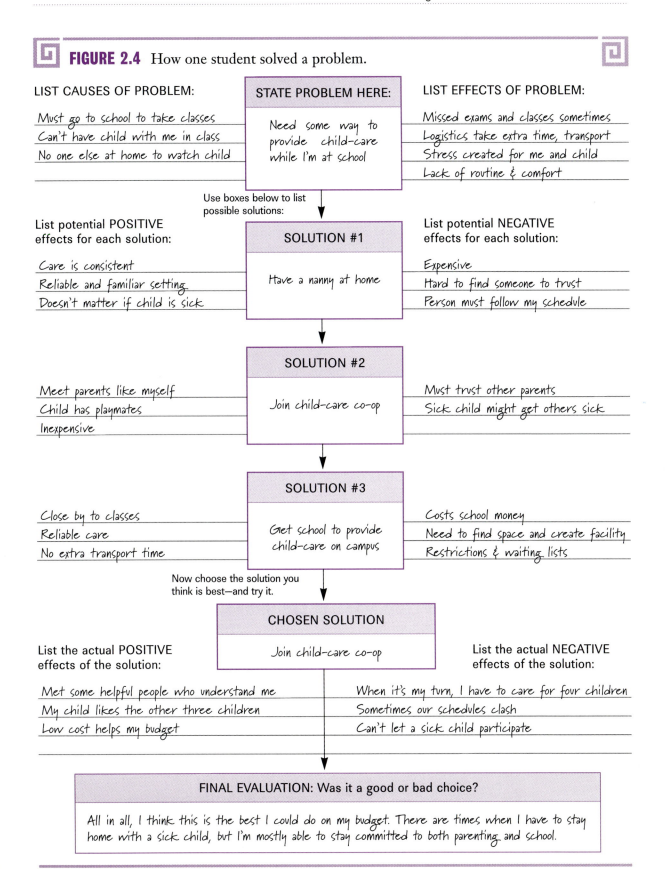

LIST CAUSES OF PROBLEM:

Must go to school to take classes
Can't have child with me in class
No one else at home to watch child

STATE PROBLEM HERE:

Need some way to provide child-care while I'm at school

LIST EFFECTS OF PROBLEM:

Missed exams and classes sometimes
Logistics take extra time, transport
Stress created for me and child
Lack of routine & comfort

Use boxes below to list possible solutions:

List potential POSITIVE effects for each solution:

Care is consistent
Reliable and familiar setting
Doesn't matter if child is sick

SOLUTION #1

Have a nanny at home

List potential NEGATIVE effects for each solution:

Expensive
Hard to find someone to trust
Person must follow my schedule

Meet parents like myself
Child has playmates
Inexpensive

SOLUTION #2

Join child-care co-op

Must trust other parents
Sick child might get others sick

Close by to classes
Reliable care
No extra transport time

SOLUTION #3

Get school to provide child-care on campus

Costs school money
Need to find space and create facility
Restrictions & waiting lists

Now choose the solution you think is best—and try it.

CHOSEN SOLUTION

Join child-care co-op

List the actual POSITIVE effects of the solution:

Met some helpful people who understand me
My child likes the other three children
Low cost helps my budget

List the actual NEGATIVE effects of the solution:

When it's my turn, I have to care for four children
Sometimes our schedules clash
Can't let a sick child participate

FINAL EVALUATION: Was it a good or bad choice?

All in all, I think this is the best I could do on my budget. There are times when I have to stay home with a sick child, but I'm mostly able to stay committed to both parenting and school.

Source: Adapted from a heuristic developed by Frank T. Lyman Jr., Ph.D., University of Maryland, 1983.

tion may drag out the process indefinitely, leading to your never getting around to solving the problem. Don't imagine there is one perfect solution. Instead, look for the *best* solution, using whatever time frame you have.

The smart-people complex. If you run into a snag while trying to solve a problem, you might get yourself off the hook by deciding that only a really smart person could solve this problem—and, of course, you refuse to define yourself as "a really smart person." This leads to both an unsolved problem and a negative assessment of your abilities. Think positive. Believe that any person, thinking critically and carefully, can solve this problem.

The first choice is the best. If you come up with a good idea right away, it's tempting to go with it. Even if you think you accomplished something, will the problem be solved effectively? If the first choice turns out not to be the best choice, you risk having to go back and start the whole process again. Be sure to give your ideas equal time, even if the first one is good. Evaluate each idea so you can be sure you have covered every angle. The more solutions you generate, the better chance you have at finding the absolute best one.

Focusing on the "easier" cause. If you aren't doing very well in a course, you may want to believe it is because your instructor is incompetent. Is that really the cause? You might feel relieved to blame someone other than yourself. If the true cause is that you aren't putting effort into your work, however, you do yourself a disservice. Blaming the instructor won't solve your difficulties in the course if the true cause lies elsewhere. Actually, it may add to the problems you already are experiencing.

Watch for these pitfalls as you work to solve the problems that come your way from day to day. Keep an eye out for them when making decisions, too.

HOW DOES CRITICAL THINKING HELP YOU MAKE DECISIONS?

Although every problem-solving process involves making a decision (when you decide which solution to try), not all decisions involve solving problems. Decisions are choices. Making a choice, or decision, requires thinking critically through all of the possible choices and evaluating which one will bring the best effects for you and for the situation. Decisions large and small come up daily, hourly, even every few minutes. Should you drop a course? Stay in a relationship? Can you work part-time while in school?

Evaluating the Decision

"Life is the sum of all your choices."
ALBERT CAMUS

Before you begin the decision-making process, evaluate the level of the decision you are making. Do you have to decide what books to bring to class (usually a minor issue) or whether to quit a good job (often a major life change)? Some decisions are little, day-to-day considerations that you can take care of quickly on your own. Others, because their effects are more significant, require thoughtful evaluation, time, and perhaps the input of others you trust.

Taking the time to evaluate your decision will help you decide how much energy to put into it. You may not need to apply the entire decision-making plan to every decision. Working too hastily through an important decision can have negative effects, though. Work it out ahead of time so you don't look back wishing you had spent more—or less—energy on a decision.

Decisions are entirely individual. Each decision is made based on **criteria** that apply to the specific decision and the people involved. To make an effective decision, you must consider the criteria when coming up with possible decisions and their potential effects.

Individual criteria can completely change a decision-making path. Say, for example, that three pregnant employees at the same company have to decide how to handle their job situations after they give birth. The company offers the exact same choices—eight weeks of unpaid maternity leave, followed by either a return to full-time or flextime with **telecommuting**— to all the women. Each woman must consider the criteria surrounding her own situation.

TERMS

Criteria
Characterizing elements or traits of a person, object, or situation.

TERMS

Telecommuting
Working from home, using the telephone, facsimile machine, and/or e-mail to communicate with the office.

- *Employee A's* spouse is self-employed and has no regular salary. She has a high-level job at the company and is the primary wage-earner in her household. *Her decision:* Return to work full time after the eight weeks, have her husband care for the child part time, and use day care for when he is working.

- *Employee B* is not married to the father of the child and will be parenting alone. She has ambitions to move up the ladder at her company. *Her decision:* Begin working flextime after six weeks of leave, and telecommute two days a week. She will care for the child when she can, and her mother will help when Employee B is working.

- *Employee C* does not really enjoy her job. Her husband earns a good living and could sustain the family alone if they cut down on spending. *Her decision:* Quit her job entirely once she is ready to give birth.

Based on these different criteria, the three employees could make three entirely different decisions and each have made the best decision for her. Criteria change the map of each individual decision. All decisions are conditional (based on particular conditions).

The Decision-Making Plan

Following are the steps for thinking critically through a decision.

1. Decide on a goal. Why is this decision necessary? What result do you want from this decision, and what is its value? Considering the *effects* you want can help you formulate your goal.

   Sample decision: A student currently attends a small private college. His goal is to become a physical therapist. The school has a good program, but his father has changed jobs and the family no longer can pay the tuition and fees.

2. Establish needs. *Recall* the needs of everyone (or everything) involved in the decision. Broaden your perspective to make sure that you consider all who will be affected.

   Sample decision: The student needs a school with a full physical therapy program; he and his parents need to cut costs; he has to be able to transfer credits.

3. Name, investigate, and evaluate available options. Brainstorm possible choices, then look at the facts surrounding each. *Evaluate* the good and bad effects of each possibility. Weigh these effects and judge which is the best course of action.

   Sample decision: Here are some possibilities that this student might consider.

   - **Continue at the current college.** *Positive effects:* I wouldn't have to adjust to a new place or to new people. I could continue my coursework as planned. *Negative effects:* I would have to find a way to finance most of my tuition and costs on my own, whether through loans, grants, or work. I'm not sure I could find time to work as much as I would need to, and I don't think I would qualify for as much aid as I now need.

   - **Transfer to the state college.** *Positive effects:* I could reconnect with people there whom I know from high school. Tuition and room costs would be cheaper than at my current school. I could transfer credits. *Negative effects:* I would still have to work some or find minimal financial aid. The physical therapy program is small and not very strong.

   - **Transfer to the community college.** *Positive effects:* The community college has many of the courses I need to continue with the physical therapy curriculum. The school is close by, so I could live at home and avoid paying housing costs. Credits will transfer. The tuition is extremely reasonable. *Negative effects:* I don't know anyone there. I would be less independent. The school doesn't offer a bachelor's degree.

4. Decide on a plan of action and pursue it. Make a choice based on your evaluation, and act on your choice.

   Sample decision: In this case the student might decide to go to the community college for two years and then transfer back to a four-year school to earn a bachelor's degree in physical therapy. Although he might lose some independence and contact with friends, the positive effects are money saved, the opportunity to spend time on studies rather than working to earn tuition, and the availability of classes that match the physical therapy program requirements.

5 Evaluate the result. Was it useful? Not useful? Some of both? Weigh the positive and negative effects.

   Sample decision: If the student decides to transfer, he may find that it can be hard being back at home, although his parents are adjusting to his independence and he is trying to respect their concerns. Fewer social distractions result in his getting more work done. The financial situation is favorable. All things considered, he evaluates that this decision was a good one.

Making important decisions can take time. Think through your decisions thoroughly, considering your own ideas as well as those of others you trust, but don't hesitate to act once you have your plan. You cannot benefit from your decision until you act upon it and follow through.

HOW CAN YOU BECOME A MORE CREATIVE THINKER?

Everyone is creative. Although the word may inspire images of art and music, **creativity** comes in many other forms, too. A creation can be a solution, an idea, an approach, a tangible product, a work of art, a system or program. Expand your concept of creativity with these examples of day-to-day creative thinking:

TERMS

Creativity
Ability to pro-
duce something
new through imag-
inative skill.

- Figuring out an alternative plan when your baby-sitter unexpectedly cancels
- Planning how to coordinate your work and class schedules
- Talking through a problem with an instructor, and working to understand each other
- Planning a budget so you can pay your monthly bills

Creative innovations continually change the world. Here are some that have had an impact:

- Susan B. Anthony and other women fought for and won the right for women to vote.
- Art Fry and Spencer Silver invented the Post-It™ note in 1980, enabling people to save paper and protect documents by using removable notes.
- Henry Ford introduced the assembly-line method of automobile construction, making cars cheap enough to be available to the average citizen.
- Rosa Parks refused to give up her seat on the bus to a white person, setting off a chain of events that gave rise to the civil rights movement.
- Alicia Diaz, director of the Center of Hispanic Policy, Research, and Development, developed corporate partnerships and internship programs that have become models for small, efficient government.

Even though these innovations have had wide-ranging effects, the characteristics of these influential innovators can be found in all people who exercise their creative capabilities.

Characteristics of Creative People

Creative people think in fresh, new ways that improve the world and increase productivity, consistently responding to change with new ideas. Roger van Oech, an expert on creativity, highlights this kind of flexibility.[6] "I've found that the hallmark of creative people is their mental flexibility," he says. "Like race-car drivers who shift in and out of different gears depending on where they are on the course, creative people are able to shift in and out of different

TABLE 2.1	CHARACTERISTICS	EXAMPLE
Characteristics of creative people.	• Willingness to take risks	• Taking a difficult, high-level course
	• Tendency to break away from customary limitations	• Entering a marathon race, particularly when physically disabled
	• Tendency to seek challenges and new experiences	• Taking an internship in an unfamiliar and high-pressure workplace
	• Broad range of interests in which he or she becomes absorbed	• Inventing new moves on the basketball court and playing guitar at an open-mike night
	• Ability to make unique things out of available materials and objects	• Making curtains out of bedsheets; writing a poem
	• Tendency to question social norms and assumptions	• Adopting a child of an ethnic background different from theirs
	• Willingness to depart from popular opinion	• Working for a small, relatively unknown political party
	• Curiosity and inquisitiveness	• Wanting to know how a computer program works; asking about the secret to a cooking trick

Source: Adapted from "What Do We Know About Creativity?" in *The Nature of Creativity,* edited by R. J. Sternberg (London: Cambridge University Press, 1988).

types of thinking depending on the needs of the situation at hand. . . . they're doggedly persistent in striving to reach their goals."

T. Z. Tardif and F. J. Sternberg[7] say that creative people are perceived as having certain characteristics. Table 2.1 provides a list of these characteristics, along with examples.

Creative people combine ideas and information in ways that form completely new solutions, ideas, processes, uses, or products. Children tend to be able to tap into this creative freedom more easily than adults. Whether they make up a new game or create forts from chairs and blankets, they often create naturally without worrying that their ideas might not be "right." See if you can retrieve some of that creative freedom from your childhood, using the suggestions you are about to read.

Enhancing Your Creativity

You are naturally creative. One way to spur creative ability is to try out new ideas and behaviors. Although these may feel uncomfortable, new experiences can reveal all kinds of possibilities. When you feel yourself resisting, remember that exploring new ideas doesn't mean that what you were doing before was wrong. You are just responding to change with flexibility and creativity.

Following are some ways to enhance your creativity, adapted from material by J. R. Hayes.[8]

Take the broadest possible perspective. At first a problem may look like, "My child won't stay quiet when I study." If you take a wider look, you may discover hidden causes or effects of the problem, such as, "I haven't chosen the best time of day to study" or, "We haven't had time together, so he feels lonely."

Choose the best atmosphere. T. M. Amabile says that people are more creative and imaginative when they spend time around other creative folk.[9] Spend time with people whose thinking inspires you. Also, if you find that a certain environment stirs your creative juices—the outdoors, a corner of the library, driving in your car—seek out that environment when you have some creative thinking to do.

Give yourself time. Rushing can stifle your creative ability. When you allow time for thought to percolate, or you take breaks when figuring out a problem, you may increase your creative output. You may not always have the luxury of extra time, but do your best to take as much time as you can. When possible, steal little moments during the day to tune your brain into something you are trying to figure out.

Don't judge yourself. Avoid evaluating ideas right away. If you criticize too soon, you tend to derail your ideas. Trust that your brain is able to come up with interesting, viable possibilities.

Gather varied input. The more information and ideas you gather as you think, the more material you will have to build a creative idea or solution. Every new piece of input offers a new perspective.

Here are a few additional creativity tips from van Oech.[10]

Don't get hooked on finding the one right answer. A question might have a lot of "right answers," depending on your point of view. Shift your perspective and come up with a few. The more possible answers you generate, the better are your chance of finding the best one.

Don't always be logical. Following strict logic may cause you to ignore hunches.

Break the rules sometimes. All kinds of creative breakthroughs have occurred because someone bypassed the rules. Women and minorities can vote and hold jobs because someone broke a rule—a law—many years ago. When necessary, challenge rules with creative ideas.

Be impractical. Ask yourself, "What if?" Use your imagination to consider what would happen if you didn't follow an accepted pattern. Too much practicality can narrow the scope of your ideas.

Let yourself play. People often hit upon their most creative ideas when they aren't trying to think at all—when they are exercising, socializing, playing around, or just relaxing. Often when your mind switches into play mode, it can more freely generate new thoughts.

Let yourself go a little crazy. It's easy to do what everyone else does. Although you may feel weird doing something different, what seems like a crazy idea might be a brilliant discovery. For example, the idea for Velcro™ came from examining how a burr sticks to clothing.

> "Problems are the cutting edge that distinguishes between success and failure. Problems create our courage and our wisdom."
> M. SCOTT PECK

Don't fear failure. Even Michael Jordan got cut from the basketball team as a high school sophomore in Wilmington, North Carolina. If you insist on getting it right all the time, you may miss out on the creative path—often paved with failures—leading to the best possible solution. Failure can open your mind to new possibilities and reveal to you the value of critical thinking.

Always consider yourself creative. Use positive self-talk. Telling yourself you are a creative person can help you act like one. Back up your talk by giving yourself opportunities to create.

Brainstorming may combine many of these strategies. Use brainstorming for problem solving, decision making, writing a paper, or whenever you need to free your mind for new possibilities.

Brainstorming Toward a Creative Answer

You are brainstorming when you approach a problem by letting your mind free-associate and come up with as many possible ideas, examples, or solutions as you can, without immediately evaluating them as good or bad. Brainstorming is also referred to as *divergent thinking*; you start with the issue or problem and then let your mind diverge, or go in as many different directions as it wants, in search of ideas or solutions. Here are some guidelines for successful brainstorming:[11]

Don't evaluate or criticize an idea right away. Write down your ideas so you remember them. Evaluate later, after you have had a chance to think about them. Try to avoid criticizing other people's ideas as well. Students often become stifled when their ideas are evaluated during brainstorming.

Focus on quantity; don't worry about quality until later. Generate as many ideas or examples as you can. The more thoughts you generate, the better is the chance that one of them may be useful. Brainstorming works well in groups. Group members can become inspired by, and make creative use of, one another's ideas.

Consider wild and wacky ideas. Trust yourself to go off the beaten track. Sometimes the craziest ideas end up being the most productive, positive, workable solutions.

Creativity can be developed if you have the desire and patience. Nurture your creativity by being accepting of your own ideas. Your creative expression will become more free with practice.

Creativity and Critical Thinking

Critical thinking is inherently creative, because it requires you to use given information to come up with ideas or solutions to problems. For example, if you were brainstorming to generate possible causes of fatigue in afternoon classes, you might come up with: lack of sleep, too much morning caffeine, an instructor who doesn't inspire you. Through your consideration of causes and solutions, you have been thinking both creatively and critically.

Creative and critical thinkers consider new perspectives, ask questions, don't hesitate to question accepted assumptions and traditions, and persist in the search for answers. Only by thinking critically and creatively can you freely question, brainstorm, and evaluate to find the most fitting ideas, solutions, decisions, arguments, and plans.

You use critical-thinking mind actions in everything you do in school and in your daily life. In this chapter and in some of the other study skills chapters, you will notice mind-action icons placed where they can help you to understand how your mind is working.

In Chinese writing, this character has two meanings: chaos and opportunity. The character communicates the belief that every challenging, chaotic, and demanding situation in life also presents an opportunity. By responding to challenges in a positive and active way, you can discover the opportunity that lies within the chaos.

Let this concept reassure you as you explore the challenges of your learning and your life as a college student. You may be going through a time of chaos and change in career, educational, and personal areas. No matter how difficult the problems and decisions you encounter, you have the ability and creativity to persevere. Developing your critical thinking skills will help you create opportunities to learn, grow, and improve.

Chapter 2   Building Thinking Skills

Name _____   Date _____

LIFE THINKING: Applying What You Learn

2.1 *Make an Important Decision*

In this series of exercises, you will use the seven mind actions and the decision-making steps presented in this chapter. First, write here the decision you need to make. Choose an important decision that has to be made soon.

_____

_____

Step 1: Name your goal. Be specific: What goal, or desired effects, do you seek from this decision? For example, if your decision is a choice between two jobs, the effects you want might be financial security, convenience, experience, or anything else that is a priority to you. It also could be a combination of these effects. Write down the desired effects that together make up your goal. Note priorities by numbering the effects in order of importance.

_____

_____

_____

_____

Step 2: Establish needs. Who and what will be affected by your decision? If you are deciding how to finance your education and you have a family to support, for example, you must take into consideration their needs as well as your own when exploring options.

   List here the people, things, or situations that may be affected by your decision and indicate how your decision will affect them.

_____

_____

_____

_____

Step 3: Check out your options. Consider any options you can imagine even if they seem impossible or unlikely; you can evaluate them later. Some decisions have only two options (to move to a new apartment or not; to get a new roommate or not); others have a wider selection of choices. For example, if you are a full-time student and the parent of a child, you must coordinate your class schedule with the child's needs. Options could be the following: (1) put the child in day-care, (2) ask a relative to care for the child, (3) hire a full-time nanny, or (4) arrange your class schedule so you can balance the duties with another parent. List three possible options for your decision. Then evaluate the potential effects of each.

Option 1 _____

Positive effects _____

Negative effects _____

Option 2 _____

Positive effects _____

Negative effects _____

Option 3 _____

Positive effects _____

Negative effects _____

Have you or someone else ever made a decision similar to the one you are about to make? What can you learn from that decision that may help you?

_____

_____

_____

Step 4: Make your decision. Taking your entire analysis into account, decide what to do. Write your decision here.

_____

_____

_____

Step 5: Act on your decision. This is perhaps the most important step.

Step 6: Evaluate the result. After you have acted on your decision, evaluate how everything turned out. Did you achieve the effects you wanted to achieve? What were the effects on you? On others? On the situation? To what extent were they positive, negative, or some of both? List three effects here. Name each effect, circle Positive or Negative, and explain that evaluation.

1. Effect   Positive   Negative

Why? _____

2. Effect   Positive   Negative

Why? _____

3. Effect   Positive   Negative

Why? _____

Final evaluation: Write one statement in reaction to the decision you made. Indicate whether you believe the decision was useful or not useful, and why. Indicate any adjustments that could have made the effects of your decision more positive.

_____

_____

_____

 TEAM THINKING: Working Together

2.2 *Group Problem Solving*

As a class, brainstorm a list of problems in your lives. Write the problems on the board or on a large piece of paper attached to an easel. Include any problems you feel comfortable discussing with others. Problems may involve school, relationships, jobs, discrimination, parenting, housing, procrastination, and others. Divide into groups of two to four with each group choosing or being assigned one problem to work on.

First use the problem investigation worksheet below to clearly *define the problem.* Make notes about perspectives, problem parts, and observations. Summarize your findings and use them to make sure the problem is worth solving. If for some reason you decide it is not, choose another problem to work on.

Once you have defined a problem worth solving, use the problem-solving flowchart below to analyze the problem in depth. Use the chapter information on problem solving as a guide.

1. *State the problem.* As a group, state your problem specifically, without causes ("I'm not attending all of my classes" is better than "lack of motivation"). Record the effects of the problem. List what causes the problem. Then analyze these causes and effects. Look for "hidden" causes (you may perceive that traffic makes you late to school, but getting up too late might be the hidden cause).

2. *Brainstorm possible solutions.* Determine the most likely causes of the problem. From those causes, derive possible solutions. Record all the ideas that group members offer. After ten minutes or so, each group member should choose one possible solution to explore independently.

3. *Explore each solution.* In thinking independently through the assigned solution, each group member should (a) weigh the positive and negative effects, (b) consider similar problems, (c) determine whether the problem requires a different strategy from other problems like it, and (d) describe how the solution affects the causes of the problem. Evaluate your assigned solution. Is it a good one? Will it work?

4. *Choose your top solution(s).* Come together again as a group. Take turns sharing your observations and recommendations, and then take a vote: Which solution is the best? You may have a tie or combine two different solutions. Either way is fine. Different solutions suit different people and situations. Although it's not always possible to reach agreement, try to find the solution that works for most of the group.

Problem-Investigation Worksheet

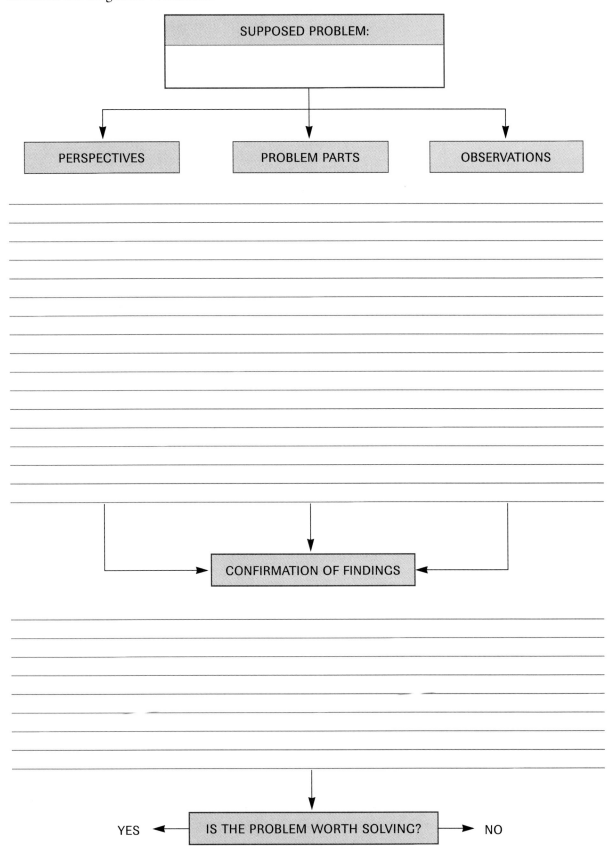

Problem-Solving Flowchart

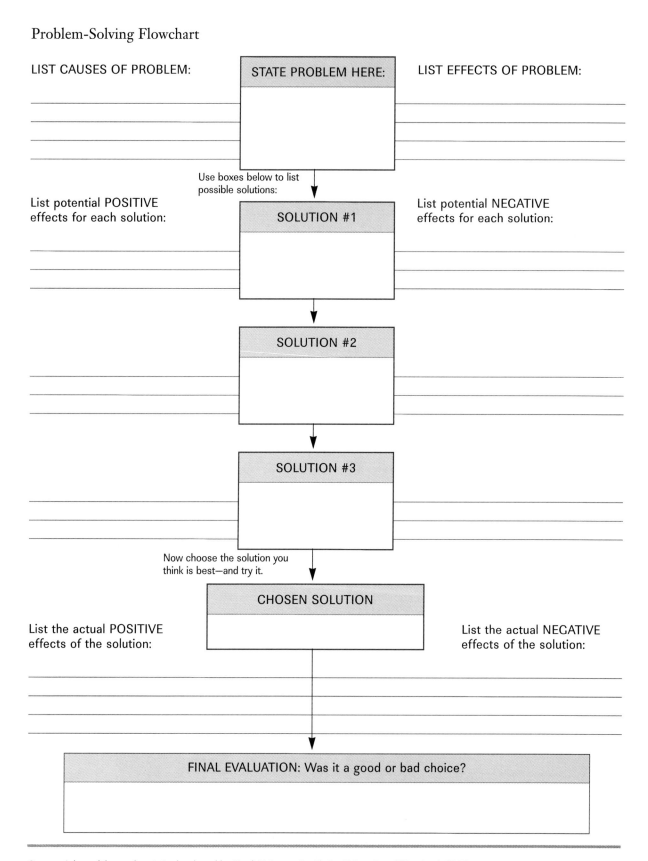

Source: Adapted from a heuristic developed by Frank T. Lyman Jr., Ph.D., University of Maryland, 1983.

5. *Evaluate the solution you decide is best.* When you decide on your top solution or solutions, discuss what would happen if you were to go through with it. What do you predict would be the positive and negative effects of this solution? Would it turn out to be a truly good solution for everyone?

 WORK THINKING: Career Portfolio

 2.3 *Find a Career on the Idea Wheel*

Your creative mind can come up with an idea when you least expect it. Many people report having brainstorms while exercising, driving, in the shower, upon waking, or even while dreaming. When the pressure is off, the mind is often more free to roam through uncharted territory and bring back treasures.

Grabbing ideas when they surface will help you make the most of your creativity. If you let ideas pass, they will roll back into your subconscious as if on a wheel. Because you never know how big the wheel is, you can't be sure when that idea will roll to the top again. That's why writers carry notebooks—they need to grab thoughts when they come to the top of the wheel.

Put your creative energy to work by engaging in a brainstorming session on what you might do for a living. Don't put a time limit on your brainstorming. Just stay aware of the thoughts that roll to the top of your wheel, seeing how what you read, hear, and experience may inspire ideas about career paths, jobs, or even specific tasks that you might want to explore. Use this chapter's information about enhancing creativity as a guide. Don't judge or discard ideas. Take advantage of free time and creative atmospheres, gather input from all sources, and get off the beaten track.

The moment an idea occurs to you, write it down. Gather your ideas together and keep a running list where you keep your other career portfolio material. You may want to keep a book by your bed to catch ideas that pop up before, during, or after sleep.

 QUESTIONING YOUR WORLD:
Information Literacy Journal

To record your thoughts, use a separate journal or the lined pages at the end of the chapter.

 2.4 *Influences on Your Decisions*

Your daily decision making comes under the influence of a constant stream of information. Television, magazines, friends, and family members pass on their opinions about what you should eat, wear, read, listen to, believe, and more. Think critically about what most influences your day-to-day decisions. Discuss your strongest influences, and why you value those influences the most.

Journal

Name _____ Date _____

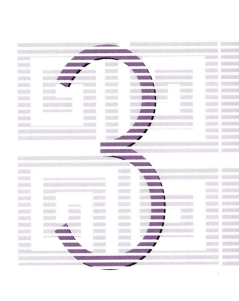

Critical Thinking

Thinking Logically

Evaluating Fact and Opinion, Assumption, and Argument

I n questioning information critically, one of your primary goals is to find out whether it is true or reliable. Based on that assessment, you can decide what value the information has to you. Information with high value leads to higher quality thinking and more effective output (solutions and ideas). For example, if you are deciding whether to take a job, a true statement about job expectations will be more useful than a false one. If you were to take a job based on what proves to be a false statement—for instance, if you were told that overtime hours are not a factor in promotions and then find out that they are—you may wish you had turned it down.

In this chapter you will explore how to question statements and assumptions, determining whether they are fact or opinion and what their value is for you. You will look at both constructing your own arguments and evaluating those of others. Finally, the chapter will cover common thinking errors that you will encounter in your own thinking and that of others.

In this chapter, you will explore answers to the following questions:

- What distinguishes fact from opinion?
- How do you identify and evaluate assumptions?
- How do you evaluate an argument?
- How do you construct an effective argument?
- What are some common errors in thinking?

WHAT DISTINGUISHES FACT FROM OPINION?

Distinguishing between fact and opinion is not as simple as it looks and often takes effort and focus. In addition, the modern onslaught of information brings with it a particular challenge. With everything that comes your way, how can you know what to believe? In a given day you can be presented with bits of information such as the following, and many more:

- Today's workplace increasingly values teamwork.
- This product will freshen your breath all day.
- The President has lied under oath.
- The gene for Rh-positive blood is dominant over the gene for Rh-negative blood.
- Social Security will be bankrupt in fifty years.
- Manx cats are born without tails.

Accepting everything you hear as true would almost certainly put you in a state of confusion. How can you reconcile opposing statements? How can you accommodate a variety of perspectives? Your key to being able to process information, and choose what you believe will be useful to you, lies in your ability to distinguish between fact and opinion and determine degrees of truth and **fallacy** in opinions.

TERMS

Fallacy
A false or
mistaken idea.

The Nature of Fact and Opinion

According to the dictionary, *fact* is information presented as objectively real and verifiable. *Opinion* is defined as a belief, conclusion, or judgment and is inherently difficult, if not impossible, to verify. Whether you are studying for a test or doing research for a paper, being able to distinguish fact from opinion is crucial to your understanding of reading material and your ability to decide what information to believe and put to use. Table 3.1 shows some paired examples of facts and opinions.

TABLE 3.1   Comparison of paired examples of fact and opinion.

TOPIC	FACT	OPINION
Library cataloging systems	Computer databases have replaced card catalogs in most college libraries.	Computer databases are an improvement over ancient card catalogs.
Stock market	In 1999 the Dow Jones Industrial average rose above 10,000 for the first time.	The Dow Jones Industrial average will continue to grow throughout the first decade of the 21st century.
Human skeletal system	A normal human body has 150 bones.	People don't appreciate the strength of the human skeleton.
Animal speed	The cheetah has been clocked at speeds that establish it as the world's fastest animal.	No animal can ever escape the speed of the cheetah.
Weather	It's raining outside.	This is the worst rainstorm I've ever seen.

The facts in the table refer to the observable or measurable, whereas the opinions involve cause-and-effect exploration. For example, the exact number that the Dow Jones reaches on any given day can be verified through research. The numbers it will hit on any future date, however, cannot possibly be verified, as future dates have not yet occurred. Anyone forming an opinion about how the Dow will perform on future dates does so by evaluating the cause-and-effect patterns of past stock market and economic activity and makes a prediction based on those patterns. That prediction will always be an opinion.

Following are some indicators that will help you determine what is fact and what is opinion. Most are from the book *Stirring Up Thinking* by Ben E. Johnson.[1]

Indicators of Opinion

Indicators of opinion include:

- *Statements that show evaluation.* Evaluation involves a judgment of value. Therefore, any statement of value—such as, "Television is bad for children"—indicates an opinion. Words such as *bad, good, ridiculous, useful, pointless,* and *beneficial* indicate these kinds of value judgments.
- *Statements that predict future events.* Nothing that will happen in the future can be proven definitively in the present. Therefore, any statement of something that will happen in the future, even if it sounds like a fact—"Population growth will level out in the year 2050"—is an opinion.
- *Statements that use abstract words.* While something like "one gallon" can be defined, something like "love" has no specific, universal definition. **Abstract** words—*wellness, strength, hate, misery, success*—usually indicate an opinion.

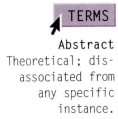

TERMS

Abstract
Theoretical; disassociated from any specific instance.

- *Statements that use emotional words.* Emotions are by nature unverifiable. Chances are that statements using words such as *delightful, nasty, miserable,* or *wonderful* will present an opinion.
- *Statements that use qualifiers.* Absolute **qualifiers**—such as *all, none, never,* and *always*—point to an opinion because statements don't often apply accurately to an entire class of subjects. For example, "All students need to work while in school" and "Teen marriages never last" are opinions. Facts using absolute qualifiers do exist—"All dogs are mammals"—but don't appear as often.

TERMS

Qualifiers
Descriptive words, such as *always, never,* or *often,* that change the meaning of another word or word group.

Indicators of Fact

Indicators of fact include:

- *Statements that deal with actual people, places, objects, and events.* If the existence of the elements involved can be verified through observation, chances are that the statement itself also can be proven true or false. "I ate three tacos for dinner" and "Jimmy Carter was a peanut farmer in Georgia" are examples of this principle.
- *Statements that use concrete words or measurable statistics.* Any statement that uses concrete, measurable terms and avoids the abstract is likely to be a fact. Examples include "Thirty-six inches constitute a yard" and "There are 2,512 full-time students enrolled this semester."

Differing Effects of Facts and Opinions

Fact and opinion generate different reactions. If you read a statement that you see as an opinion, you may focus on deciding whether you agree with that opinion according to how it is supported. If, in an article, you were to come upon the statement, "Working part-time is beneficial to college students," and you decide that this is an opinion, you probably would read further to see what facts (in this case, effects) the author uses to support that opinion. Based on the presentation of facts, you would decide whether you agree with the opinion.

Conversely, if you see a statement as fact, your focus probably will move toward evaluating the truth of that fact and how well it is used to support other ideas or opinions. Say you read, in the same article, the statement, "At ABC University, 74% of students who work part-time move immediately into the workforce after graduation, compared to 42% of nonworking students." First you might check the reference to see if you trust how the statistic was compiled. Then you might focus on seeing how well you think this statement supports the relative "goodness" of working part-time. You might even think it provides poor support—for example, you might question whether all college students actually want to go into the workforce right away or whether the students like the jobs they enter right after graduation.

You can put facts and opinions to use in your own communication when you want to create certain effects. Decide how you want to use them when writing or speaking persuasively (see Chapter 8).

Fact and Opinion Versus Truth and Falsehood

It's important to separate the concepts of "fact" and "opinion" from those of "true" and "false." Neither a fact nor an opinion is automatically true or false. Actually, a fact can be false and an opinion can be true. The status of any statement as fact or opinion has to do with how it is presented, not the inherent truth or falsehood of what it says. Noting particular characteristics of facts and opinions can help you to separate them from your idea of "true" and "false."

Facts Can Be Wrong

You may recognize that the third fact in Table 3.1—regarding the number of bones in the human body—is incorrect (actually, the normal adult human has 206 bones). A fact, or factual statement, does not necessarily have to be correct. Its status as fact is determined by how it is stated. The definition of a fact says that it is a statement *presented* as objectively real. Whether it is actually true is up to individual evaluation and investigation.

Here's an example: If someone tells you class is at 10:00, and upon checking your course catalog, you discover that it is actually at 11:00, that person has given you an incorrect statement of fact. In court, a witness for the prosecution often states facts that contradict other facts given by a witness for the defense. One may say that the man he saw running away from the car had short brown hair, for instance, and the other may say that the man was not running and that his hair was past the shoulder.

Opinions Can Seem Like Facts

A statement of opinion can masquerade as a fact, such as when it is accompanied by the kinds of definitive language and assertive tone that you might associate with a statement of fact. The following are opinions, even though they look like facts:

- The new "dress-down Fridays" policy has had no effect on office morale.
- A program of twenty to thirty minutes of vigorous exercise three to five times a week is essential for good health.

Factual-seeming statements like these may be revealed to be opinions if investigation shows any part of them to be unverifiable. But each one of the statements has an element that cannot be determined definitively:

- Whether absolutely no employees have experienced a morale boost from dressing down
- The chance that the same frequency and level of exercise would have the same effect on all people

At times you will encounter a statement of opinion that you think is a fact, such as when you find yourself agreeing strongly with the opinion. Don't discount your feelings; "not verifiable" is not the same as "inaccurate." Opinions are not necessarily wrong even if you cannot prove them. Stay aware, however, of how you evaluate the statement. In your mind, separate the statement from your feeling about it. Even if you agree with an opinion, it retains its status as an opinion.

Using Questions to Investigate Truth and Accuracy

Once you label a statement as a fact or opinion, explore its degree of truth. Both facts and opinions require investigation through questioning. Investigating the truth and accuracy of information, whether it is presented as fact or opinion, is the mark of an awake critical thinker. Critical-thinking experts Sylvan Barnet and Hugo Bedau state that when you test for the truth of a statement, you "determine whether what it asserts corresponds with reality; if it does, then it is true, and if it doesn't, then it is false."[2] Asking questions using the mind actions will help you determine in what ways or to what degree a statement is similar to, or different from, reality.

Questions you may ask include the following:

- What facts or examples provide evidence of the truth of this statement?
- How does the maker of the statement know this to be true?
- Is there another fact that contradicts this statement or information?
- How reliable are the sources of information?
- What about this statement is similar to other facts?
- Are the stated effects of this information the real effects?
- What might be the effects of treating this statement as true—or as false?
- How could I test the validity of this statement or information?

You may not always arrive at a definitive decision about the truth of a statement, especially if it is an opinion. No matter what you ultimately decide, however, the process of questioning will help you to determine the value of the statement to you. Even if you cannot verify an opinion, for example, looking at its source, similar or different opinions, and the effects of adopting that particular opinion will help you to decide if that opinion is of worth to you.

Another crucial part of investigating truth is questioning the assumptions that you and others hold, and that are the underlying force in shaping opinions.

 ## HOW DO YOU IDENTIFY AND EVALUATE ASSUMPTIONS?

"If it's more expensive, it's better." "The most effective studying takes place in a library." These statements reveal assumptions—evaluations or generalizations influenced by values and based on observing cause and effect—that often hide within seemingly truthful statements. Basically, any time you believe or disbelieve something automatically, without investigating it through questioning, you are making an assumption. An assumption is a kind of opinion.

An **assumption** can influence choices: Assuming that you should earn a certain college degree or own a car can lead you to the college registrar or to

TERMS

Assumption
An idea or statement accepted as true without examination or proof.

the auto dealer. Often, people neither question whether their assumptions make sense nor challenge the assumptions of others. It's easier and faster just to assume and move on. This, however, isn't always beneficial to the person who is making the assumption—or to anyone about whom the assumption is being made.

Types of Assumptions

Briefly, there are two different types of assumptions.[2]

1. *Reality assumptions* *refer to assumptions about how things are.* These usually are presented as facts. Reality assumptions are based on cause-and-effect reasoning (when you observe certain effects, you assume the cause). "Students with higher SATs do better in class" is one example of a reality assumption (observing that students with higher SATs tend to do better in class, the assumption is made that those SAT scores cause the better performance).

2. *Value assumptions* *refer to assumptions about how people believe something ought to be.* These usually are presented as opinions. For example, "Children are better off having two parents" is a value assumption. Like reality assumptions, value assumptions are based on evaluation of effects. Reality assumptions often underlie value assumptions—for example, a reality assumption such as, "Children from two-parent families perform better in school" may underlie the value assumption, "Children are better off having two parents."

You can remember the two types by linking them to what you know about fact and opinion. When a statement you assume to be true is a fact, you probably are making a reality assumption. When a statement you assume to be true is an opinion, you probably are making a value assumption. Both kinds of assumptions require the same kind of questioning, and both can be equally harmful if accepted or rejected without investigation. Table 3.2 presents some examples of reality and value assumptions.

TABLE 3.2   Examples of reality and value assumptions.

REALITY ASSUMPTIONS	VALUE ASSUMPTIONS
Drinking bland soda reduces stomach acid.	Upset stomach sufferers should drink ginger ale.
Newspaper readers are ten times more likely to vote than people who don't read newspapers.	People should read a newspaper every day.
Half of gun purchasers intend to use their guns illegally.	Gun purchasers should be subject to background checks.
Fewer breast-fed babies develop asthma than do bottle-fed babies.	Babies need to be fed breast milk.

Sources of Assumptions

Assumptions can come from many different sources. Throughout your life, as you learn and grow, you are exposed to ideas and perspectives. It's common to absorb these without evaluating them, especially if you learn them when you are young. Sources of assumptions include:

- *Parents and relatives.* Your family members make assumptions about all sorts of things, and chances are they passed many assumptions to you early on. Assumptions can cover a wide range of opinion. A few sample assumptions that parents have passed on to their children are: "It's important to go to college." "College is a waste of money—you're better off getting a job." "You should work to earn your college tuition." "You shouldn't work during college because that will take time away from your studies." Assumptions like these are all evaluations based on selected causes and effects.

- *Television and other media.* Watch an evening of television, switching channels from time to time, and you will hear and see assumptions about everything from cooking utensils to characteristics of different human races to the American way of marriage to what kids should read in school. Statements based on assumptions can be just as convincing coming from a situation comedy as they can from the six o'clock news. Every TV program or advertisement comes from someone's perspective, and that person might be trying to communicate an opinion based on an assumption.

- *Friends.* Everyone is susceptible to the influence of friends. You tend to trust the opinions of people you like. Therefore, your friends' assumptions may find their way into your life. Look at the way you dress, the entertainment you prefer, the lifestyle you enjoy. Chances are you picked up some of your choices from your favorite people.

- *Personal experiences.* Experiences leave a strong impression. Reading about a tornado, for example, is not as affecting as going through one yourself. For this reason, personal experience can easily lead to assumptions. It can be difficult, for example, for a person who has been mugged on a city street not to assume that all urban environments are dangerous. When you experience one memorable effect, you might assume it to be lurking everywhere.

It's possible that the assumptions you make about the world around you are appropriate and are based on reliable evidence and investigation. It's just as possible, though, that your assumptions can close your mind to opportunities and even cause harm. For example, the assumption that people who speak with a regional or foreign accent are less intelligent or less qualified has caused a great deal of harm through opinions expressed and actions taken. The key is to investigate each assumption as you would any statement of fact or opinion. Make sure that what you assume is based on an accurate, balanced analysis of cause and effect. If it isn't, be willing to make a change.

Investigating with Questions

The first step in uncovering any assumptions that underlie a statement is to look at the cause-and-effect pattern of the statement, seeing if the way reasons move to conclusions is supported by evidence or involves a hidden assumption.[3] If you discover an assumption, ask these questions to investigate it:

1. In what cases is this assumption valid or invalid? What examples prove or disprove it?
2. Has making this assumption had positive effects on me or others? Has it had negative effects? In what ways?
3. What is the source of this assumption? How reliable is the source (i.e., can the sources be counted on to have investigated this assumption)?
4. What harm could be done by always taking this assumption as fact?

Take this statement: "The most productive schedule involves getting started early in the day." First of all, a cause-and-effect evaluation shows that this statement reveals the following assumption: "The morning is when people have the most energy and are most able to get things done." Here's how you might use the questions to investigate that assumption:

1. This assumption might be generally true for people who enjoy early morning hours and have high energy during that part of the day. But the assumption may be not true for people who work best in the afternoon or evening hours.
2. Society's basic standard of daytime classes and 8:00 a.m. to 5:00 p.m. working hours supports this assumption. Therefore, the assumption may work for people who have early jobs and classes. It may not work, however, for people who work shifts or who take evening classes.
3. Maybe people who believe this assumption were raised to start their days early. Perhaps they merely go along with what seems to be society's standard, based on earlier centuries when almost everyone had to get up early and work all day just to provide food and shelter for themselves and their families. Still, plenty of people operate on a different schedule and enjoy successful, productive lives.
4. Taking this assumption as fact could hurt people who don't operate at their peak in the earlier hours. For example, if a "night owl" tries to take early classes, he or she may experience concentration problems that would not necessarily be the case later in the day. In situations that favor their specific characteristics—later classes and jobs, career areas that don't require early morning work—these people have just as much potential as anyone else to succeed.

Be careful to question all assumptions, not just those that seem problematic from the start. An assumption may have different effects in different situations. An example of an assumption with varied effects is, "We should keep finding new uses for computers." Computers indeed have improved industry and communication. Many people, however, have lost jobs because the computer does what they used to do by hand. In addition, some people become addicted to computers and neglect their responsibilities. After investigating the positive and negative effects of a situation, evaluate and form your opinion.

Don't just stop at your own assumptions, either. Respectfully question the assumptions of family, friends, and coworkers. Ask them why they believe what they believe, and offer alternatives. Question the assumptions of organizations by investigating their policies and voicing your opinion. Your state and national governments make assumptions all the time. Your Representative and Senator may vote yes or no on a bill based on what they assume voters want. Investigate where they stand on the issues, and if they have made an incorrect assumption about your wants, challenge that assumption with a letter or e-mail. Bring a message of questioning into the world of automatically accepted assumptions.

> "The human mind is our fundamental resource."
> JOHN F. KENNEDY

HOW DO YOU EVALUATE AN ARGUMENT?

In this case, *argument* refers to a persuasive case that you make to prove or disprove a point. It is a set of connected ideas (often opinions) supported by examples. Arguments pop up in textbook reading, articles in newspapers and magazines, television shows, lectures from instructors, speeches, and discussions with supervisors, coworkers, and friends. Any time a statement is presented and supported, an argument is taking place.

It's easy—and common—to accept or reject an argument outright, according to whether it fits with one's own opinions and views. If you ask questions about an argument, however, you will be able to determine its validity and will learn more from it. Furthermore, critical thinking will help you avoid accepting opinions and assumptions that are not supported by evidence.

The Structure of an Argument

TERMS

Premise
Something supposed as a basis of argument; a preliminary assumption.

Essentially, an argument is structured according to deductive reasoning principles (see Chapter 1). Based on a particular topic and issue, it starts with an idea or **premise**, gives examples to support that premise, and finally asserts a conclusion. It's helpful to establish the issue of the argument—what the argument is about, minus the bias of its premise—to see the structure more clearly. Here's one example:

The topic:	Herbal supplements
The issue:	Whether to take herbal supplements
The premise:	Herbal supplements can be a health hazard when they are taken in larger and unadvised amounts.
The evidence:	Statistics about the potential side effects of three sample herbal supplements, and verifiable stories about people who have died or suffered severe health problems because of overuse of a supplement.
The conclusion:	Herbal supplements should be treated as medication and regulated by the Federal Drug Administration.

Types of Evidence

Evidence—the examples an argument presents to support an idea and persuade the audience that it is valid—comes in many forms. Explore what forms tend to persuade an audience and the structure that these forms of evidence take.

What Persuades an Audience

To **persuade** is to influence the reader or listener to accept the message. Many different techniques and tactics can be used to persuade. Some include:[4]

- *Knowledge*—Exhibiting knowledge can impress and inform.
- *Honesty*—Appearing honest can promote respect, which inspires attention.
- *Bias*—If similar to the bias of the audience, this can win people over.
- *Likability*—An audience is more likely to consider the opinions of someone it likes.
- *Motivational thoughts*—Feeling energized and motivated might encourage acceptance.
- *Rational appeal*—A logical argument can lead a thinking audience to appreciation.
- *Emotional appeal*—An audience is likely to be persuaded by something that stirs strong emotions.

What works with one person or audience may not work with another. You may read an article and think it's right on target, whereas someone else may think it's way off base. Reaction depends on the audience's perspective, background, bias, personality traits, or personal opinions. For example, a political speech made by a Democrat, if it adheres to principles the Democratic party commonly accepts, most likely will appeal more to Democrats than to Republicans.

TERMS

Persuade
To convince some-
one through
argument or
reasoning to
adopt a belief,
position, or
course of action.

Structure of Evidence

Ways to structure evidence are as individual as the person making the argument. You might see an argument that presents the evidence up front with a list of statistics. You might read an article that weaves evidence in later. You might hear a speech that is so confusing to you that you can't discern where the evidence appears at all.

Look for two major structures of evidence—*separate support* and *chain support*.[5] Knowing them will help you understand what the evidence is saying and evaluate whether the evidence adequately supports the argument. Figure 3.1 shows visual representations of each structure.

Separate support. In this case, the argument presents different pieces of evidence, not necessarily related, yet shows each of them to support the argument. Their element of similarity is in how they provide support. For example, a teenager arguing for more independence at home might cite examples of having done well in school, kept up with family responsibilities, and adhered to curfews.

FIGURE 3.1 Types of argument support.

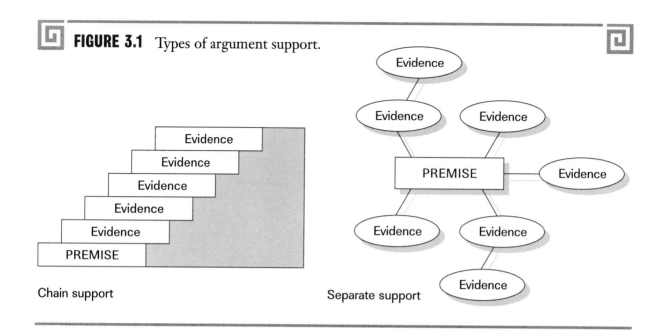

Chain support

Separate support

Chain support. Here the argument uses a set of reasons that build on one another. For example, an argument about what caused the dinosaurs to become extinct may work its way through a chronological series of ecological events that occurred at the time the dinosaurs died out. Or an argument about what caused a person to commit a crime may detail a connected series of events in that person's life prior to the crime.

Evaluating the Evidence

The center of thinking critically about an argument involves evaluating the evidence. Your evaluation should consist of two parts:

1. Evaluating the quality of the evidence itself
2. Evaluating whether the evidence adequately supports the premise

These two considerations will give you a fairly good idea of whether the argument works. If good-quality evidence (true input) combines with good-quality use of evidence (valid reasoning), you get a solid argument (true output). Generally, a "good" or successful argument:[6]

- Makes clear premises and conclusions.
- Persuades based on evidence, not on unsupported claims that appeal to emotion.
- Shows credible and sufficient evidence.
- Considers the other side.

Quality of evidence. To see whether the evidence itself is valid, ask the following questions:

- What type of evidence is it—fact or opinion?

- How is the evidence similar to, or different from, what I already believe to be true?
- Where is the evidence from? Are those sources reliable and free of bias? (examples of sources include intuition, authorities, personal experience, and observation)

Quality of support. To determine whether you think the evidence successfully makes the argument, ask these questions:

- Do examples logically follow from ideas, and ideas logically lead to given examples?
- Does the evidence show any similarity to what I consider common sense?
- Are there enough pieces of evidence to support the conclusion well?
- Do I know of any competing views or pieces of evidence that differ from this evidence and lead to another, different idea?
- Does any piece of this evidence seem to contradict another piece—i.e., do they seem to lead to different conclusions, or do they seem to be causes of different effects?
- Do the examples connect to the idea?
- Does the argument reveal any hidden assumptions masquerading as factual evidence?
- If the evidence includes first-hand accounts of events or testimonials, how are they similar to or different from your own experience? If they are different, do they ring true anyway?
- Has the argument evaluated all of the positive and negative effects involved? Is there any unconsidered negative effect to what the conclusion is arguing? For whom, and why?
- Do these examples point to a different conclusion than the argument makes, or might more than one possible conclusion logically be drawn?

The more you read and listen to arguments, the more adept you will become at evaluating their effectiveness. Make a habit of reading a newspaper and listening to public radio stations. Pay attention to the views of people around you. Make an effort not to take anything as true or false without spending some time asking questions about it first. These efforts will prepare you for constructing your own effective arguments.

 ## HOW DO YOU CONSTRUCT AN EFFECTIVE ARGUMENT?

You often will encounter situations in which your success depends on your ability to persuade someone, either verbally or in writing, to agree with you. You might have to write a paper persuading the reader that a certain scientific idea changed the world, for example, or you might have to persuade a prospective employer that you are the one for the job.

FIGURE 3.2 The structure of an argument.

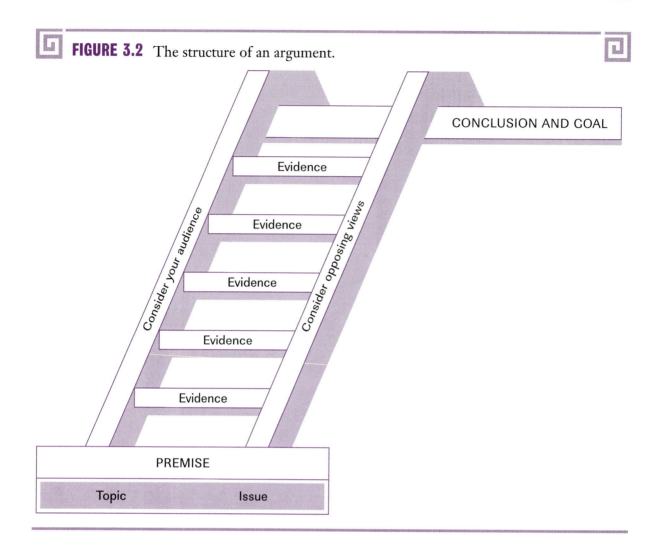

When you decide to work toward a major life goal—admission to a college, winning a job, committing to a relationship—building a persuasive argument or case through critical thinking can help you achieve what you want. Use the following strategies to put the mind actions to work. Figure 3.2 illustrates the structure and purpose of an argument.

Establish the Premise

First, define a premise, or idea—what you want to argue. This is your basic framework for the entire argument and will give you a context in which to fit the rest of the structure. Set up a foundation for your premise by establishing the topic of your argument and the issue at hand. *Topic* refers to the subject being discussed, independent of any opinion or question, and *issue* refers to the question that your premise and argument will answer in a certain way. Here are two examples:

Topic: Grading
Issue: Whether courses should be graded on a curve
Premise: Courses should never be graded using a curve.

Topic:	Computer maintenance
Issue:	When virus-detection programs should be updated
Premise:	Virus-detection programs should be updated the instant a new version of the software appears.

In addition, define what goal you want to reach by making your argument. If you are writing a paper, you may want to achieve a level of knowledge and a good grade from your instructor. With other arguments, you may want to achieve a job offer, a change in the status of a relationship, votes in your favor, a special privilege, or simply the satisfaction of knowing you have made people think. No argument provides an absolute guarantee of achieving a goal, but establishing the goal ahead of time will allow you to focus on it and will give you your best shot.

Gather and Organize Examples, or Evidence, in Support

What will support your request? Gather as much evidence as you can first, and then evaluate what evidence is best and decide how you can best use it. Use the following strategies.

Organize and clearly express your evidence. Using separate support or chain support, put your evidence in some sort of logical order. Consider your work carefully to make sure you have not committed any common thinking errors (see discussion later in this chapter).

Anticipate questions. Think of the argument from the audience's point of view. What do you think the other person or people might ask you to explain? Address those questions in how you choose and present your evidence.

Consider the other side. How might someone argue the complete opposite of your premise? What could someone bring up that argues against what you want to conclude? To be thorough about covering your bases, think it through from the other side. To defend against opposing points, decide what you will say. You might even want to address the other side directly, without being asked, showing that you understand its points and presenting well-supported ways in which you disagree with them.

Be flexible. You never know what will happen as you present your argument, or what questions someone reading your paper will raise. You might win your audience over easily—or it may turn out to be tougher than you thought. If you are making your argument in person, rehearse your responses to questions, so you will be as prepared as possible to handle any twists and turns the conversation takes.

Consider your audience. When you know what you want to prove, consider to whom you are proving it. With each piece of evidence you gather and evaluate, keep your audience in mind. If you acknowledge where the audience is starting from, you can move them more effectively from their own set of ideas to a place where they can consider yours. What perspective does your audi-

ence come from, and what biases may the audience hold? What assumptions might the audience make, and what values underlie these assumptions? What moves the audience—facts and figures, appeals to values or emotions, or information that takes the audience's needs into consideration? A varied audience might complicate matters. Still, whatever information you have on whom you are trying to persuade will help you formulate your argument.

You might need more, stronger, or more tailored evidence to back up a less common or controversial premise than you would to support a commonly held idea. During a football game, for example, an advertising company will have an easier time selling the merits of consuming beer than it will selling wine. Similarly, convincing an instructor that you should be allowed to retake a test might take more work than asking for a chance to do an extra-credit assignment.

Draw a Conclusion

After you have presented your evidence, formulate a conclusion that summarizes how this evidence supports the initial premise you made. Include any new insights you had in the process of presenting your evidence.

Keep your goal in mind and let that inform your conclusion. For example, if your goal is to fulfill the requirements of an assignment, make sure that you have done so and that your conclusion clearly shows it. If your goal is to persuade an audience to adopt your point of view, formulate a conclusion that hits your most persuasive points.

A Sample Argument

As an example, imagine that you want a raise and promotion to a new position at work. Here is one way to present your argument:

Your topic:	Job status
Your issue:	What role you should have at this point in your career
Your premise:	You deserve a raise and promotion
Your audience:	Your supervisor (who may or may not be receptive to your argument, depending on your relationship)

As supporting evidence, you have consistently received good performance reviews and you have ideas for the position you want. You believe that your experience and high level of motivation will have positive effects for the company. You feel a bit stifled in your current job, and bored, and you believe that increased job happiness on your part will lead to increased productivity—for you, as well as for the others with and for whom you work.

Questions you anticipate include: What have you achieved in your current position? What do you know about the position you want to take? What new and creative ideas do you have?

Your supervisor might say that you may not be able to handle the new position's longer hours because of your part-time school schedule. In preparation, you could look into what it would take to reschedule classes and make adjustments in your other commitments. Your supervisor might say that you are more valuable where you are now. In response, you could emphasize the positive effects (value) that you plan to bring to the company in your new position.

> *Your conclusion:*   Promoting you would have positive effects for both you and the company.

Above all, work to remain flexible. You never know what turn a conversation will take, or how a reader will interpret a written argument. Keep your mind active and ready to address any surprises that come your way, and watch out for errors in thinking—on your part or on the part of your audience.

WHAT ARE SOME COMMON THINKING ERRORS?

Trying to think clearly, critically, and effectively about everything you encounter is a tall order. Human fallibility leads everyone to commit thinking errors from time to time. In some situations, flawed thinking may make your day harder than it has to be. In others, however, it can cause harm, from a small setback to grand catastrophe. False assumptions about Africans and Jews, for example, played a large part in the slave trade of the 1700s and 1800s and the Holocaust of World War II.

Common thinking errors can be divided into two categories: errors involving the information used in the argument, or *input errors*, and errors involving how that information is structured, or *output errors*.

Input Errors

In making input errors, people mishandle the facts or evidence before they begin to use it in a thinking process. Following are common input errors.

False premise. If, in making assumptions, you base an argument on an incorrect premise, your thinking will be flawed from the start. For example, certain ancient scientists, assuming that the sun revolved around the earth, made flawed arguments about the solar system and universe.

Leaving out information (also called *selective perception* or *selective omission*). Here, the person making the argument uses only the evidence that can most effectively support his or her point. Sometimes intentional, other times unconscious, a person can leave out information because of personal bias or of ignorance. For example, an argument in support of raising the minimum wage might deliberately omit the potential negative effects of the raise so as to be more convincing. At the same time, a person could make this argument and simply not be aware of, or not have explored, the down side, and for that reason not indicate it in the argument.

Either/or thinking (also called *black/white thinking, false dilemma*, and *polarization*). This refers to a simplistic argument presenting only two opposing perspectives or choices—i.e., "Either we put students in uniforms or we set the stage for chaos in the schools" or, "Either you take this course or you won't graduate." In its attempt to simplify an issue, either/or thinking ignores any other possible solutions. For example, in the second situation above, a little problem solving might reveal that an internship could earn you the same kind of credit that the course would give. Some situations do only have two alternatives—for example, a student can either attend or not attend class—but most have gray areas or other possibilities that deserve attention.

False or misidentified cause (also called *post hoc ergo propter hoc*, which means "after it therefore because of it" in Latin). In looking to form a cause-and-effect explanation, people might link a cause and effect that are unrelated. "Juvenile delinquents fall into trouble because they come from broken homes" is one example. To assume that having divorced parents is necessarily a direct cause of delinquency is mistaken. Further examination would reveal many children of divorced parents who avoid trouble, as well as others who get into trouble despite intact homes.

Distracting or irrelevant information (also called a *red herring*). One common argumentation tactic is to try to distract the audience with information that throws it off the track of the argument (especially useful when the argument is poorly constructed). An example is: "Gun control laws should be repealed. The Constitution says we have a right to bear arms, and this country is not upholding its Constitution. Recent violations of the First Amendment are really getting out of hand." This argument detracts from the effects of uncontrolled guns by setting the audience to thinking about violations of the right-to-freedom of speech or of the press.

Output Errors

With output errors, people mishandle the way they connect facts to ideas in the structure of their thinking. The following are some common output errors.

Slippery slope. This error has an element of false cause. It occurs when the assumption is that an extreme condition will follow automatically from a less extreme occurrence or situation. For example, a slippery-slope argument about Internet shopping might state that within ten years no one will ever again leave their homes to shop or bank and that people will become completely sedentary. Although a slippery-slope argument often has some valid elements, the conclusion is exaggerated and won't necessarily follow directly from the cause.

Circular reasoning (also called *begging the question*). Here the argument uses, as its supporting reasons, restatements of the argument itself. This results in the argument having no valid support. For example: "You and I aren't getting along because we always fight." Not getting along and fighting are essentially different ways of stating the same issue. Nowhere are causes given for the fighting.

Overgeneralization (including forms of *stereotyping*). People commonly use generalizations to process information. When you overgeneralize, however, you take your opinion of a part and judge the whole based on that opinion, moving carelessly from example to idea. Such a generalization does not necessarily apply. Stereotyping is a good example, such as if someone knows one studious Asian person and then generalizes that all Asian people are studious. As another example, if you were to do poorly on an essay test, you would assume, or generalize, that you can't take essay tests well. Some assumptions are hasty generalizations.

Appealing to authority. To cite an authority when trying to make a point sounds impressive. Not every authority is reliable, though. When you see an authority cited or want to cite one, ask questions: What expertise or training does this authority have? Does this authority have reason to know the facts? Is this authority as free as possible of bias? For example, a movie advertisement might run quotes such as, "Brilliant!" "An incredible film!" "Stunning!" Then, when you look closely, you find that the sources quoted are unrecognizable newspapers or radio disk jockeys, and not the *New York Times* or nationally known film critics.

Appeal to emotions. To react to an emotional appeal is human, and many arguments take advantage of this—often, unfortunately, to distract from a poorly supported argument. You might see an appeal to pity—"Can you help these poor people?"; fear—"Do you want your children meeting this man on the street?"; pride—"Give your family the best!"; or flattery—"It costs more, but you're worth it." These statements may or may not be based on truth. The point is that no reasons or effects are given to support them.

Appeal to tradition. Bringing long-standing tradition into the discussion can be effective—and distracting. People often believe that a way of seeing or doing something is good just because that's the way it's been done for a long time. Traditions die hard. An advertisement that says "just like your grandma made," for example, appeals to tradition.

Attacking the person (also called *ad hominem*, meaning "to the man" in Latin, or *name calling*). Someone who doesn't have a solid defense against an opposing argument might attack the person making that argument, to distract from the ineffective defense. Politicians often do this during a political race. One may discount another's views because he didn't serve in the armed services or because she was investigated by the IRS, even though these factors don't necessarily have any bearing on what that person could accomplish in office.

Appeal to ignorance. Often, the audience does not know enough about the topic to be able to question the reasoning. Therefore, if no one can prove it wrong, an argument is assumed to be right. The person making the argument might try to present unverifiable evidence as support for an argument so no one will challenge it. This thinking error is often used in political situations, such as in discussions of economics.

Appeal to majority (also called *peer pressure* and the *bandwagon appeal*). People are naturally susceptible to their perception of people around them. It's easy to assume that if a large number of people are doing, saying, or thinking something, it therefore must be valid. Advertisements often imply that "everyone's got one" or "everybody's doing it" and thereby try to convince you to get or do it too. This fallacy is part of why it is difficult to dislodge a practice or idea that has been around for a long time. For example, when African-Americans had never voted before, it took a great deal of effort to shift public opinion in favor of giving them the right to vote.

No one thinks flawlessly all the time, so you won't always be able to avoid making errors. The more informed you are about thinking errors, however, the more likely you will be to recognize them, in your own thinking and that of others. Once you recognize them, you can make the effort to address them and to improve your thinking.

> "Education should convert the mind into a living fountain and not a reservoir."
> JOHN M. MASON

ཤེས་ར་ཡེང་ཞིག

In Sanskrit, the written language of India and other Hindu countries, the characters above read *sem ma yeng chik*, meaning, "Do not be distracted." This advice can refer to the focus for a task or job at hand, the concentration required to think critically and talk through a problem, the mental discipline of meditation, and many other situations.

Think of this concept as you strive to evaluate the truth of information, construct and analyze arguments, and weed out thinking errors. Focus on the task or the information at hand. Try not to be led astray by the ease of assumptions, the emotional pull of an argument, or pressure to think too quickly. Be present in the moment to comprehensively evaluate input and construct output. Do not be distracted.

Chapter 3   Building Thinking Skills

Name _____   Date _____

LIFE THINKING: Applying What You Learn

3.1   *Fact and Opinion*

For a warm-up, identify the following statements as fact or opinion.

The new formula freshens your breath all day.

_____

Students are permitted to transfer credits within thirty days of registration.

_____

Senators have no term limits.

_____

Dog owners should keep their dogs leashed at all times.

_____

In New York, dog owners must keep their dogs leashed in all outdoor public spaces not officially designated as dog runs.

_____

Next, in the space below, write five facts that affect your life and five opinions of yours concerning anything you encounter in your day-to-day activities.

FACTS:

1. _____
2. _____
3. _____
4. _____
5. _____

OPINIONS:

1. _____
2. _____
3. _____
4. _____
5. _____

Finally, if you have time, join with a partner and look at each other's lists of facts and opinions. If you disagree with each other's identification of what is fact and what is opinion, exchange your thoughts and work together to clarify the statements.

3.2 *Thinking Errors*

For each of the following statements, identify the thinking error.

If it rains, the Knicks will win—that's how it's happened all season.

Don't be the last one on your block to get digital cable.

If you sail in a boat toward the horizon, you eventually will fall off.

I should be permitted to skip that required course. I'm already halfway toward completing my major.

We've always used this computer system. If it ain't broke, don't fix it.

Video games are bad for children because they're damaging.

How can you approve a person who has admitted to drug use as a nominee to the Supreme Court?

Four in five dentists recommend sugarless gum for their patients who chew gum.

The launch will work because the drag coefficient has been corrected and the left side exoskeleton repaired.

How can we possibly put up with this kind of insult? Let's take a stand!

The dominance of African Americans in the music business shows that all African Americans are musically gifted.

If we let her begin to date, the next thing you know, she'll be moving out of the house and getting an apartment with some guy.

If the nation doesn't eliminate pesticides, the entire food supply will be contaminated.

 TEAM THINKING: Working Together

 3.3 *Opposing Arguments*

As a class, brainstorm issues that are a part of your college life—student-instructor relations, interaction among students, class size, declaring majors, transportation, anything that is important to you. Stop when you have five issues.

Then divide into groups of four. Each group of four should choose one issue and name two opposing premises for that issue. Here are two examples:

Issue:	Whether students should be able to make up for missed classes with extra assignments
Opposing premises:	"Students should be allowed" versus "Students shouldn't be allowed"
Issue:	Bridging the gap among ethnicities
Opposing premises:	"Students should be put in situations where they have to interact" versus "Students should be left alone to associate with whomever they prefer"

Within your groups, divide into two pairs. One pair takes one premise, and the other pair takes the other. Meet with your partner and spend some time coming up with an argument that supports your premise.

Finally, rejoin with the rest of your group and take turns presenting your arguments to each other. Challenge each other's arguments with questions. Explore both sides of your issue in as much detail as you can.

 WORK THINKING: Career Portfolio

 3.4 *Letters of Recommendation*

Letters of recommendation from people who know and respect you are important. You will use them when you apply for jobs, internships, scholarships, or academic programs.

Think critically about who in your life will make a positive, logical, convincing argument in your favor. Choose people who know you well and who have seen you in action, either in school or at work. You will want your references to emphasize your strengths and to discuss qualities such as open-mindedness, ability to be a team player, and interpersonal relations. Letters also should contain references to your specific skills, capabilities, and style of working and thinking.

Furthermore, evaluate every possible person in the audience for their recommendation—prospective employers, scholarship administrators, and so on. For example, a former employer might be more convincing to a prospective employer, and an instructor might be a persuasive resource for a scholarship director.

Create a list of people who have served, or could serve, as references for you. Brainstorm names from all areas of your human resources. Possibilities are:

instructors	friends	present/former employers
administrators	family members	mentors
counselors	present/former coworkers	students

After critical consideration of who would be most appropriate to have as your references, make a chart, on a separate piece of paper, that looks like the one below. Add as many rows as you need. Fill in the information for each reference you have chosen.

NAME	ADDRESS	PHONE NUMBER	ASSOCIATION
Jo Trenholm	727 Mercury Way Boston, MA	(617) 555-2808	Current Supervisor

Update the information on this chart as you meet potential references or lose touch with old ones. Keep it on hand for occasions in which you need a new letter or want to cite a reference on a resume.

If you have a specific purpose for your letter right now, choose three people you would like to approach to write letters that suit that purpose. If you don't, keep the information on hand until you do, and use it then.

When references write letters for you, thank them right away for their help and keep them up-to-date on your activities. Always let a reference know when you have sent a letter so he or she may be prepared to receive a call from the person, company, or program to which you have applied.

 QUESTIONING YOUR WORLD:
Information Literacy Journal

To record your thoughts, use a separate journal or the lined pages at the end of the chapter.

3.5 *Looking for Assumptions*

Find an edition of a major newspaper from this past week. Look at the editorial pages, and choose one editorial to read. Describe its topic briefly, and analyze the assumptions underlying its argument or opinion. Do you agree with them? Why or why not? Did this editorial change your mind about anything?

Journal

Name _____   Date _____

Journal

Name _____   Date _____

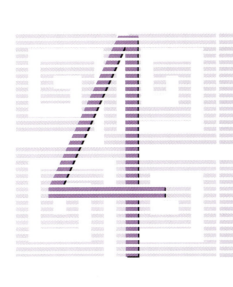

Thinking About Your World

Recognizing Perspectives

Everything you do, see, hear, and experience contributes to how you view the world. Daily you encounter information in varied forms—television, newspapers and magazines, radio, and conversation—that influences you. With the barrage of data in this "information age," it is easy to accept what you encounter, or reject it, without thinking through what it really means. You may figure that if an advertisement, your best friend, or a web site says so, it must be true.

A critical thinker, though, will step back from information and wait to judge. If you can take the time and energy to ask questions about information, you will be able to make well-examined choices about what to believe. This chapter will lead you through a discussion of how people develop values and perspectives and the positive effects of thinking critically about them. You also will explore approaches toward information in the sections on information literacy and library use.

In this chapter, you will explore answers to the following questions:

- What are values and how do they develop?
- Why should you explore perspectives?
- What is information literacy?
- How can you make the most of the library?

WHAT ARE VALUES AND HOW DO THEY DEVELOP?

Before thinking about why it is important to open your mind to perspectives other than your own, you should become aware of your own current views. One direct route to your perspectives is to explore your values. Values underlie perspectives, forming a basis for how you look at the world and influencing your opinions.

Personal values are basic assumptions about what is worthwhile, or valuable, in life. Examples include education, caring for others, justice, and freedom of choice. **Values** form the bedrock of decision making, guiding each choice you make. The sum total of all your values is often referred to as your *value system*. You demonstrate the effects of your value system in your actions, the priorities you set, how you communicate with others, your family life, your educational and career choices, and your lifestyle. Use a tree image to envision your value system with its sources and effects (see Figure 4.1).

Living according to a given set of values means making two specific choices:

1. *What to value.* When you think about your life—in terms of both what you do daily and what you plan for the future—what is important to you? Values show what you believe in. For example, you may believe in honesty, hard work, healthy living, and organization.

2. *How to be true to those values.* Equally important is how you put your values into action. When you make choices that demonstrate your values, you strengthen their roles in your life. The values mentioned in the previous paragraph might inspire these actions.

   - *Honesty*—admitting mistakes on the job, or expressing your feelings to your parents
   - *Hard work*—putting out 100% at your job, or being committed to a certain amount of study time each day
   - *Healthy living*—eating five servings of fruits and vegetables a day, or subscribing to a healthy cooking magazine
   - *Organization*—wearing a watch, or keeping a date book

To explore your values, begin by looking at their sources.

TERMS

Values
Principles or qualities that one considers important, right, or good.

FIGURE 4.1   The value system.

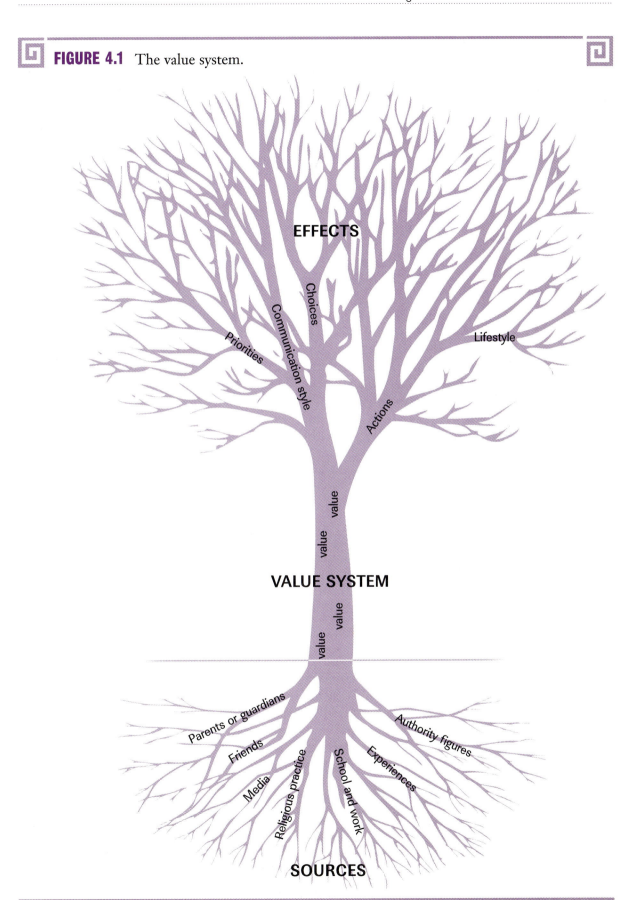

EFFECTS

Choices

Communication style

Priorities

Lifestyle

Actions

value
value
value
value
value
value

VALUE SYSTEM

Parents or guardians

Friends

Authority figures

Media

Religious practice

School and work

Experiences

SOURCES

Sources of Values

Have you ever thought about why you value what you do? Although you are ultimately in control of choosing what to value, you may often feel influenced by the choices of others, because all values have their roots in your reaction to outside information. A value system evolves over time, built from information that comes from many different sources. Such sources are the roots of your values. Sources of values include the following:

Parents, guardians, or relatives. Your father may have instilled in you the importance of being handy around the house. Your grandmother may have corrected your grammar when you spoke. Your baby-sitter might have made sure you brushed your teeth after your late night snacks. All of these people, through their words and actions, have communicated values (self-sufficiency, communication, health) to you.

Friends and peers. From your friends, current and former alike, you may have picked up all kinds of values. One friend may have taught you how to treat others by treating you a certain way. Another may have helped you establish your workplace values. A third may have been involved in a certain area of study or personal belief that you then adopted as your own.

Books, magazines, television, and other media. With the prevalence of today's media, it is easy to adopt the values that swirl around you. People may dress a certain way because a magazine says it's the latest style, drink a certain kind of soda because a TV advertisement advocates it, change their career path based on what a TV show character does for a living, or adopt a particular political point of view that they hear discussed on the radio.

Instructors, supervisors, mentors, and other authority figures. Authority figures you respect might influence you just as family members can. You may be drawn to a particular major because of an instructor whom you like. You might choose a spiritual path similar to one followed by a coworker or supervisor whom you respect. You might even speak or act like a mentor who is important in your life, "trying out" a certain behavior to see if it fits you.

Religious belief and study. The world's religions teach values to their followers. If you study or follow one or more religions, you learn both its values and the actions you should take to live by those values. For example, the Hindu reverence for animals, especially cows, leads Hindu followers to avoid eating beef.

Workplace and school. The environments in which you live influence your value system. If your company requires a specific dress code, it may become important to you to dress that way even off the job. Your school might have an "honor system" that forbids specific actions, and you may find that you begin to live by the rules of the honor system even when you are off-campus.

Your own experiences. What happens to you may lead to changes in your values both subtle and drastic. For example, if you become close to an alcoholic, your experience as that person's friend may lead you to value drinking in moderation or not drinking at all. Sometimes losing something, either temporarily or permanently, can lead you to value it far more than you did before. If you experience a medical crisis, for example, you may begin to strongly value your health, and you may change your day-to-day actions based on this new value.

Values may come from more than one source. For example, a student may value education (sources: parents and high school teachers) and music (sources: media and friends). Another student may have abandoned all of the values that he or she grew up with and adopted values from three important people—a mentor, a best friend, and an important relative.

Examining the sources of your values can help you define those values and trace their origins. More important, however, is the process of thinking critically about the values themselves. For example, although certain sources (parents, school) may have a better reputation than others (TV, friends), the values they pass on may not reflect their reputations. For example, you may have learned the value of close friendship—supposedly a "good" value—from watching a TV show. You also may have a parent who, by example, led you to value smoking as a relaxation strategy—perhaps a "not so good" value.

Choosing Values Critically

Values are born of your interaction with the world. As with any other choice that requires critical thinking, the process should involve taking in information, thinking critically about it, and acting on it. Almost everyone, however, has adopted some values without thinking. Often an assumption will lead to a value that isn't so appropriate for a given person, such as if you were to assume that a friend's values should fit you because you like that friend.

The influence of peers or the media can lead to uncritical value choices. People may choose values based on what others value or what society or the media seem to value. One example is the prevalence of thin models in magazine advertisements and articles. Many young women, automatically assuming that they should value this kind of appearance, have fought their own natural body types and developed dangerous illnesses such as anorexia or bulimia.

Each individual value system is unique, even if many values originally come from other sources. Your responsibility is to make sure that your values are your own choice and not primarily the choice of others. Make value choices based on what seems right for you, for your life, and for others around you. Do this by using your ability to think critically.

Take in information objectively. Try to take in what you see, hear, read, and experience without automatically judging it. See it as it is, without making any assumptions about it. For example, if your on-the-job supervisor emphasizes teamwork and being on time to meetings, you might take in that the values being presented to you are cooperation and promptness.

Evaluate information critically. This is the core of smart value choices. Ask important questions about what positive and negative effects adopting this value may have on you. For example, a fellow student values social time over studying. Ask yourself: If I chose this value, would it be to please my friend or would it be truly my choice? What effects might this behavior have on my studies, my opinion of myself, my progress toward a career, or my daily schedule? Are the positive effects of this value, for me, more than the negative effects?

Put your evaluation into action. Finally, once you have taken the time to evaluate a value, make your choice and find ways to incorporate it into your daily life. For example, if your lifeguard son has convinced you that you should value healthy skin, taking action might mean applying a sunscreen every day or going yearly to the dermatologist to have your skin examined.

Values are not "good" or "bad" in and of themselves. Each value must be evaluated according to the individual and the situation at hand. No matter what you may think of a value at first, it is crucial that you let go of your assumptions and evaluate the positive and negative effects on your own life and on the lives of those around you. Think critically about where any value leads you. Is it where you want to—or ought to—go?

Take the previous example of a friend who values social time over studying. According to what you think about how you "should" behave as a student, you might assume this value to have negative effects. There may be situations, however, in which this value is important. Perhaps a student previously became ill because of the intense pressure to succeed that she put on herself. Or perhaps a student has no family to lean on and therefore has a need to stay close to his friends. In either of these cases, what seems at first like a "bad" value can have some important positive effects.

On the flip side, consider a value that traditionally seems "good"—spending time with family. This value is extremely important to many people. Some people, however, have families that are difficult, judgmental, or even abusive. In these cases, spending time with family might cause more harm than good, and this value would have bad effects.

Changing Values

Because you, your needs, and the world around you are in a fairly constant state of change, you should adjust your value system accordingly. This doesn't mean that you should swing from one extreme to the other at the drop of a hat. Rather, it means that you will benefit from staying aware of the changes around you and evaluating your values periodically to see if they still suit your circumstances.

Certain life changes may cause your value system to shift. For example, the difficulty of a divorce may result in an increased value of independence and individuality, or entering a long-term relationship may create an emphasis on sharing and compromise. New experiences may herald newly emphasized, or even new, values. A student who goes to college away from home and meets other students from unfamiliar backgrounds, for example, may come to value living in a diverse community. If you continue to be open to new ideas and to think them through, your values will grow and develop as you do.

The work you do in looking at your values and their effects on your life will prepare you for the challenge of exploring and shifting your perspectives.

WHY SHOULD YOU EXPLORE PERSPECTIVES?

Perspective is complex and unique to each individual. You have your own way of looking at everything you encounter, from your big-picture perspective on the world to your general opinion on an infinite number of specifics such as ideas, activities, people, and places. The thoughts you have on a day-to-day basis, ranging from "I think that people should use water-saver shower heads" to "I think that the United States should support democracy in the Slavic states," reflect your individual perspectives—and your perspectives reflect who you are. Figure 4.2 represents a view of the complex composition of perspective: You can think of perspective as the view through a telescope, with all of the mirrors and lenses inside representing the various elements that affect the view.

Seeing the world *only* from your perspective—and resisting any challenges to or differences from that perspective—can be inflexible, limiting, and frustrating to both you and others. You probably know how difficult it can be when someone cannot understand your point of view. Perhaps an instructor doesn't like the fact that you leave early on Thursdays for physical therapy, or a friend can't understand why you would date someone of a race different from yours.

Exploring perspectives critically will introduce you to new ideas, improve your communication with others, and encourage mutual respect.

A Critical Thinking Approach to Perspectives

The most effective way to evaluate perspectives involves taking in information, evaluating it with questions, then acting upon it in whatever way seems appropriate to you.

TERMS

Perspective
A point of view or outlook based on a cluster of related assumptions, incorporating values, interests, experience, and knowledge.

FIGURE 4.2 The elements of perspective.

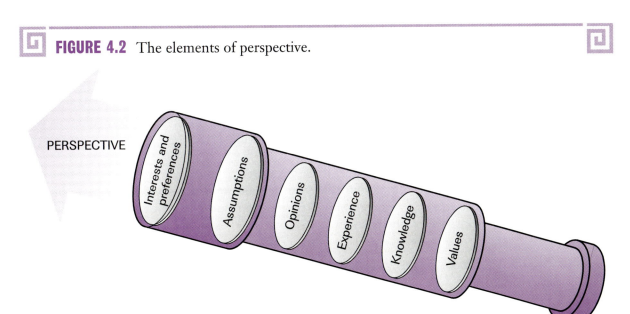

Take in New Information

The first step is to take in new perspectives and simply acknowledge that they exist without immediately judging, rejecting, or even accepting them. It's easy to feel so strongly about a topic—for example, whether the government should allow capital punishment—that you don't even give a chance to anyone with an opposing view. Resist your own strong opinions and listen. One of the most important qualities of critical thinkers is the ability to allow for the existence of perspectives that differ from, and even completely negate, their own.

Evaluate the Perspective

Asking questions will help you maintain flexibility and openness.

- What is similar and different about this perspective and my own perspective? What is similar and different about the person holding this perspective and me? What experiences have we had that may have led to our perspectives?

- What examples, evidence, or reasons could be used to support or justify this perspective? Do some reasons provide good support even if I don't agree with the reasons?

- What positive and negative effects may come from this different way of being, acting, or believing? Are the effects different on different people and different situations? Even if this perspective seems to have negative effects for me, how might it have positive effects for others, and therefore have value?

- What can I learn from this different perspective? Could I adopt anything from it for my own life—something that would help me improve who I am or what I do? Is there anything I wouldn't do myself but that I can still respect and learn from?

Accept or Perhaps Take Action

On the one hand, perhaps your evaluation will lead you simply to a recognition and appreciation of the other perspective, even if you decide that it is not right for you. On the other hand, thinking through the new perspective may lead you to believe that it would be worthwhile to try out or to adopt as your own. You may think that what you have learned has led you to a new way of seeing yourself or your life.

Thoughtful consideration of all perspectives is important, whether they are your own that you have long held fast to or those of others that you have just encountered. Figure 4.3 illustrates some aspects of the critical thinking approach to perspectives.

Use Analogies to Communicate Perspectives

Understanding a new perspective isn't always easy. You may have had difficulty putting yourself in someone else's shoes, or you may have had trouble communicating an idea to someone else. Sometimes it feels like the concept just won't "get through."

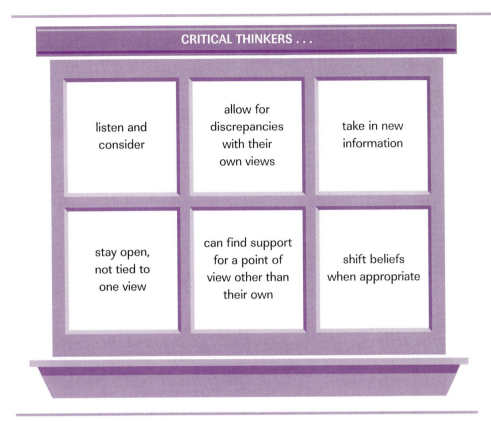

Adapted from Donald E. P. Smith, Glenn M. Knudsvig, and Timothy L. Walter, *Critical Thinking: Building the Basics.* Belmont, CA: Wadsworth, 1998, p. 51.

Using an **analogy** can bring about the common understanding that could lead to comprehension of a different perspective. An analogy can create a shift in context, bringing in a new idea or scenario that may help to explain a confusing concept. When people have no context with which to understand a situation, explaining how the situation is similar to something they are familiar with will help them get a grasp of what is happening. When you are the one having trouble understanding, trying to think of something similar in your own life, experience, or understanding may help you understand it. Some cause-and-effect examples are found in:

TERMS

Analogy
A comparison based on a resemblance in some aspects between things otherwise unlike.

- *Medicine.* To explain to addicts the effect an illness has on the body, a doctor might use a war analogy, showing how the illness attacks healthy cells.
- *History.* To explain the way nations interacted in a historical event, an instructor could compare the nations to individual people, using human relations logic to show why the nations took the actions that they did.
- *Human relations.* To explain to a friend how divorce feels, a person might compare the situation to that friend's experience with being estranged from a parent or sibling.

A first step in helping another person see your perspective is having him or her understand concepts and cause-and-effect patterns the way you understand them. Using an analogy, as in the above examples, helps to increase understanding. Although better understanding won't change or shift someone's perspective by itself, it is a necessary step on the way to that shift. Only when people have a concrete understanding of different perspectives can they consider these critically and have the ability, if they choose, to shift their own views.

The Value of Seeing Other Perspectives

Seeing beyond one's own perspective can be difficult. Why put in the effort? Some of the very real benefits of being able to see and consider other perspectives are:

- *Improved communication.* The ability to see other perspectives is at the heart of all successful communication. When you consider another person's perspective, you open the lines of communication. For instance, if you want to add or drop a course and your advisor says it's impossible before listening to everything you have to say, you might not feel much like explaining. But if your advisor asks to hear your perspective on the matter, you may sense that your needs are respected. Feeling respected may encourage you to respond or even to change your mind.

- *Mutual respect.* Think about when someone takes the time and energy to understand how you feel about an issue. You probably feel respected and in return offer respect to the person who made the effort. When people respect one another, relationships become stronger and more productive, whether they are personal, workplace, or educational.

- *Continued learning.* Every time you shift your perspective, you can learn something new. Worlds of knowledge and possibilities exist outside your life's experience. You may learn, for example, that what you eat daily may be against someone else's religious beliefs. You might meet people who have found fulfillment in careers that you perceive as impossible. You may find completely different, yet equally valid, ways of getting an education, living as a family, or relating to others. Above all else, you may see that each person is entitled to his or her own perspective, no matter how foreign it may be to you.

Even a group of people similar to yourself will have a variety of perspectives. Each one you consider helps you invite communication, build respect, and increase your knowledge. The connection with others that you foster by being able to accept and shift perspective could mean the difference between success and failure in today's world. This becomes more true as the information age introduces you to more and more perspectives every day.

 ## WHAT IS INFORMATION LITERACY?

Do you believe everything you hear from people around you, read in magazines, or see on television? Think about it for a moment. If you were to trust every advertisement, you would believe that at least four fast-food restaurants serve "the best burger around." If you were to agree with every newspaper article, you would know that Elvis passed away many years ago and still believe that he was shopping for peanut butter last week in Oklahoma. If you were to believe what everyone told you, you would be utterly confused about the best way to do just about anything from applying for a loan to packing up your recycling materials. It is impossible to believe everything without becoming totally confused about what is real.

If literacy refers to the ability to read, information literacy can be seen as the ability to read information critically. Information literacy is the ability to respond with thought to the information you encounter. It is essential for a realistic understanding of the data that bombard you daily. Information literacy also is often referred to as *media literacy*, because so much of the information that comes your way is through the various **media.** Essentially, information literacy means that instead of accepting anything a person, newspaper article, magazine advertisement, or TV announcer says is fact, you take time to question the information, using your mind actions and critical thinking processes.

The people who founded the Center for Media Literacy work to encourage others to think critically about the media. They have put forth what they call the "Five Core Concepts of Media Literacy."[1] These concepts apply to any information you encounter.

TERMS

Media
The agencies of mass communication—television, film, and journalism (magazines and newspapers).

1. *All media are constructions.* Any TV show or advertisement, for example, is not a view of actual life or fact but, rather, a carefully constructed presentation designed to have a certain effect on the viewer—to encourage you to feel a certain emotion, develop a particular opinion, or buy the product advertised. For example, an article that intends the reader to feel good about the President will focus on his strengths rather than his shortcomings.

2. *Media use unique "languages."* The people who produce media carefully choose wording, background music, colors, images, timing, and other factors to produce the effect they want. The next time you go to a movie, listen carefully to the music that plays behind an emotional scene or a high-speed chase.

3. *Different audiences understand the same media message differently.* Individual people understand media in the context of their own unique perspectives. For this reason, people often interpret media quite differently. A child who has not experienced violence might be frightened by violent scenes on television, whereas a child who has witnessed or experienced violence might accept these images as normal and acceptable.

4. *Media have commercial interests.* Rather than being driven by the need to tell the truth, media are driven by the intent to sell you something. Television programs, newspapers, and magazines make sure that the advertisers who support the show or publication get a chance to convey a message or perspective to the consumer. Advertising is chosen to appeal most to those most likely to be reading or seeing that specific kind of media. For example, ads for toys usually come on during children's programming, and ads for beer and cars dominate the airwaves during major sports events.

5. *Media have embedded values and perspectives.* Any media product carries the values of the people who created it. No medium is free of someone's perspective of what deserves the most attention. Through assigning and choosing articles, for example, an editor conveys a magazine's perspective of what is important. *Runner's World* thinks that how to stay warm on a winter run is important, for example, whereas *Parenting* emphasizes what to do when your child has a fever.

The whole point of information literacy is to approach with thought and consideration what you see, hear, and read. The following strategies will help you use your mind actions and critical thinking processes to analyze information and develop an informed opinion.

- *Ask questions about the information, based on the mind actions.* Is what you read in an article similar to something you already know to be true? Does a newspaper ad show something that differs from your own experience? Do you evaluate a magazine article to be useful or not? Do you agree with the causes or effects that are cited, and do you agree with the importance, or value, given to each?

- *Question the source of the information.* Who wrote or presented the information? Do you trust the source as an authority? Why? Has other information from that source been reliable or not? Has contradictory information come from a more reliable source?

- *Search for assumptions.* Does the information have a basis in any assumptions? If so, do you agree or disagree with these assumptions? Does believing in or agreeing with the information require you to accept certain assumptions?

- *Evaluate the truth of the argument.* If a TV ad argues that a car is the best on the road, evaluate this information the way you would any argument. With what facts does the advertiser back up its claims (premises)? How can you test the validity of the facts or claims? Does assuming the claims to be true cause any harm? From what you know about constructing an argument, what appeals is the advertiser using to persuade you to adopt its idea?

- *Be aware of, and investigate, other perspectives.* It is just as important to avoid rejecting media messages automatically as it is to avoid accepting the messages automatically. Any media offering has its own perspective, which comes from the person or people who created it. Take the time to define this perspective and the underlying values. Then decide whether you should accept it (even if it may be different from your own). Ask what positive and negative effects adopting this perspective might have on you. For instance, if a cigarette ad in a magazine encourages you to adopt the perspective that you should smoke, this may have harmful effects on your health. Or if a newspaper article introduces a new way to get enough calcium in your diet, adopting that perspective might have positive effects.

Becoming an information-literate person will help you become a smart consumer of the media, a shrewd listener to those around you, and a person who ultimately is able to be responsible for your own actions. Don't let a rumor or a TV ad tell you what to do. Take in the message, evaluate it critically, and make your own decision. Information literacy is a key to a responsible, self-powered life.

 ## HOW CAN YOU MAKE THE MOST OF THE LIBRARY?

A library is a home for information. Consider it the "brain" of your college. Libraries contain a world of information—from every novel Toni Morrison ever wrote to scholarship and financial-aid directories to online job listings to medical journal articles on breast cancer research. It's all there waiting for you. Your job is to find what you need as quickly and efficiently as you can.

Start with a Road Map

Most college libraries are bigger than high school and community libraries. You may feel lost on your first visit, or even a few visits after that. You can make your life easier right away by learning how your library is organized. Although every library has a different layout, all libraries have certain areas in common.

Reference area. In the reference area you'll find reference books, including encyclopedias, public- and private-sector directories, dictionaries, almanacs, and atlases. You'll also find librarians and other library employees who can direct you to the information you need. Computer terminals, containing the library's catalog of holdings, as well as online bibliographic and full-text databases, usually are part of the reference area.

Book area. Books—and, in many libraries, magazines and journals in bound or boxed volumes—are stored in the *stacks*. A library with "open stacks" allows you to search for materials on your own. In a "closed-stack" system a staff member retrieves materials for you.

Periodicals area. In the periodicals area you'll find recent issues of popular and scholarly magazines, journals, and newspapers. Most college libraries collect **periodicals,** ranging from *Time* to *Advertising Age* to the *New England Journal of Medicine*. Because you usually can't check out unbound periodicals, you may find photocopy machines nearby, where you can copy the pages you need.

Audio/visual materials areas. Many libraries have specialized areas for video, art and photography, and recorded music collections.

Computer areas. Computer terminals, linked to databases and the Internet, are found increasingly in libraries. These might be scattered throughout the building or set off in special areas. You might be able to access these databases and the Internet from the college's computer labs and writing centers, or even from your own computer, if you have one.

"The very spring and root of honesty and virtue lie in good education."
PLUTARCH

▲ TERMS

Periodicals Magazines, journals, and newspapers published on a regular basis throughout the year.

TERMS

Microfilm
A reel of film on
which printed
materials are
photographed at
greatly reduced
size for ease of
storage.

Microfiche
A card or sheet
of microfilm that
contains a con-
siderable number
of pages of
printed matter.

Microform areas. Most libraries have microform reading areas or rooms. Microforms are materials printed on film, either **microfilm** or **microfiche,** that is read through special viewing machines. Many microform reading machines can print hard copies of stored images and text.

To learn about your college library, take a library tour or a training session. You also might ask for a pamphlet giving the layout, and then take some time for a self-tour. Almost all college libraries offer some kind of orientation on how to use their books, periodicals, databases, and Internet hookups. If your school has a network of libraries, including one or more central libraries and other smaller, specialized libraries, explore each one you intend to use.

Learn How to Conduct an Information Search

The most successful and time-saving library research involves following a specific *search strategy*—a step-by-step method for finding information that takes you from general to specific sources. Starting with general sources usually works best because they provide an overview of your research topic and can lead you to more specific information and sources.

For example, an encyclopedia article on the archaeological discovery of the Dead Sea Scrolls—manuscripts written between 250 B.C. and A.D. 68 that trace the roots of Judaism and Christianity—might mention that one of the most important books on the subject is *Understanding the Dead Sea Scrolls*, edited by Hershel Shanks (New York: Random House, 1992). This book, in turn, will lead you to 13 experts who wrote text chapters.

Defining your exact topic is critical to the success of your search. Although the topic "The Dead Sea Scrolls" may be too broad for your research paper, possibilities of narrower topics may include:

- How the Bedouin shepherds discovered the Dead Sea Scrolls in 1947
- Historical origins of the scrolls
- The process archaeologists used to reconstruct scroll fragments

A *keyword search*—a search for information through the use of specific words and phrases related to the information—will help you narrow your topic. Use your library's computer database for keyword searches. For instance, instead of searching through the broad category *Art*, you can use a keyword search to narrow your focus to *French Art* or, more specifically, to *French Art in the nineteenth century.*

Keyword searches are relatively easy because they use natural language rather than specialized classification vocabulary. Table 4.1 includes some tips that will help you use the keyword system.

As you search, keep in mind that

- Double quotes around a word or phrase will locate the term exactly as you entered it ("financial aid").
- Using upper or lower case will not affect the search (*Scholarships* will find *scholarships*).
- Singular terms will find the plural (*scholarship* will find *scholarships*).

TABLE 4.1   How to perform an effective keyword search.

IF YOU ARE SEARCHING FOR . . .	DO THIS	EXAMPLE
A word	Type the word normally	aid
A phrase	Type the phrase in its normal word order (use regular word spacing) or surround the phrase with double quotation marks	financial aid or "financial aid"
Two or more keywords without regard to word order	Type the words in any order, surrounding the words with quotation marks (use "and" to separate the words)	"financial aid" and "scholarships"
Topic A or topic B	Type the words in any order (use "or" to separate the words)	"financial aid" or "scholarships"
Topic A but not topic B	Type topic A first and then topic B (use "not" to separate the words)	"financial aid" not "scholarships"

Conduct Research Using a Search Strategy

Knowing where to look during each phase of your search will help you find information quickly and efficiently. A successful search strategy often starts with general reference works, then moves to more specific reference works, books, periodicals, and electronic sources such as the Internet (see Figure 4-4).

Use General Reference Works

Begin your research with *general reference works*. These works cover hundreds—sometimes thousands—of different topics in a broad, nondetailed way. General reference guides often are available online or on **CD-ROM.**

TERMS

CD-ROM
a compact disk ("read-only memory") capable of holding millions of words and images that can be read by a computer.

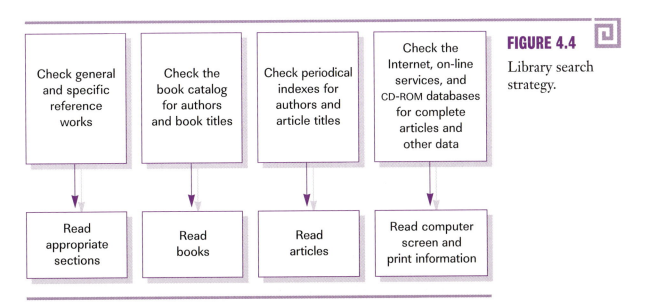

FIGURE 4.4

Library search strategy.

General reference works include:

- Encyclopedias such as the multivolume *Encyclopedia Americana*
- Almanacs such as the *World Almanac and Book of Facts*
- Yearbooks such as the *McGraw-Hill Yearbook of Science and Technology*
- Dictionaries such as *Webster's New World College Dictionary*
- Biographical reference works such as *American Writers* and *Who's Who*
- Bibliographies such as *Books in Print* (especially the *Subject Guide to Books in Print*)

Scan these sources for an overview of your topic. Bibliographies at the end of encyclopedia articles also may lead to other important sources.

Search Specialized Reference Works

After you have an overview of your topic, *specialized reference works* will help you find more specific facts. Specialized reference works include encyclopedias and dictionaries that focus on a narrow field. Although the entries you find in these volumes are short summaries, they present the critical ideas and the key words you will need to conduct additional research. Bibliographies that accompany the articles point to the names and works of recognized experts. Examples of specialized reference works, organized by subject, are:

- Fine Arts (including music, art, film, television, and theater), such as the *International Encyclopedia of Music and Musicians*
- History, such as the *Encyclopedia of American History*
- Science and Technology, such as the *Encyclopedia of Computer Science and Technology*
- Social Sciences, such as the *Dictionary of Education*
- Current Affairs, such as the *Social Issues Resources Series (SIRS)*

Browse Through Books on Your Subject

"The best effect of any book is that it excites the reader to self-activity."
THOMAS CARLYLE

Use the *library catalog* to find books and other materials on your topic. The catalog tells you which publications the library owns and where they can be found. Before computers, most library catalogs consisted of endless cards filed in tiny drawers. Today most of these "card catalogs" have been replaced by online computer catalogs. When general and specialized reference works lead to a dead end, the catalog may provide a good topic overview.

The library catalog contains a list of every library holding, searchable by author, title, and subject. For example, a library that owns *The Artist's Way: A Spiritual Path to Higher Creativity* by Julia Cameron may list the book in the author catalog under Cameron, Julia (last name first); in the title catalog, under *Artist's Way* (articles such as *the*, *a*, and *an* are dropped from the beginnings of titles and subjects); in the subject catalog under "Creative Ability—problems, exercises, etc.," and "Creation—literary, artistic, etc." If you are using a keyword search, you may be able to find this book using "Art" and "Creativity" or "Art" and "Spirituality."

Each catalog listing refers to the library's classification system, which tells you exactly where the publication can be found. Taking a moment to familiarize yourself with your library's system will save time and trouble in your research because you will know more quickly where to go to find what you need. The Dewey decimal and the Library of Congress systems are among the most common classification systems.

Dewey decimal system. The Dewey decimal system classifies materials into ten major subject categories and assigns each library holding a specific *call number.* For example, publications with call numbers between 100 to 199 deal with philosophy. Successive numbers and decimal points divide each major category into subcategories. The more specific the call number, the more targeted is your search. For example, a book with a call number of 378 falls into the general social science category and into the subcategory of higher education. Student finances, a narrower topic, uses the call number 378.3.

Library of Congress system. The Library of Congress uses a letter-based classification system to divide library holdings according to subject categories. Figure 4.5 shows the call letters that correspond to each category. Each category is divided further into specialized subgroups through the addition of letters and numbers.

Become familiar with these classification systems. The more you know about how a library is organized, the more you can focus your research and avoid hours of needless effort.

CALL LETTER	MAIN CLASSIFICATION CATEGORY	CALL LETTER	MAIN CLASSIFICATION CATEGORY
A	General works	N	Fine arts
B	Philosophy and religion	P	Language—Literature (nonfiction)
C	History—Auxiliary sciences	Q	Sciences
D	History—Topography	R	Medicine
E–F	American history—Topography	S	Agriculture
G	Geography—Anthropology	T	Technology
H	Social sciences	U	Military science
J	Political sciences	V	Naval science
K	Law	Z	Bibliography and library science
L	Education	P–Z	Literature (fiction)
M	Music		

FIGURE 4.5

Library of Congress subject classification system.

Use Periodical Indexes to Search for Periodicals

Because of their frequent publication, periodicals are a valuable source of current information. *Journals* are periodicals written for readers with special knowledge and expertise. *Newsweek* magazine may run a general-interest article on AIDS research, whereas the *Journal of the American Medical Association* may print the original scientific study and direct the article to physicians and scientists. Many libraries display periodicals that are up to a year or two old and convert older copies to microfilm or microfiche. Some libraries also bind recent issues into volumes.

Periodical indexes lead you to specific articles. The *Reader's Guide to Periodical Literature*, available on CD-ROM and in book form, provides general information. The *Reader's Guide* indexes articles in more than 240 general-interest magazines and newspapers. Many libraries also carry the *Reader's Guide Abstracts*, which print article summaries. Look in the *Infotrac* family of databases, online or on CD-ROM, for other periodical indexes such as Health Reference Center and General Business File.

Because there is no all-inclusive index for technical, medical, and scholarly journal articles, you'll have to search indexes that catalog articles in narrow subject areas such as history, art, and psychology. Many specialized indexes also include *abstracts* (article summaries) and can be found in electronic or book form. Just a few of the indexes you might run across are:

- Business Periodicals Index
- ERIC (Educational Resources Information Center)
- Hispanic American Periodicals Index
- Index to United States Government Periodicals
- Psychological Abstracts

Almost no library owns all the publications listed in these and other specialized indexes. You might find separate newspaper indexes at your library, in print, microform, CD-ROM, or online. Some of these indexes include many different newspapers, such as the Index to Black Newspapers, whereas others index a single publication, such as the Chicago Tribune Index. In addition, journals not found in your library or online might be available through *interlibrary loan*, by which you can have your library request materials from another library. You then can use the materials at your library, but you must return them by a specified date. Although interlibrary loans can be helpful, the amount of time you will have to wait for the materials is unpredictable and might stretch out for weeks.

Search the Internet

In many ways, the Internet is a student researcher's dream come true. You'll find sites that teach you how to write a business plan; others that list job openings at major companies; others that provide health, wellness, and nutritional information; and still others that analyze different theories of child development. The special appendix at the end of this book, entitled "Researching Information and Student Resources on the Internet," will help you learn how to find information on the Internet and judge its value in the same way that you evaluate any other material you read.

Ask the Librarian

Librarians are information experts who can help you solve research problems.* They can help you locate unfamiliar or hard-to-find sources, as well as navigate computer catalogs and databases. Say, for example, you are researching a gun-control bill that is currently before Congress and you want to contact lobbying organizations on both sides of the issue. The librarian may lead you to the *Encyclopedia of Associations*, which lists the National Rifle Association and Handgun Control Inc. (two groups with opposing perspectives). By calling or e-mailing these groups or visiting their Web sites, you will get their information on current legislation.

Among the specific services librarians provide are search services and information sources.

Search services. Some tips on getting the best advice are to:

- *Be prepared.* Know what you're looking for so you can make a specific request. Instead of asking for information on the American presidency, focus on the topic you expect to write about in your American history paper—for example, how President Franklin D. Roosevelt's physical disability may have affected his leadership during World War II.
- *Be willing to reach out.* Don't think you have to do it all yourself. Librarians will help you, whether with basic sources or more difficult problems. Asking questions is a sign of willingness to learn, not a weakness.
- *Ask for help when you can't find a specific source.* For example, when a specific book is not on the shelf, the librarian may direct you to another source that will work just as well.

Information services. Most libraries answer phone inquiries that can be researched quickly. For example, if you forget to write down the publisher and date of publication of Renee Blank and Sandra Slipp's book, *Voices of Diversity: Real People Talk about Problems and Solutions in a Workplace Where Everyone Is Not Alike*, call a staff member with the title and author.

Interlibrary loans. If a publication is not available in your library, the librarian can arrange for an interlibrary loan.

Use Critical Thinking to Evaluate Every Source

If all information were equal, you could trust the accuracy of every book and article. Information from the Internet home page of the National Aeronautics and Space Administration (NASA) would have the same value as information

---

*Librarians are not the only helpful people in the library. For simplicity's sake, this book uses the word *librarian* to refer to librarians as well as other staff members who are trained to help.

from "Bob's Home Page on Aliens and Extraterrestrials." As that isn't the case, use critical-thinking skills to evaluate research sources. Some critical-thinking questions to ask about every source are:

- *Is the author a recognized expert?* A journalist who writes his or her first article on child development does not have the same credibility as an author of three child-development texts.
- *Does the author write from a certain perspective?* An article evaluating liberal Democrat policies written by a conservative Republican would almost certainly take the perspective that such policies are problematic.
- *Is the source recent enough for your purposes?* Whereas a history published in 1990 on the U.S. Civil War probably will be accurate in the year 2000, a 1990 analysis of current computer technology will be hopelessly out of date at the turn of the century.
- *Are the author's sources reliable?* Where did the author get the information? Check the bibliography and footnotes not only for the number of sources listed but also for their quality. Find out whether they are reputable, established publications. If the work is based on *primary evidence*, the author's original work or direct observation, do the examples given fit the author's primary idea? If it is based on *secondary evidence*, an analysis of the works of others, are the conclusions well-supported by the evidence given?

As you will see in the Internet research appendix at the end of the text, critical thinking skills are especially important when using the Internet. Accepting information you find there at face value—no matter the source—is often a mistake and may lead to incorrect conclusions.

The library is one of your college's most valuable resources, so take advantage of it. Your library research and critical-thinking skills will give you the ability to collect information, weigh alternatives, and make decisions. These skills will last a lifetime.

Gestalt

The German word *gestalt* refers to a whole that is greater than the sum of its parts. When you can think in terms of *gestalt*, you are able to see both the whole picture and how each individual part contributes to it. To refer to a common phrase, *gestalt* is seeing the whole forest as well as individual trees.

Think of this concept as you consider values, perspectives, and the information that you encounter from day to day. Although it can be easier to focus on your own particular view of the world, stepping back to evaluate the whole *gestalt*—to take in different perspectives and carefully consider information in its broader context—will build your knowledge and help you become an open-minded person. As important as individual facts and perspectives may seem, the *gestalt* is what helps you see that everything takes its place as a part of, and in relation to, the whole.

Chapter 4   Building Thinking Skills

Name _____   Date _____

LIFE THINKING: Applying What You Learn

4.1 *Your Values*

Begin to explore your values by rating the following values on a scale from 1 to 4, 1 being least important to you and 4 being most important. If you have values that you don't see in the chart, list them in the blank spaces and rate them.

RATING	VALUE	RATING	VALUE
_____	Knowing yourself	_____	Mental health
_____	Physical health	_____	Fitness/exercise
_____	Spending time with family	_____	Close friendships
_____	Helping others	_____	Education
_____	Being well paid	_____	Being employed
_____	Being liked by others	_____	Free time/vacations
_____	Enjoying entertainment	_____	Time to yourself
_____	Spiritual/religious life	_____	Reading
_____	Keeping up with news	_____	Staying organized
_____	Financial stability	_____	Intimate relationship
_____	Creative/artistic pursuits	_____	Self-improvement
_____	Lifelong learning	_____	Facing your fears

Considering your priorities, write your top five values here:

1. _____
2. _____
3. _____
4. _____
5. _____

Evaluating Information in the Media

Choose a specific information source to evaluate. It can be a television show, an article in a magazine or newspaper, a web site, an advertisement, or any other source. Name it here:

_____

_____

Now evaluate the source using the following questions, based on what you know about information literacy.

What effect does this information source intend to have on you?

_____

_____

_____

How does this source use a particular language (images, music, wording, etc.) to communicate? What does this language intend to convey to you?

_____

_____

_____

Does this information source have a commercial interest? Does it want to sell something to you? If so, what?

_____

_____

_____

What values does this information source carry?

_____

_____

_____

Do you accept the information from this source as true or valid? Why or why not?

_____

_____

_____

Does the information contain hidden assumptions? If so, what are they? Do you agree with them?

_____

_____

_____

_____

Do you trust the source itself? Why or why not?

_____

_____

_____

_____

 TEAM THINKING: Working Together

4.3 *Analyzing Perspectives*

Divide into groups of three or four. With your group, choose one of the following topics.

- Financial aid for education
- Salary caps for athletes
- Health care
- Child care
- Computer technology

Brainstorm differing perspectives on the topic you have chosen—enough so each group member has one. For example, if the topic were "Recycling," some perspectives might be:

- All recyclable materials should be recycled
- Recycling is more trouble and takes more energy than it's worth
- Government should assume the financial responsibility for recycling
- Citizens should pay a fine if they do not recycle

After you brainstorm perspectives, each group member should write a brief discussion of the elements of that perspective, noting the values, experiences, opinions, assumptions, and preferences that may lie behind it (see Figure 4-2).

Then meet again as a group, when each group member has a chance to present his or her perspective to the other group members. With what you now know about each perspective, discuss as a group their individual effects. Come to a conclusion (if you can) about what perspective seems to have the most positive effects.

WORK THINKING: Career Portfolio

4.4 *Research a Career*

Activate your research skills by doing research on one career that interests you. Put together an informal "research paper" that catalogs all of the basics you think you would need to know to make a decision on whether to pursue this career past an initial interest. Use these sources:

- General and specific reference works
- Periodicals (especially current newspapers, where you can find updated information on the status of your particular career)
- The Internet
- Any sources found at your school's career center

Include the following topics (as well as any others that seem pertinent to you):

- Recent growth status of your career (whether opportunities are increasing or decreasing)
- Strength of this career where you live or want to live
- Educational requirements (degrees, certificates, and tests)
- Estimated salaries
- Potential benefits
- General duties and skills required
- Opportunities for advancement
- Time and location flexibility, if any

Keep this information on hand for when you are ready to start pursuing your career in earnest.

QUESTIONING YOUR WORLD:
Information Literacy Journal

To record your thoughts, use a separate journal or the lined pages at the end of the chapter.

4.5 *Investigating a Statement*

Consider the following: "Nine times more back surgeries are performed in the United States than in Canada." Evaluate this statement according to what you know about information literacy and the nature of fact and opinion. Is this fact? What is the context? Why might this be the case? What impression might someone want to make with this statement?

_____

_____

_____

_____

_____

_____

_____

Journal

Name _____ Date _____

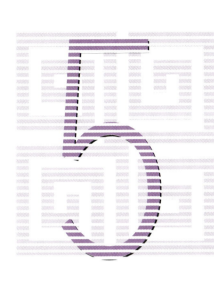

5

Thinking Strategically

Setting Goals and Planning Your Time

People dream of what they want out of life, but not everyone knows how to turn dreams into reality. Often, dreams and goals seem far off in time, too difficult, or obscured by life's day-to-day details. Thinking strategically will help you see where you want to go and identify the individual steps you will have to take to get there. When you set goals, prioritize, and manage your time effectively, you increase your ability to realize your dreams.

This chapter explains how to think critically about your goals. You will see how to create a framework for your life's goals—a personal mission statement—and how to set long-term and short-term goals. You will discover how setting priorities and managing time effectively can give shape to your goals by translating them into daily, weekly, monthly, and yearly steps. Finally, you will explore the topic of procrastination and how to minimize its negative effects.

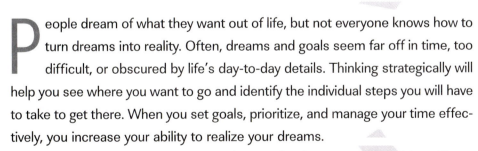

In this chapter, you will explore answers to the following questions:

- Why plan strategically?

- How do you set and achieve goals?

- What are your priorities?

- How can you manage your time?

- Why is procrastination a problem?

WHY PLAN STRATEGICALLY?

If you've ever played a game of chess, participated in a martial arts match, or made a detailed plan of how to reach a specific goal, you have had experience with **strategy**. Strategy is the plan of action, the method, the "how" behind any goal you want to achieve.

Strategic planning means looking at the next week, month, year, or ten years and exploring the positive and negative effects that current choices and actions may have in the future. You have planned strategically just by being in school. You made a decision that the effort of attending college is a legitimate price to pay for the skills, contacts, and opportunities you receive that will help you during school and beyond.

Even though competitive games are good examples of strategy, you don't have to compete against someone else to be strategic. You can be strategic on your own or even in a cooperative situation. As a student, for example, you are continually challenging yourself to achieve. You are learning to analyze what you want in the long term, set goals that will help you achieve what you want, and increase your career options. Here are some more examples of strategic planning:

- Packing for a trip (*the strategy:* considering the potential effects of bringing or not bringing certain items)
- Drafting a proposal for a new law (*the strategy:* considering the effects that the law may have on how people live)
- Making a long-term commitment to a relationship (*the strategy:* considering the effects that you and your partner may have on each other's lives)

Being strategic means challenging yourself as you would challenge a competitor, demanding that you work to achieve your goals with conviction and determination. It means using your decision-making skills to choose how to best accomplish tasks. It means asking questions.

Strategy and Critical Thinking

Strategic planning is a critical thinking process. The mind actions run like a thread through all of your strategic planning. In situations that demand strategy, think critically by asking questions like these:

- If you aim for a certain goal, what actions might cause you to achieve that goal?
- What are the potential effects, positive or negative, of different actions or choices?
- What can you learn from previous experiences that may inspire similar or different actions in current situations?
- What can you recall about what others have done in similar situations?
- Which set of effects would be most helpful or desirable to you?

For any situation that would benefit from strategic planning, from getting ready for a study session to aiming for a career, you can follow these steps (similar to the decision-making process in Chapter 2). They will help you to make choices that bring about the most positive effects.

1. *Establish a goal.* What do you want to achieve? When do you want to achieve it?

2. *Brainstorm possible plans.* What are some ways you can get where you want to go? What steps toward your goal will you have to take one year, five years, ten years, or twenty years from now?

3. *Anticipate all possible effects of each plan.* What positive and negative effects may occur, both soon and in the long term? What approach seems as if it will best help you achieve your goal? Here you may also want to:

   - *Experiment.* If you have the time and opportunity, try different plans and evaluate their positive and negative effects first hand. For example, you might try two different kinds of date books to help you plan your semester, and eventually decide that one works better for you than the other.

   - *Use human resources.* Talk to people who are where you want to be, whether professionally or personally. What caused them to get there? Ask them what they believe are the important steps to take, degrees to have, training to experience, or knowledge to gain.

4. *Put your plan into action.* Act on the decision you have made.

5. *Evaluate continually, and be prepared to change.* Keep evaluating your progress, especially if the goal you are working toward is a long-term one that may take a year or more. The strategies you choose might not have the effects you predicted. If you discover that things are not going the way you planned, for any reason, reevaluate and change your strategy. Making the change will benefit you and keep you on the road to growth.

The most important critical thinking question for successful strategic planning is: How? *How* do you achieve your goals? *How* do you remember what you learn? *How* do you develop a productive idea at work? *How* do you make your mark at school? Strategic planning, in a nutshell, helps you find the best answer to "how."

Benefits of Strategic Planning

Strategic planning has many positive effects. Following are a few from which you can benefit.

Strategy is an essential skill at school and at work. A student who wants to do well in a course has to plan study sessions during which to complete assignments. A lawyer has to anticipate how to respond to points raised in court. A manager has to predict how a specific business plan will serve the company. Strategic planning creates a vision into the future that allows the planner to anticipate possibilities and to be prepared for them.

Strategic planning powers your short-term and long-term goal setting. Once you have set goals, thinking strategically helps you see how to achieve them over time. For example, a student who wants to contribute to his tuition in a year's time might decide to work toward that goal by driving a used car and holding a part-time job during the year.

Strategic planning helps you keep up with technology. As technology develops, new jobs spring up and other jobs become obsolete. The rapid advancement in technological developments over the last decade has increased the rate of change in the job market. Thinking strategically about job opportunities may lead you to a broader range of courses or a major and career in a growing career area, making it more likely that your skills will be in demand when you graduate.

Strategic planning means using critical thinking to develop a vision of your future. Although you can't predict with certainty what will happen, you can ask questions about the potential effects of your actions. With what you know from exploring these questions, you can make plans that you believe will bring the best possible effects for you and others.

After you establish your vision, setting concrete goals will help you use action to realize that vision.

HOW DO YOU SET AND ACHIEVE GOALS?

A **goal** can be something as concrete as buying a health insurance plan or as abstract as controlling your temper. From major life decisions to the tiniest day-to-day activities, setting goals will help you define how you want to live and what you want to achieve.

Paul Timm, an expert in self-management, believes that focus is a key ingredient in setting and achieving goals: "Focus adds power to our actions. If somebody threw a bucket of water on you, you'd get wet . . . But if water was shot at you through a high-pressure nozzle, you might get injured. The only difference is focus."[1] Focus your goal-setting energy by defining a personal mission statement, placing your goals in long-term and short-term time frames, evaluating goals in terms of your values, and exploring different types of goals.

Identify Your Personal Mission Statement

If you choose not to set goals or explore what you want out of life, you may look back on your past with a sense of emptiness, not knowing what you've done or why you did it. You can avoid the emptiness by thinking broadly about where you've been and where you want to be.

> "I have always thought that one man of tolerable abilities may work great changes, and accomplish great affairs among mankind, if he first forms a good plan."
>
> BENJAMIN FRANKLIN

TERMS

Goal
An end toward which effort is directed; an aim or intention.

One way to determine your general direction is to write a personal mission statement. Stephen Covey, author of *The Seven Habits of Highly Effective People*, defines a mission statement as a philosophy outlining what you want to be (character), what you want to do (contributions and achievements), and the principles by which you live. Dr. Covey compares the personal mission statement to the Constitution of the United States, a statement of principles that guides the country:

> A personal mission statement based on correct principles becomes the same kind of standard for an individual. It becomes a personal constitution, the basis for making major, life-directing decisions, the basis for making daily decisions in the midst of the circumstances and emotions that affect our lives.[2]

Your personal mission isn't written in stone. It should change as you move from one phase of life to the next—from single person to spouse, from student to working citizen. Stay flexible and reevaluate your personal mission from time to time.

Here is an example of author Carol Carter's personal mission statement:

> My mission is to use my talents and abilities to help people of all ages, stages, backgrounds, and economic levels achieve their human potential through fully developing their minds and their talents. I also aim to balance work with people in my life, understanding that my family and friends are a priority above all else.

A company, like a person, has to establish standards and principles that guide its many activities. Companies often have mission statements so that each member of the organization clearly understands what to strive for. If a company fails to identify its mission, a thousand well-intentioned employees might focus their energies in just as many different directions, creating chaos and low productivity.

Here is a mission statement from the company that publishes this text:

> To provide the most innovative resources—books, technology, programs—to help students of all ages and stages achieve their academic and professional goals inside the classroom and out.

You will have an opportunity to write your own personal mission statement at the end of this chapter. Thinking through your personal mission can help you begin to take charge of your life. It can put you in control instead of allowing circumstances and events to control you. If you frame your mission statement carefully so that it truly reflects your goals, it can be your guide in everything you do.

Place Goals in Time

Everyone has the same twenty-four hours in a day, but it often doesn't feel like enough. Have you ever had a busy day flash by so quickly that it seems you accomplished nothing? Have you ever felt that way about a longer time—a month or even a year? Your commitments can overwhelm you unless you plan steps toward achieving your goals.

If developing a personal mission statement establishes the big picture, placing your goals within time frames allows you to bring individual areas of that picture into the foreground. Planning your progress step by step will help you maintain your efforts over the extended time often needed to accomplish a goal. Goals fall into two categories: long-term and short-term.

Setting Long-Term Goals

Establish first the goals that have the largest scope, the long-term goals that you aim to attain over a lengthy period, up to a few years or more. As a student, you know what long-term goals are all about. You have set a goal to attend school and earn a degree or certificate. Becoming educated is an admirable goal that often takes years to reach.

Some long-term goals are lifelong, such as a goal to continually learn more about yourself and the world around you. Others have a more definite end, such as a goal to complete a course successfully. To determine your long-term goals, think about what you want out of your professional, educational, and personal life. Here is Carol Carter's long-term goal statement.

> *Carol's Goals:*   To accomplish my mission through writing books, giving seminars, and developing programs that create opportunities for students to learn and develop. To create a personal, professional, and family environment that allows me to manifest my abilities and duly tend to each of my responsibilities.

For example, you may establish long-term goals such as:

- I will graduate from school and know that I have learned all that I could, no matter what my GPA is.
- I will build my leadership and teamwork skills by forming positive, productive relationships with classmates, instructors, and coworkers.

Long-term goals don't have to be lifelong goals. Think about your long-term goals for the coming year. Considering what you want to accomplish in a year's time will give you clarity, focus, and a sense of what has to take place right away. When Carol thought about her long-term goals for the coming year, she came up with the following:

1. Develop programs to provide internships, scholarships, and other quality initiatives for students.
2. Allow time in my personal life to eat well, exercise five days a week, and spend quality time with family and friends. Allow time daily for quiet reflection and spiritual devotion.

In the same way that Carol's goals are tailored to her personality and interests, your goals should reflect who you are. Personal missions and goals are as unique as each individual. Continuing the example above, you might adopt these goals for the coming year:

1. I will earn passing grades in all my classes.
2. I will join two clubs and make an effort to take a leadership role in one of them.

Setting Short-Term Goals

When you divide your long-term goals into smaller, manageable goals that you hope to accomplish within a relatively short time, you are setting short-term goals. Short-term goals narrow your focus, helping you to maintain your progress toward your long-term goals. They are the steps that take you where you want to go, and the answers to the question, "How do I reach that long-term goal?" Imagine that you have set the two long-term goals you just read in the previous section. To stay on track toward those goals, you may want to accomplish these short-term goals in the next six months:

1. I will pass Business Writing I so I can move on to Business Writing II.
2. I will attend four of the monthly meetings of the Journalism Club.

These same goals can be broken down into even smaller parts, such as one month.

1. I will complete five of the ten essays for Business Writing I.
2. I will write an article for next month's Journalism Club newsletter.

In addition to monthly goals, you may have short-term goals that extend for a week, a day, or even a couple of hours in a given day. Take as an example the article you have planned to write for the next month's Journalism Club newsletter. Short-term goals may include the following:

1. Three weeks from now: Final draft ready. Submit it to editor of newsletter.
2. Two weeks from now: Second draft ready. Give it to one more person to review.
3. One week from now: First draft ready. Ask my writing instructor if he will review it.
4. By end of today: Freewrite about subject of article, and narrow down to a specific topic.
5. By 3:00 P.M. today: Brainstorm ideas for the article [Chapter 8 includes a discussion on brainstorming and freewriting].

As you consider your long-term and short-term goals, notice how all of your goals are linked. As Figure 5.1 shows, your long-term goals establish a context for the short-term goals. In turn, your short-term goals make the long-term goals seem clearer and more reachable. The whole system works to keep you on track.

Link Goals With Values

Keeping your values in mind will help you set goals, because goals enable you to put values into practice. When you set and pursue goals that are based on values, you demonstrate and reinforce values by taking action. The strength

FIGURE 5.1 Linking goals together.

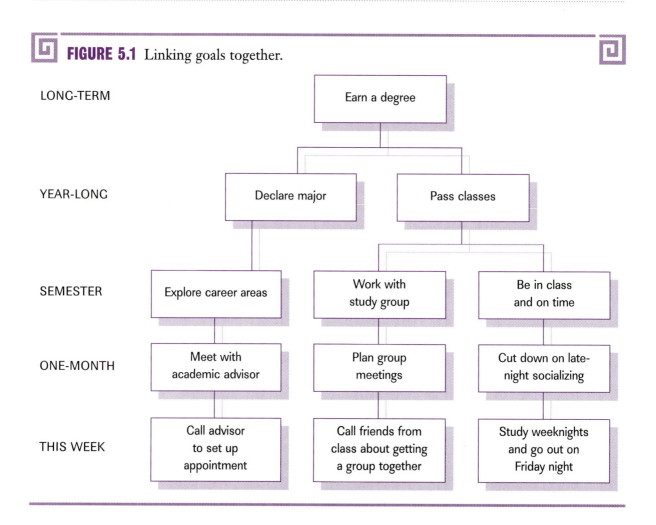

of those values, in turn, reinforces your goals. If you build goals around what is most important to you, you will have a stronger drive to achieve. (See Chapter 4 for more about values.)

If you value health, for example, your mission statement might emphasize your commitment to staying in shape throughout your life. Your long-term goal might be to run a marathon, while your short-term goals might involve your weekly exercise and eating plan.

When you use your values as a compass for your goals, make sure the compass is pointed in the direction of your real feelings. Watch out for the following two pitfalls.

Setting Goals According to Other Peoples' Values

Friends and family might encourage you to strive for what they think you should value. Of course, you might share their values—but, then again, you might not. If you follow advice that you don't believe in, you may have a harder time sticking to your path. For example, someone who attends school primarily because a parent thought it was right could well have less motivation than someone who has his own reasons for pursuing an education. Staying in tune with your own values will help you make decisions that are right for you.

Setting Goals that Reflect Values You Held in the Past

Life changes can alter your values. The best goals reflect what you believe today. For example, a person who has been through a near-fatal car accident may experience a dramatic increase in how she values time with friends and family and a drop in how she values material possessions. Someone who survives a serious illness might value healthy living above all else. Keep in touch with your life's changes so your goals can reflect who you are.

Different Kinds of Goals

People have many different goals, involving different parts of life and different values. As school is currently a focus in your life, examine your educational goals.

Identifying Educational Goals

First, to define a context for your school goals, explore why you have decided to pursue an education. Ask yourself, "Why am I here?" Your answer may include one or more of the following.

- I want to earn a higher salary.
- I want to build marketable skills in a certain career area.
- My supervisor at work says a degree will help me move ahead in my career.
- Most of my friends were going.
- I want to be a student and learn all I can.
- It seems like the only option for me right now.
- I'm recently divorced and need to find a way to earn money.
- Everybody in my family goes to college; it's expected.
- I don't feel ready to jump into the working world yet.
- I got a scholarship.
- My friend loves her job and encouraged me to take courses in the field.
- My parent (or a spouse or partner) pushed me to go to college.
- I need to get better skills so I can provide for my kids.
- I don't really know.

All of these answers are legitimate, even the last one. Being honest with yourself is crucial if you want to discover who you are and what life paths make sense for you. Whatever your reasons are for being in school, you are at the gateway to a journey of discovery.

It isn't easy to enroll in college, pay tuition, decide what to study, sign up for classes, gather the necessary materials, and actually get yourself to the school and into the classroom. Many people give up along the way, but somehow your reasons have been compelling enough for you to have arrived at this point. Thinking about why you value your education will help you stick with it.

"Even if you're on the right track, you'll get run over if you just sit there."
WILL ROGERS

After considering why you are here, start thinking about your educational goals—what you want out of being here. Consider what is available to you—classes, instructors, class schedule, and available degrees or certificates. Think about your commitment to academic excellence and whether honors and awards are goals. If you have an idea of the career you want to pursue, consider the degree(s), certificate(s), or test(s) that may be required. Consider, too, what you want out of your time in school in terms of learning, relationships, and personal growth.

Goals in Your Career and Personal Life

Establish your long-term and short-term goals for your other two paths—career and personal life—as well as for your educational path. Remember that all your goals are interconnected. A school goal is often a step toward a career goal and can affect a personal goal.

Career. Think of your career goals in terms of both *job* and *financial* goals.

- First, consider the job you want after you graduate: career area, requirements, job duties, hours, coworkers, salary, transportation, and company size and style. How much responsibility do you want? Do you want to become a manager, a supervisor, an independent contractor, a business owner?
- Then, consider your financial goals. How much money do you need to pay your bills, live comfortably, and save for the future? Do you need to borrow money for school or a major purchase such as a car? Do you need to reduce your bills? Compare your current financial picture to how you want to live, and set goals that will help you bridge the gap.

Personal life. Consider personal goals in terms of *self*, *family*, and *lifestyle*.

- First look at yourself—character, personality, health/fitness, and conduct. Do you want to gain confidence and knowledge? Get in shape? Change your social circle? Examine the difference between who you are and who you want to be.
- Then consider your family goals. Do you want to stay single, marry, be a parent, or expand a family you've already started? Do you want to improve relations with a mate or other family members? Do you want to live near relatives or far away?
- Finally consider your ideal lifestyle—where you want to live, in what kind of space, and with whom. How do you want to participate in your community? What do you like to do in your leisure time? Consider goals that allow you to live the way you want to live.

Setting and working toward goals can be frightening and difficult at times. Just like learning a new physical task, it takes a lot of practice and repeated efforts. As long as you do all you can to achieve a goal, you haven't failed, even if you don't achieve it completely or in the time frame you had planned. Even one step in the right direction is an achievement. For example, if you wanted to raise your course grade to a B from a D, and you ended up with a C, you still have accomplished something important.

Achieving goals becomes easier when you are realistic about what is possible. Setting priorities will help you make that distinction.

WHAT ARE YOUR PRIORITIES?

When you set a **priority,** you identify what's important at a given moment. Prioritizing helps you focus on your most important goals, especially when the important ones are the most difficult. Human nature often leads people to tackle easy goals first and leave the tough ones for later. The risk is that you might never reach for goals that are crucial to your success.

To explore your priorities, think about your personal mission and look at your school, career, and personal goals. Do one or two of these paths take priority for you right now? In any path, which goals take priority? Which goals take priority over all?

You are a unique individual, and your priorities are yours alone. What may be top priority to someone else may not mean that much to you, and vice versa. You can see this in Figure 5.2, which compares the priorities of two very different students. Each student's priorities are listed in order, with the first priority at the top and the lowest priority at the bottom.

First and foremost, your priorities should reflect your goals. In addition, they should reflect your relationships with others. For example, if you are a parent, your children's needs will probably be high on the priority list. You might be in

> **TERMS**
>
> Priority
> An action or intention that takes precedence in time, attention, or position.

FIGURE 5.2 Comparison of two students' priorities.

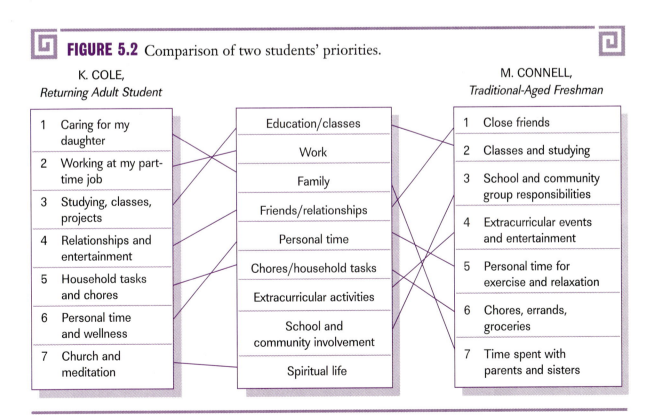

school so you can get a better job and give them a better life. If you are in a committed relationship, you might schedule your classes so you and your partner are together as often as possible. Even as you consider others' needs, though, be true to your own goals and priorities so you can make the most of who you are.

Setting priorities moves you closer to accomplishing specific goals. It also helps you begin planning to achieve your goals within specific time frames. Being able to achieve your goals is directly linked to effective time management.

HOW CAN YOU MANAGE YOUR TIME?

Time is one of your most valuable and precious resources. Time doesn't discriminate. Everyone has the same twenty-four hours in a day, every day. Your responsibility and your potential for success lie in how you use yours. Even though you cannot change how time passes, you can spend it wisely by taking steps to achieve your goals. Efficient time management helps you achieve your goals in a steady, step-by-step process.

People have a variety of approaches to time management. Your learning style (see Chapter 6) can help you understand how you use time. For example, students with strong logical-mathematical intelligence tend to organize activities within a framework of time. Because they stay aware of how long it takes them to do something or travel somewhere, they usually are prompt. By contrast, less logical learners with perhaps stronger visual or interpersonal intelligence are more likely to neglect details such as how much time they have to complete a task. They often are late without meaning to be.

Time management, like physical fitness, is a lifelong pursuit. No one can plan a perfect schedule or build a terrific physique and then be "done." Throughout your life, your ability to manage your time will vary with your stress level, how busy you are, and other factors. Don't expect perfection— just keep at it. Above all, maintain a critical thinking view of your time-management strategies, periodically asking questions about the effects of your actions and investigating how you might make changes and improvements. Time management involves building a schedule, taking responsibility for how you spend your time, and being flexible.

Build a Schedule

Just as a road map helps you travel from place to place, a schedule is a time-and-activity map that helps you get from the beginning of the day (or week or month) to the end as smoothly as possible. Schedules help you gain control of your life in two ways:

1. They allocate segments of time for the fulfillment of your daily, weekly, monthly, and longer-term goals.
2. They serve as a concrete reminder of tasks, events, due dates, responsibilities, and deadlines.

Few moments are more stressful than suddenly realizing you have forgotten to take a test or to be at your job. Scheduling can help you avoid events like these.

Keep a Date Book

Gather the tools of the trade: a pen or pencil and a date book (sometimes called a planner). A date book is indispensable for keeping track of your time. Some of you have used date books for years. Others have had no luck with them or have never tried. Even if you don't think you would benefit from one, give it a try. Paul Timm says, "Most time management experts agree that rule number one in a thoughtful planning process is: Use some form of a planner where you can write things down."

The two major types of date books are:

1. *Day-at-a-glance.* This version devotes a page to each day. Although it gives you ample space to write the day's activities, it's harder to see what's ahead.

2. *Week-at-a-glance.* This date book gives you a view of the week's plans but has less room to write per day.

If you write detailed daily plans, you might like the day-at-a-glance version. If you prefer to remind yourself of plans ahead of time, try the book that shows a week's schedule all at once. Some date books contain sections for monthly and yearly goals. You also can create your own sheets for yearly and monthly notations in a notepad section, if your book has one, or on plain paper that you then can insert into the book.

Another option to consider is an *electronic planner*, a compact minicomputer that can hold a large amount of information. You can use it to schedule your days and weeks, make to-do lists, and create and store an address book. Electronic planners are powerful, convenient, and often fun. They certainly cost more than the paper version, though, and you can lose a lot of important data if something goes wrong with the computer inside. Evaluate your options and decide what works best for you.

Set Weekly and Daily Goals

The most ideal time management starts with the smallest tasks and builds to bigger ones. Setting short-term goals that tie in to your long-term goals has the following benefits:

- Increased meaning for your daily activities
- Shaping your path toward achievement of your long-term goals
- A sense of order and progress

For college students, as well as working people, the week is often the easiest unit of time to consider at one shot. Weekly goal setting and planning allows you to keep track of day-to-day activities while giving you the larger perspective of what is coming up during the week. Take some time before each week starts to remind yourself of your long-term goals. Keeping long-term goals in mind will help you determine related short-term goals that you can accomplish during the week to come. Figure 5.3 shows parts of a daily schedule and a weekly schedule.

FIGURE 5.3

Daily and weekly
schedules.

Monday, March 22		1999
Time	Tasks	Priority
7:00 AM		
8:00	Up at 8am — finish homework	*
9:00		
10:00	Business Administration	
11:00	Renew driver's license @ DMV	*
12:00 PM		
1:00	Lunch	
2:00	Writing Seminar (peer editing today)	*
3:00	↓	
4:00	check on Ms. Schwartz's office hrs.	
5:00	5:30 work out	
6:00	└→6:30	
7:00	Dinner	
8:00	Read two chapter for Business Admin.	
9:00	↓	
10:00		
11:00		

Monday, March 22			
8		Call: Mike Blair	1
9	BIO 212	Finanical Aid Office	2
10		EMS 262 *Paramedic*	3
11	CHEM 203	role-play	4
12			5
Evening	6pm yoga class		

Tuesday, March 23			
8	Finish reading assignment!	Work @ library	1
9			2
10	ENG 112	(study for quiz)	3
11	↓		4
12			5
Evening		↓ until 7pm	

Wednesday, March 24			
8		Meet w/advisor	1
9	BIO 212		2
10		EMS 262	3
11	CHEM 203 *Quiz		4
12		Pick up photos	5
Evening	6pm Aerobics		

Link Daily and Weekly Goals With Long-Term Goals

After you evaluate what you need to accomplish in the coming year, semester, month, week, and day to reach your long-term goals, use your schedule to record those steps. Write down the short-term goals that will enable you to stay on track. Here is how a student might map out two different goals over a year's time.

This year:	Complete enough courses to graduate.
	Improve my physical fitness.
This semester:	Complete my accounting class with a B average or higher.
	Lose 10 pounds and exercise regularly.
This month:	Set up study-group schedule to coincide with quizzes.
	Begin walking and weight lifting.
This week:	Meet with study group; go over material for Friday's quiz.
	Go for a fitness walk three times; go to weight room twice.
Today:	Go over Chapter 3 in accounting text.
	Walk for 40 minutes.

Prioritize Goals

Prioritizing enables you to use your date book with maximum efficiency. On any given day, your goals will have varying degrees of importance. Record your goals first, and then label them according to their level of importance, using these categories: Priority 1, Priority 2, and Priority 3. Identify these categories by using any code that makes sense to you. Some people use numbers, as above. Some use letters (A, B, C). Some write activities in different colors according to priority level. Some use symbols (*, +, –).

Priority 1 activities are the most important things in your life. They might include, for instance, attending class, picking up a child from day care, and paying bills.

Priority 2 activities are part of your routine. Examples include grocery shopping, working out, participating in a school organization, and cleaning. Priority 2 tasks are important but more flexible than priority 1's.

Priority 3 activities are those you would like to do but can reschedule without much sacrifice. Examples might be a trip to the mall, a visit to a friend, a social phone call, or a sports event. As much as you would like to do them, you don't consider them urgent. Many people don't enter priority 3 tasks in their date books until they are sure they have time to get them done.

Prioritizing your activities is essential for two reasons.

1. Some activities are more important than others, and effective time management requires that you focus most of your energy on priority 1 items.

2. Looking at all your priorities helps you plan when you can get things done. Often, it's not possible to get all your priority 1 activities done early in the day, especially if they involve scheduled classes or meetings. Prioritizing helps you set priority 1 items and then schedule priority 2 and 3 items around them as they fit.

Keep Track of Events

Your date book also enables you to schedule events. Think of events in terms of how they tie in with your long-term goals, just as you would your other tasks. For example, attending a wedding in a few months will contribute to your commitment to spending time with your family. Being aware of quiz dates, due dates for assignments, and meeting dates will aid your goals to achieve in school and become involved.

Note events in your date book so you can be aware of them ahead of time. Write them in daily, weekly, monthly, or even yearly sections, where a quick look will remind you that they are approaching. Following are some kinds of events worth noting in your date book:

- Due dates for papers, projects, presentations, and tests
- Important meetings, medical appointments, and due dates for bill payments
- Birthdays, anniversaries, social events, holidays, and other special occasions
- Benchmarks for steps toward a goal, such as due dates for sections of a project or a deadline for losing five pounds on your way to twenty

One other positive effect of writing down events is that it will help you plan strategically how to fit them in among your other activities. For example, if you have three big tests and a presentation all in one week, you'll want to take time in the weeks preceding to prepare for them.

Take Responsibility for How You Spend Your Time

When you plan your activities with an eye toward achieving your most important goals, you are taking responsibility for how you live. The following strategies will help you stay in charge of your choices.

Plan your schedule each week. Before each week starts, note events, goals, and priorities. Decide where to fit activities such as studying and priority 3 items. For example, if you have a test on Thursday, you can plan study sessions on the preceding days. If you have more free time on Tuesday and Friday than other days, you can plan workouts or priority 3 activities at those times.

Make and use to-do lists. Use a to-do list to record what you want to accomplish. If you generate a daily or weekly to-do list on a separate piece of paper, you can look at all tasks and goals at once. This will help you consider time frames and priorities. You might want to prioritize your tasks and transfer them to appropriate places in your date book. Some people create daily to-do lists right on their date book pages. You can tailor a to-do list to an important event such as exam week or an especially busy day. This kind of specific to-do list can help you prioritize and accomplish an unusually large task load.

Post monthly and yearly calendars at home. Keeping a calendar on the wall will help you stay aware of important events. You can purchase one or draw it yourself, month by month, on plain paper. Use a yearly or a monthly version (Figure 5.4 shows part of a monthly calendar), and keep it where you can refer

FIGURE 5.4 Monthly calendar.

AUGUST 1999

SUNDAY	MONDAY	TUESDAY	WEDNESDAY	THURSDAY	FRIDAY	SATURDAY
1	2 WORK	3 Turn in English paper	4 Dentist 2pm	5 Chem. test	6	7
8 Frank's B-day	9 Psych test	10 6:30 pm Meeting at Student Center	11 Statistics quiz WORK	12 History study group	13 WORK	14 WORK
15	16 WORK	17	18 WORK	19	20	21
22	23	24	25	26	27	28
29	30	31				

to it often. If you live with family or friends, make the calendar a group project so that you stay aware of each other's plans. Knowing each other's schedules also can help you avoid problems such as two people needing the car at the same time.

Schedule down time. When you're wiped out from too much activity, you don't have the energy to accomplish as much. Some **down time** will refresh you and improve your attitude. Even half an hour a day will help. Fill the time with whatever relaxes you—eating a snack, reading, watching television, playing a game or sport, walking, writing, or just doing nothing. Make down time a priority.

Shake off the judgments of others. A student who thinks no one will hire him because of his weight may not search for jobs. A student who believes her instructor is prejudiced against her might not study for that instructor's course. Instead of letting **judgments** like these rob you of your control of your time, choose actions that improve your circumstances. If you lose a job, for example, spend an hour a day investigating other job opportunities. If you have trouble with an instructor, address the problem with that instructor directly. Try to find an active option that will allow you to be in control.

Be Flexible

No matter how well you plan your time, the changes that life brings can make you feel out of control. One minute you seem to be on track, and the next minute chaos hits—in forms as minor as a room change for a class or as major as a medical emergency. Coping with changes can cause stress. As your stress level rises, your sense of control dwindles.

TERMS

Down time
Quiet time set aside for relaxation and low-key activity.

TERMS

Judgments
Considered opinions, assessments, or evaluations.

Although you cannot always choose your circumstances, you might have some control over how you *handle* them. Use the following ideas to cope with changes large and small.

Day-to-Day Changes

A small change any time can result in priority shifts that jumble your schedule. On Monday, a homework assignment due in a week might be priority 2. Then if you haven't gotten to it by Saturday, it becomes priority 1. Sometimes a class is canceled, so you have extra time on your hands. Perhaps your baby-sitter doesn't show up, and you have to figure out how to provide care for your child.

If you accept change as part of life, you will be more prepared to reschedule tasks. For changes that occur frequently, you can make a backup plan ahead of time (such as having a friend on call for emergency child care). For unexpected free time, you could keep some work or reading with you. For other situations, the best you can do is to keep an open mind about possibilities and to remember to call on your resources in a pinch. Your problem-solving skills (see Chapter 2) will help you build your ability to adjust to whatever changes come your way.

Life Changes

"Obstacles are what people see when they take their eyes off the goal."

NEW YORK
SUBWAY
BULLETIN
BOARD

Sometimes changes are more serious than a shift in class schedule. Your car breaks down; your relationship falls apart; you fail a class; you or a close family member develops a medical problem; you get laid off at work. These changes call for more extensive problem solving. They also require an ability to look at the big picture. Whereas a class change affects your schedule for a day, a medical problem may affect your schedule for much longer.

When life hands you a major curve ball, first remember that you still have some choices about how to handle the situation. Then use your problem-solving skills to think critically about what you can do. If possible, talk with people who can help you. Before choosing and implementing a solution, carefully explore all of your options. Finally, make use of your resources. Your academic advisor, counselor, dean, financial aid advisor, or instructors may have ideas and assistance to offer you, but they can help only if you let them know what you need.

No matter how well you schedule your time, you will have moments when it's hard to stay in control. Knowing how to identify and avoid procrastination will help you get back on track.

WHY IS PROCRASTINATION A PROBLEM?

TERMS

Procrastination
The act of putting off a task until another time.

When you postpone tasks, you are engaging in **procrastination.** People procrastinate for different reasons. Having trouble with goal setting is one reason. People might project goals too far into the future, set unrealistic goals that are too frustrating to reach, or have no goals at all. People also procrastinate because they don't believe in their ability to complete a task or don't believe in themselves in general. Procrastination is human, and not every instance of procrastination means trouble. If it is taken to the extreme, however, procrastination can develop into a habit that will dominate a person's behavior and cause problems at school, on the job, and at home.

Jane B. Burka and Lenora M. Yuen, authors of *Procrastination: Why You Do It and What To Do About It*, say that habitual procrastinators are often perfectionists who create problems by using their ability to achieve as the only measure of their self-worth:

> The performance becomes the only measure of the person; nothing else is taken into account. An outstanding performance means an outstanding person; a mediocre performance means a mediocre person . . . As long as you procrastinate, you never have to confront the real limits of your ability, whatever those limits are.[3]

For the procrastinator, the fear of failure prevents taking the risk that could bring success.

Following are some ways to fight your tendencies to procrastinate.

Think critically about positive and negative effects. What effects lie ahead if you get it done? What will be the effects if you continue to put it off? Which situation has better effects? Chances are that you will benefit more in the long term from facing the task head-on.

Set reasonable goals. Plan your goals carefully, allowing enough time to complete them. Unreasonable goals can be so intimidating that you do nothing at all. "Pay off the credit-card bill next month" could throw you. But, "Pay off the credit-card bill in ten months" might inspire you to take action.

Break the task into smaller parts. Look at the task in terms of its parts. How can you approach it step by step? If you can concentrate on achieving one small goal at a time, the task might become less of a burden. In addition, setting concrete time limits for each task might help you feel more in control.

Get started whether or not you "feel like it." Going from doing nothing to doing something is often the hardest part of avoiding procrastination. Tell yourself that you have to take only one step at a time. Once you start, you might find it easier to continue.

Ask for help with tasks and projects at school, work, and home. Once you identify what's holding you up, see who can help you face the task. For example, if you have put off an assignment, ask your instructor for guidance. If you avoid a project because you dislike the employee with whom you work, talk to your supervisor about adjusting tasks or personnel. If you need accommodations because of a disability, don't assume that others know about it.

Don't expect perfection. No one is perfect. Most people learn by starting at the beginning and wading through mistakes and confusion. It's better to try your best than to do nothing at all.

Procrastination is natural, but it can cause you problems if you let it get the best of you. When it does happen, take some time to think about the causes. What is it about this situation that frightens you or puts you off? If you discover what causes lie underneath the procrastination, you might be able to use your problem-solving skills to address those causes.

In Hebrew, the word *chai* means "life," representing all aspects of life—spiritual, emotional, family, educational, and career. Individual Hebrew characters have number values. Because the characters in the word *chai* add up to 18, the number 18 has come to be associated with good luck. The word *chai* is often worn as a good-luck charm. As you plan your goals, think about your view of luck. Many people think that a person can create his or her own luck by pursuing goals persistently and staying open to possibilities and opportunities. Canadian novelist Robertson Davies once said, "What we call luck is the inner man externalized. We make things happen to us."

Consider that your vision of life might largely determine how you live. You can prepare the way for luck by establishing a personal mission and forging ahead toward your goals. If you believe that the life you want awaits you, you will be able to recognize and make the most of luck when it comes around. *L'Chaim*—to life, and good luck.

Chapter 5 Building Thinking Skills

Name _____   Date _____

LIFE THINKING: Applying What You Learn

5.1 Discover How You Spend Your Time

In the chart on the following page, estimate the total time you think you spend per week on each listed activity. Then add the hours. If your number is above 168 (the number of hours in a week), rethink your estimates and recalculate so the total is equal to or below 168. Then subtract your total from 168. Whatever is left over is your estimate of hours that you spend in unscheduled activities.

$$168$$

Minus total _____

Unscheduled time _____

ACTIVITY	ESTIMATED TIME SPENT
Class	
Work	
Studying	
Sleeping	
Eating	
Family time/child care	
Commuting/traveling	
Chores and personal business	
Friends and important relationships	
Telephone time	
Leisure/entertainment	
Spiritual life	
Total	

Now spend a week recording exactly how you spend your time. The following chart has blocks showing half-hour increments. As you go through the week, write in what you do each hour, indicating when you started and when you stopped. Don't forget activities that don't feel like "activities," such as sleeping, relaxing, and watching TV. Also, be honest—record your actual activities instead of how you *want* to spend your time or how you think you *should* have spent your time. There are no wrong answers.

MONDAY		TUESDAY		WEDNESDAY		THURSDAY	
TIME	ACTIVITY	TIME	ACTIVITY	TIME	ACTIVITY	TIME	ACTIVITY
5:00 AM		5:00 AM		5:00 AM		5:00 AM	
5:30 AM		5:30 AM		5:30 AM		5:30 AM	
6:00 AM		6:00 AM		6:00 AM		6:00 AM	
6:30 AM		6:30 AM		6:30 AM		6:30 AM	
7:00 AM		7:00 AM		7:00 AM		7:00 AM	
7:30 AM		7:30 AM		7:30 AM		7:30 AM	
8:00 AM		8:00 AM		8:00 AM		8:00 AM	
8:30 AM		8:30 AM		8:30 AM		8:30 AM	
9:00 AM		9:00 AM		9:00 AM		9:00 AM	
9:30 AM		9:30 AM		9:30 AM		9:30 AM	
10:00 AM		10:00 AM		10:00 AM		10:00 AM	
10:30 AM		10:30 AM		10:30 AM		10:30 AM	
11:00 AM		11:00 AM		11:00 AM		11:00 AM	
11:30 AM		11:30 AM		11:30 AM		11:30 AM	
12:00 PM		12:00 PM		12:00 PM		12:00 PM	
12:30 PM		12:30 PM		12:30 PM		12:30 PM	
1:00 PM		1:00 PM		1:00 PM		1:00 PM	
1:30 PM		1:30 PM		1:30 PM		1:30 PM	
2:00 PM		2:00 PM		2:00 PM		2:00 PM	
2:30 PM		2:30 PM		2:30 PM		2:30 PM	
3:00 PM		3:00 PM		3:00 PM		3:00 PM	
3:30 PM		3:30 PM		3:30 PM		3:30 PM	
4:00 PM		4:00 PM		4:00 PM		4:00 PM	
4:30 PM		4:30 PM		4:30 PM		4:30 PM	
5:00 PM		5:00 PM		5:00 PM		5:00 PM	
5:30 PM		5:30 PM		5:30 PM		5:30 PM	
6:00 PM		6:00 PM		6:00 PM		6:00 PM	
6:30 PM		6:30 PM		6:30 PM		6:30 PM	
7:00 PM		7:00 PM		7:00 PM		7:00 PM	
7:30 PM		7:30 PM		7:30 PM		7:30 PM	
8:00 PM		8:00 PM		8:00 PM		8:00 PM	
8:30 PM		8:30 PM		8:30 PM		8:30 PM	
9:00 PM		9:00 PM		9:00 PM		9:00 PM	
9:30 PM		9:30 PM		9:30 PM		9:30 PM	
10:00 PM		10:00 PM		10:00 PM		10:00 PM	
10:30 PM		10:30 PM		10:30 PM		10:30 PM	
11:00 PM		11:00 PM		11:00 PM		11:00 PM	
11:30 PM		11:30 PM		11:30 PM		11:30 PM	

FRIDAY		SATURDAY		SUNDAY	
TIME	ACTIVITY	TIME	ACTIVITY	TIME	ACTIVITY
5:00 AM		5:00 AM		5:00 AM	
5:30 AM		5:30 AM		5:30 AM	
6:00 AM		6:00 AM		6:00 AM	
6:30 AM		6:30 AM		6:30 AM	
7:00 AM		7:00 AM		7:00 AM	
7:30 AM		7:30 AM		7:30 AM	
8:00 AM		8:00 AM		8:00 AM	
8:30 AM		8:30 AM		8:30 AM	
9:00 AM		9:00 AM		9:00 AM	
9:30 AM		9:30 AM		9:30 AM	
10:00 AM		10:00 AM		10:00 AM	
10:30 AM		10:30 AM		10:30 AM	
11:00 AM		11:00 AM		11:00 AM	
11:30 AM		11:30 AM		11:30 AM	
12:00 PM		12:00 PM		12:00 PM	
12:30 PM		12:30 PM		12:30 PM	
1:00 PM		1:00 PM		1:00 PM	
1:30 PM		1:30 PM		1:30 PM	
2:00 PM		2:00 PM		2:00 PM	
2:30 PM		2:30 PM		2:30 PM	
3:00 PM		3:00 PM		3:00 PM	
3:30 PM		3:30 PM		3:30 PM	
4:00 PM		4:00 PM		4:00 PM	
4:30 PM		4:30 PM		4:30 PM	
5:00 PM		5:00 PM		5:00 PM	
5:30 PM		5:30 PM		5:30 PM	
6:00 PM		6:00 PM		6:00 PM	
6:30 PM		6:30 PM		6:30 PM	
7:00 PM		7:00 PM		7:00 PM	
7:30 PM		7:30 PM		7:30 PM	
8:00 PM		8:00 PM		8:00 PM	
8:30 PM		8:30 PM		8:30 PM	
9:00 PM		9:00 PM		9:00 PM	
9:30 PM		9:30 PM		9:30 PM	
10:00 PM		10:00 PM		10:00 PM	
10:30 PM		10:30 PM		10:30 PM	
11:00 PM		11:00 PM		11:00 PM	
11:30 PM		11:30 PM		11:30 PM	

Now go through the following chart and look at how many hours you actually spent on the activities for which you estimated your hours before. Tally the hours in the boxes in the following table using straight tally marks; round off to half hours and use a short tally mark for a half-hour spent. In the third column, total the hours for each activity. Leave the "ideal time in hours" column blank for now.

ACTIVITY	TIME TALLIED OVER ONE-WEEK PERIOD	TOTAL TIME IN HOURS	IDEAL TIME IN HOURS
Example: Class	‖‖‖ ‖‖‖ ‖‖‖ ‖	16.5	
Class			
Work			
Studying			
Sleeping			
Eating			
Family time/child care			
Commuting/traveling			
Chores and personal business			
Friends and important relationships			
Telephone time			
Leisure/entertainment			
Spiritual life			
Total			

Add the totals in the third column to find your GRAND TOTAL:

Compare your grand total to your estimated grand total; compare your actual activity hour totals to your estimated activity hour totals. What matches and what doesn't? Describe the most interesting similarities and differences.

_____

_____

_____

_____

What is the one biggest surprise about how you spend your time?

_____

_____

_____

_____

Name one change you would like to make in how you spend your time.

_____

_____

_____

_____

Think about what kinds of changes might help you improve your ability to set and achieve goals. Ask yourself important questions about what you do daily, weekly, and monthly. On what activities do you think you should spend more or less time? Go back to the chart on p. 128 and fill in the Ideal Time in Hours column. When you think about the changes you want to make in your life, consider the difference between actual hours and ideal hours.

5.2 *Think Critically About Procrastination*

Name one situation in which you habitually procrastinate.

_____

_____

What are the effects of your procrastination? Discuss how procrastination can affect the quality of your work, motivation, productivity, ability to be on time, grades, or self-perception.

_____

_____

_____

_____

What you would like to do differently in this situation? How can you achieve what you want? Brainstorm three possible solutions to the problem and write them below. On a separate piece of paper, use your problem-solving plan (see p. 50) to evaluate solutions and choose one.

1. _____

2. _____

3. _____

TEAM THINKING: Working Together

5.3 *Individual Priorities*

In a group of three or four, brainstorm long-term goals and have one member of the group write them down. From that list, pick out ten goals that everyone can relate to most. Each group member then should take five minutes alone to evaluate the relative importance of the ten goals and rank them in the order that he or she prefers. Use a 1-to-10 scale, with 1 being the highest priority and 10 the lowest.

Display the rankings of each group member side by side. How many different orders are there? Discuss why each person has a different set of priorities, and be open to different views. What factors in different people's lives have caused them to select particular rankings? If you have time, discuss how priorities have changed for each group member over the course of a year, perhaps by having each person re-rank the goals according to his or her needs a year ago.

 WORK THINKING: Career Portfolio

5.4 *Strategic Career Planning*

The most reasonable and reachable career goals are ones that are linked to your school and life goals. First, name a long-term career goal of yours.

_____

_____

Then imagine that you will begin working toward it. Indicate a series of steps you can take—from short-term to long-term—that you think will help you achieve this goal. Write what you hope to accomplish in the next year, the next six months, the next month, the next week, and the next day.

TIME FRAME	CAREER GOAL
One Year	_____
	_____
	_____
Six Months	_____
	_____
	_____
One Month	_____
	_____
	_____

This Week   _____
          _____
          _____

Today   _____
          _____
          _____

Now explore your job priorities. How do you want your job to benefit you? Note your requirements in each of the following areas.

Salary/wage level _____

Time of day _____

Hours per week (part-time versus full-time) _____

Duties _____

Location _____

Flexibility _____

Affiliation with school or financial aid program _____

What kind of job, in the career area for which you listed your goals, might fit all or most of your requirements? List two possibilities here. Briefly note any positive or negative effects you predict either job may have for you.

1. _____

Potential effects _____
_____
_____

2. _____

Potential effects _____
_____
_____

QUESTIONING YOUR WORLD:
Information Literacy Journal

To record your thoughts, use a separate journal or the lined pages at the end of the chapter.

5.5 *Personal Mission Statement*

Using the personal mission statement examples in the chapter as a guide, consider what you want out of your life and create your own personal mission statement. You can write it in paragraph form, in a list of long-term goals, or in the form of a think link. Take as much time as you need to be as complete as possible. Write a draft on a separate sheet of paper and take time to revise it before you write the final version here. If you have created a think link rather than a verbal statement, attach it separately.

After you have created your personal mission statement, analyze it in terms of the information you encounter in your life. What information sources have influenced your mission? What values lie behind your mission, and where do you think you got them? If any aspect of your mission came from something you read, saw on TV, heard on the radio, or saw on the Internet that affected you strongly, name the source and discuss why you think it had that effect on you.

Journal

Name _____ Date _____

Journal

Name _____   Date _____

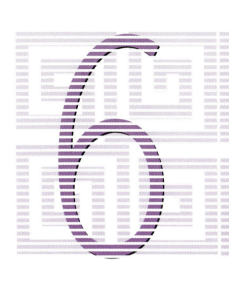

6

Thinking About How You Learn

Learning Styles

earning in college and throughout your life can help you keep up with the rapid pace at which technology is changing the world. The Internet allows people to send documents and photographs over phone lines in the blink of an eye. Cameras, cars, stereos, and all kinds of other items have computer chips inside them that control their operation. Medical science has discovered how to isolate the genes that cause certain genetic diseases and characteristics.

If you begin to think critically about the factors surrounding learning—individual tendencies, particular environments, certain teaching styles—you will be able to make the most of what helps you learn most effectively. In this chapter you will become aware of your learning style by completing an assessment based on the Multiple Intelligences theory. You then will explore other important

135

elements of self: your self-perception, your preferences, your habits, and your abilities.

In this chapter, you will explore answers to the following questions:

- What are some common assumptions about learning?
- How can you discover your learning style?
- What are the benefits of knowing your learning style?
- How do you explore who you are?
- How can you start thinking about choosing a major?

WHAT ARE SOME COMMON ASSUMPTIONS ABOUT LEARNING?

The human mind is a powerful tool. Each person has a unique capacity to take in and process information. Certain common assumptions about learning, however, can prevent people from making the most of their abilities. Here are three such assumptions.

1. There is one "best" way to learn, and the most successful people are those who learn that way. It may seem that the educational system favors the verbal learner, and that the workplace favors the organized, detail-oriented worker. A design course might emphasize the visual, however, and a psychology course might emphasize interpersonal interaction. Furthermore, success in the workplace is not limited to one kind of learner. A software salesperson may use communication savvy to ride the wave to success, and a hospice worker may be valued most for personal integrity and caring.

2. Everyone has a set capacity for learning. The way people are often labeled reinforces the idea that everyone has the same capacity for learning. You go through your educational experience being given a place in line (97th in your class, a C on a scale of A to F), or being categorized (learning disabled, gifted and talented, developmental English, Advanced Placement History), based on your performance. These labels can lead you and others to form assumptions about your learning capacity. Such assumptions, however, can limit students to levels far below what they actually can achieve. Winston Churchill (Prime Minister of England during World War II) failed the sixth grade, for example, and Louis Pasteur (master chemist) was a poor student in chemistry.

3. If you don't have a clear talent for something, you shouldn't pursue it. It might seem that people who have certain talents don't even have to lift a finger to find success. Remember, though, that the information you receive about successful people sometimes is limited to what the media want to communicate. You might not hear about how hard these people work each day or the tough road that they traveled to get where they are. Ask questions of the people around you whom you consider to be successful. Did they have an immediate aptitude for what they do? What obstacles did, or do, they have to overcome? What kind of day-to-day hard work and learning lies behind the more visible side of what they do?

Think critically about these assumptions and any others you know of, using what you learned in Chapter 3. Ask questions: What examples support or negate this statement? Does what I already know support it or not? Is it fact or opinion? What positive or negative effects might result from assuming this to be true?

There are many ways to learn, and different strategies are suited to different tasks and situations. Each person's learning style is unique. Like any other personality trait, **learning style** is part of your individual set of personal characteristics.

TERMS

Learning style
A particular way in which the mind receives and processes information.

 ## HOW CAN YOU DISCOVER YOUR LEARNING STYLE?

Many different assessments—by exploring strengths and weaknesses, abilities and limitations—help people discover how they learn. This chapter focuses on one assessment. If you want to explore learning styles further, see the two additional assessments in Appendix A. You also can find information about other assessments, such as the widely used Myers-Briggs Type Indicator (MBTI) and the Keirsey Sorter (a shorter version of the MBTI), through your career or counseling center or even online.

After you complete the assessment, you will read about strategies that can help you make the most of certain aspects of your style, both in school and beyond. Knowing how you learn will help you to improve your understanding of yourself—how you function at school, in the workplace, and in your personal life.

Multiple Intelligences Theory

There is a saying, "It is not how smart you are, but how you are smart." In 1983, Howard Gardner, a Harvard University professor, published his theory of multiple intelligences and changed the way people perceive **intelligence** and learning. Gardner believes all people possess at least eight distinct intelligences, and that every person has developed some intelligences more fully than others. Most people have at one time learned something quickly and comfortably. Most also have had the opposite experience: No matter how hard they tried, something they wanted to learn just would not sink in. According to the multiple intelligences theory, when you find a task or subject easy, you probably are using a more fully developed intelligence; when you have more trouble, you may be using a less developed intelligence.[1]

Following are brief descriptions of the focus of each of the intelligences. Study skills that reinforce each intelligence are described later in the chapter.

TERMS

Intelligence
As defined by H. Gardner, an ability to solve problems or fashion products that are useful in a particular cultural setting or community.

- *Verbal–linguistic intelligence*—ability to communicate through language (listening, reading, writing, speaking)

TERMS

Kinesthetic
Describes physi-
cal sensation
caused by body
movements and
tensions.

- *Logical–mathematical intelligence*—ability to understand logical reasoning and problem solving (math, science, patterns, sequences)
- *Bodily–**kinesthetic** intelligence*—ability to use the physical body skillfully and to take in knowledge through bodily sensation (coordination, working with the hands)
- *Visual–spatial intelligence*—ability to understand spatial relationships and to perceive and create images (visual art, graphic design, charts and maps)
- *Interpersonal intelligence*—ability to relate to others, noticing their moods, motivations, and feelings (social activity, cooperative learning, teamwork)
- *Intrapersonal intelligence*—ability to understand one's own behavior and feelings (self-awareness, independence, time spent alone)
- *Musical intelligence*—ability to comprehend and create meaningful sound (music, sensitivity to sound, understanding patterns)
- *Naturalistic intelligence*—ability to understand features of the environment (interest in nature, environmental balance, ecosystem, stress relief brought by natural environments)

The multiple intelligences reach beyond helping you understand how you learn. They help you to see how you operate in every arena of life: how you think, how you relate to others, how you understand yourself, and more. Because this chapter focuses on learning styles, however, your collective set of scores will be referred to here as your "learning style." Elsewhere in the text you will find references that illustrate how the intelligences influence other skills and life areas.

Pathways to Learning

The following assessment (pp. 139–140) of your multiple intelligences, *Pathways to Learning*, will help you determine the levels to which your intelligences are developed. Don't be concerned if some of your scores are low (that is true of almost everyone, even your instructors and the authors). To rate each statement, think critically. Evaluate how similar or different to your own behavior you consider the statement to be. The more closely you can see who you are today, the more effectively you can set goals for where you want to go from here.

The Reasonable Approach to Learning Style

No learning style assessment can give you the final word on who you are and what you can and cannot do. It's human to want an easy answer—a one-page printout of the secret to your identity—but this kind of quick fix does not exist. You are a complex person who cannot be summed up by a test or evaluation.

The most reasonable way to approach any assessment of learning style is as a reference point rather than a label. There are no "right" answers, no "best" set of intelligences scores. Instead of boxing yourself into one or more categories, which limits you, approach your learning style assessment as a tool with which you can expand your idea of yourself. Think of it as a new set of eyeglasses for a person with somewhat blurred vision. The glasses will not

(text continued on pg. 141)

PATHWAYS TO LEARNING[3]

Directions: Rate each statement as follows: rarely 1; sometimes 2; usually 3; always 4.

Write the number of your response (1–4) in the box next to the statement and total each set of the six questions.

Developed by Joyce Bishop, Ph.D., and based upon Howard Gardner, *Frames of Mind: The Theory of Multiple Intelligences.*

- ☐ 1. I enjoy physical activities.
- ☐ 2. I am uncomfortable sitting still.
- ☐ 3. I prefer to learn through doing.
- ☐ 4. When sitting, I move my legs or hands.
- ☐ 5. I enjoy working with my hands.
- ☐ 6. I like to pace when I'm thinking or studying.
- ☐ **TOTAL for Bodily–Kinesthetic**

- ☐ 7. I use maps easily.
- ☐ 8. I draw pictures/diagrams when explaining ideas.
- ☐ 9. I can assemble items easily from diagrams.
- ☐ 10. I enjoy drawing or photography.
- ☐ 11. I do not like to read long paragraphs.
- ☐ 12. I prefer a drawn map over written directions.
- ☐ **TOTAL for Visual–Spatial**

- ☐ 13. I enjoy telling stories.
- ☐ 14. I like to write.
- ☐ 15. I like to read.
- ☐ 16. I express myself clearly.
- ☐ 17. I am good at negotiating.
- ☐ 18. I like to discuss topics that interest me.
- ☐ **TOTAL for Verbal–Linguistic**

- ☐ 19. I like math in school.
- ☐ 20. I like science.
- ☐ 21. I problem-solve well.
- ☐ 22. I question how things work.
- ☐ 23. I enjoy planning or designing something new.
- ☐ 24. I am able to fix things.
- ☐ **TOTAL for Logical–Mathematical**

- ☐ 25. I listen to music.
- ☐ 26. I move my fingers or feet when I hear music.
- ☐ 27. I have good rhythm.
- ☐ 28. I like to sing along with music.
- ☐ 29. People have said I have musical talent.
- ☐ 30. I like to express my ideas through music.
- ☐ **TOTAL for Musical**

- ☐ 31. I like doing a project with other people.
- ☐ 32. People come to me to help settle conflicts.
- ☐ 33. I like to spend time with friends.
- ☐ 34. I am good at understanding people.
- ☐ 35. I am good at making people feel comfortable.
- ☐ 36. I enjoy helping others.
- ☐ **TOTAL for Interpersonal**

- ☐ 37. I need quiet time to think.
- ☐ 38. I think about issues before I want to talk.
- ☐ 39. I am interested in self-improvement.
- ☐ 40. I understand my thoughts and feelings.
- ☐ 41. I know what I want out of life.
- ☐ 42. I prefer to work on projects alone.
- ☐ **TOTAL for Intrapersonal**

- ☐ 43. I enjoy nature whenever possible.
- ☐ 44. I think about having a career involving nature.
- ☐ 45. I enjoy studying plants, animals, and oceans.
- ☐ 46. I avoid being indoors except when I sleep.
- ☐ 47. As a child I played with bugs and leaves.
- ☐ 48. When I feel stressed, I want to be out in nature.
- ☐ **TOTAL for Naturalistic**

Below are eight empty bars, corresponding to the eight intelligences. For each intelligence, draw a line at your score and fill in the bar below the line.

SCORE	BODILY–KINESTHETIC	VISUAL–SPATIAL	VERBAL–LINGUISTIC	LOGICAL–MATHEMATICAL	MUSICAL	INTERPERSONAL	INTRAPERSONAL	NATURALISTIC
24								
23								
22								
21								
20								
19								
18								
17								
16								
15								
14								
13								
12								
11								
10								
9								
8								
7								
6								
5								
4								
3								
2								
1								
0								

This chart will help you see visually which of your intelligences are most developed. You may have obvious strong and weak areas, or your chart may reveal a relative balance among the intelligences. There is no right answer—your strengths are simply your strengths! Take advantage of them!

create new paths and possibilities for you, but they will help you see more clearly the paths and possibilities that already exist. They give you the power to explore, choose, and move ahead with confidence.

You will continually learn, change, and grow throughout your life. Any evaluation is simply a snapshot, a look at who you are at a given moment. The answers can, and will, change as you change and as circumstances change. They provide an opportunity for you to identify a moment and learn from it by asking questions: Who am I right now? How does this compare to who I want to be?

Using Multiple Intelligences for Understanding

Understanding your multiple intelligences will help you understand yourself. Avoid labeling yourself narrowly by using one intelligence, such as if you were to say, "I'm no good in math." Anyone can learn math, but some people learn math more efficiently through intelligences other than logical-mathematical. For example, a visual-spatial learner may want to draw diagrams of a math problem.

People are a blend of all the multiple intelligences, in proportions unique to them, with one or two being dominant. When material is difficult or when you are feeling insecure about learning something new, use your most developed multiple intelligences. When something is easy for you, it provides an opportunity for you to improve your less developed multiple intelligences. All of your multiple intelligences will continue to develop throughout your lifetime. Learn as much as you can about your preferences and how you can maximize your learning.

In addition, you may change which multiple intelligences you emphasize, depending on the situation. For example, a student might find it easy to take notes in outline style when the instructor lectures in an organized way. If another instructor jumps from topic to topic, however, the student might choose to use the Cornell system or a think link (see Chapter 7).

WHAT ARE THE BENEFITS OF KNOWING YOUR LEARNING STYLE?

Although determining your learning style takes work, the understanding you develop can have positive effects on studying, in classroom situations, and elsewhere.

Study Benefits

Most students aim to maximize learning while minimizing frustration and time spent studying. If you know your most and least developed multiple intelligences, you can use techniques that take advantage of your highly developed areas while helping you through your less developed ones. Say you perform better in smaller, discussion-based classes. When you have the opportunity, choose a course section that is smaller or is taught by an instructor who prefers group discussion. You also might apply specific strategies to improve your retention in a large-group lecture.

Use mind actions and critical thinking processes to stay aware of how you learn, build on what you already know from your assessment, and improve your learning potential and environment.

- Consider what is similar about academic situations in which you have had good (or bad) experiences.

- See how you might have different reactions to different courses or teaching styles.

- Determine what positive or negative effects various academic situations have on you.

- Judge the value of your academic situations and choices based on those effects.

- Use your problem-solving ability to make changes when you are experiencing too many negative effects.

- Challenge the assumptions you or others have about you as a learner by showing that the examples of how you learn don't always fit the idea that others might have of you.

- Continually evaluate your state of mind and your progress, and make strategic plans to improve or to achieve your most important school goals.

This section describes the techniques that tend to complement the strengths and shortcomings of each intelligence. Keep in mind that you have abilities in all multiple intelligence areas, even though some are dominant. Therefore, you might see useful suggestions under any of the headings. What's important is that you use what works. Try different study techniques, evaluate their effects, and keep those you find to be useful.

Bodily–Kinesthetic Learners

Bodily–kinesthetic learners like to apply information to the real world. Rather than just reading about something or looking at a visual representation of it, they learn best by taking in information through their own hands-on actions and experiences.

Strategies suggested by students for bodily–kinesthetic learners:

- Study in a group in which members take turns explaining topics to each other and then discussing them.
- Think of practical uses of the course material.
- Pace and recite while you learn.
- Act out material or design games.
- Use flash cards with other people.
- Teach the material to someone else.

Visual–Spatial Learners

Visual–spatial learners remember best what they see: diagrams, flowcharts, timelines, films, and demonstration. They tend to forget spoken words and ideas. Classes typically don't include that much visual information. Note that although words written on paper or shown with an overhead projector are something you see, visual learners learn best from visual cues that don't involve words.

Strategies suggested by students for visual–spatial learners:

- Add diagrams to your notes whenever possible. Draw dates on a timeline; graph math functions; draw percentages in a pie chart.
- Organize your notes so you can clearly see main points and supporting facts and how things are connected. You will learn more about different styles of note taking in Chapter 6.
- Connect related facts in your notes by drawing arrows.
- Color-code your notes with differently colored highlighters so everything relating to a topic is the same color.

Verbal–Linguistic Learners

Verbal–linguistic learners remember much of what they hear and more of what they hear and then say. They benefit from discussion, prefer verbal explanation to visual demonstration, and learn effectively by explaining things to others. Because written words are processed as verbal information, verbal learners learn well through reading. Most classes, because they present material through the written word, lecture, or discussion, are geared to verbal learners.

Strategies suggested by students for verbal–linguistic learners:

- Talk about what you learn. Work in study groups so you have an opportunity to explain and discuss what you are learning.
- Read the textbook and highlight no more than 10 percent.
- Rewrite your notes.
- Outline chapters.
- Recite information or write scripts and debates.

Logical–Mathematical Learners

Logical–mathematical learners retain and understand information better after they have taken time to analyze it carefully. They prefer to organize facts into some kind of system or structure. They also learn information more effectively when it is presented in a structured way.

Strategies suggested by students for logical–mathematical learners:

- Organize material logically.
- Explain information sequentially to someone.

- Develop systems and find patterns within groups of information.
- Write outlines and develop charts and graphs.
- Write short summaries of the key points of the material.

Musical Learners

Musical learners have a strong memory for rhymes and can be energized by music. They often have a song running through their mind and find themselves tapping a foot or snapping their fingers when they hear music. They tend to learn information well when it is organized into patterns, similar to musical patterns.

Strategies suggested by students for musical learners:

- Create rhymes out of vocabulary words.
- Beat out rhythms while studying.
- Organize information into structured patterns.
- Play instrumental music while studying if it does not distract you, but first determine what type of music improves your concentration the most.
- Take study breaks and listen to music.
- Write a song or rap about your topic, or put new words (containing study information) to a tune you already know.

Interpersonal Learners

Interpersonal learners learn effectively when interacting with others. They enjoy and benefit from discussing information with others or explaining to others what they have learned. They often prefer discussion-based classroom environments.

Strategies suggested by students for interpersonal learners:

- Study in a group in which members take turns explaining topics to one another and then discuss them.
- Whenever possible, choose classes that include extensive use of discussion.
- With one or more other students, use flash cards to quiz each other.
- Teach the material to someone, or have that person teach it to you.

Intrapersonal Learners

Intrapersonal learners retain and understand information better after they have taken some time to think about it. They benefit from solo reading and studying and tend to process information over time. They might prefer lecture settings or courses that involve independent study and individual research projects.

Strategies suggested by students for intrapersonal learners:

- Study in a quiet setting.

- When you are reading, stop periodically to think about what you have read.
- Reflect on the personal meaning of information. Keep a journal.
- Don't just memorize material; think about when it is important and what it relates to, considering the causes and effects involved.
- Write short summaries of what the material means to you.

Naturalistic Learners

Naturalistic learners feel energized when they are connected to nature. Their career choices and hobbies often reflect their love of nature. They often understand information when it is organized into categories, similar to how plant and animal species are categorized.

Strategies suggested by students for naturalistic learners:

- Study outside whenever practical but only if it is not distracting.
- Explore subjects that reflect your love for nature. Learning is much easier when you have a passion for it.
- Relate abstract information to something concrete in nature.
- Put new information into categories whenever possible.
- Take breaks with something you enjoy from nature—a walk, watching your fish, or viewing a nature video. Use nature as a reward for getting other work done.

Classroom Benefits

Knowing your learning style does more than help you adjust to different kinds of material. It also can help you make the most of the teaching styles of your instructors. Your personal learning style might work better with the way some instructors teach and be a mismatch with other instructors. The first step is to understand the various teaching styles you encounter (an instructor's teaching style often reflects his or her learning style). The next step is to make adjustments so that you can maximize your learning.

After perhaps two class meetings, you can make a fairly good assessment of any instructor's teaching styles (instructors may exhibit more than one). Figure 6.1 presents some common styles.

After you have an idea of what you're working with, you can assess how well your own styles match the teaching styles. If your styles mesh well with an instructor's teaching style, you're in luck. If not, you have some options.

1. You can bring extra focus to your weaker intelligences. Although it's not easy, working on your weaker points can help you break new ground in your learning. For example, if you're a verbal person in a math- and logic-oriented class, you can increase your focus and concentration during class so you will get as much as you can from the presentation. Then you can spend extra study time on the material, make a point to ask others from your class to help you, and search for additional supplemental materials and exercises that might reinforce your knowledge.

FIGURE 6.1

Teaching styles.

- **Lecture:** Instructor speaks to the class for the entire class period; little to no class interaction
- **Group discussion:** Instructor presents material but encourages class discussion throughout
- **Small groups:** Instructor presents material and then breaks class into small groups for discussion or project work
- **Visual focus:** Instructor uses visual elements such as diagrams, photographs, drawings, transparencies
- **Verbal focus:** Instructor relies primarily on words, either spoken or written on the board or overhead projector
- **Logical presentation:** Instructor organizes material in a logical sequence, such as by time or importance
- **Random presentation:** Instructor tackles topics in no particular order, jumps around a lot, or digresses

2. You can ask your instructor for additional help. For example, if you are a visual person, you might ask your instructor if he or she can recommend any visuals that would help to illustrate the points made in class. If the class breaks into smaller groups, you might ask the instructor to divide those groups roughly according to learning style so the visual students can help each other understand the material.

3. You can "convert" class material during study time. As an example, an interpersonal learner takes a class with an instructor who presents big-picture information in a lecture format. This student might organize study groups and, in those groups, focus on filling in the factual gaps by reading materials assigned for that class. Likewise, a visual student might rewrite notes in various colors to add a visual element—for example, assigning a different color to each main point or topic or using one color for central ideas and another for supporting examples.

Instructors are as individual as students. Taking time to focus on their teaching styles and on how to adjust will help you learn more effectively and avoid frustration. And you can take advantage of your instructor's office hours when you have an issue stemming from a learning style that is causing you difficulty.

"To be what we are, and to become what we are capable of becoming, is the only end of life."

ROBERT LOUIS STEVENSON

General Benefits

Although teaching styles and school curricula traditionally have favored verbal–linguistic learners, one style has no general advantage over another. The only advantage is in discovering your profile through accurate and honest analysis. Three benefits of knowing your learning styles are as follows.

1. You will have a better chance of avoiding problematic situations. If you don't explore what works best for you, you risk forcing yourself into career or personal situations that will stifle your creativity, development, and happiness. Knowing how you learn and how you relate to the world can help you plan strategically and make smarter choices.

2. You will be more successful on the job.   Your learning style is essentially your working style. If you know how you learn, you will be able to look for an environment that suits you best and you'll be able to work effectively on work teams. This will prepare you for successful employment in the twenty-first century.

3. You will be more able to target areas that need improvement. The more you know about your learning styles, the more you will be able to pinpoint the areas that are more difficult for you. That has two advantages. First, you can begin to work on difficult areas, step by step. Second, when a task requires a skill that is tough for you, you either can take special care with it or suggest someone else whose style may be better suited to it.

Your learning style is one important fact of self-knowledge. Next you will explore other important factors that help to define you.

HOW DO YOU EXPLORE WHO YOU ARE?

You are an absolutely unique individual. Although you may share individual characteristics with others, your combination of traits is one of a kind. Furthermore, it could take a lifetime to learn everything there is to know about yourself because you are constantly changing. You can start, however, by asking questions about these facets of yourself: self-perception, interests, habits, and abilities, including strengths and limitations.

Self-Perception

Having an accurate image of yourself is difficult. Unfortunately, many people err on the side of negativity. Feeling inadequate from time to time is normal, but a constantly negative **self-perception** can have destructive effects. Look at people you know who think they are less intelligent, capable, or attractive than they really are. Observe how that shuts down their confidence and motivation. You do the same to yourself when you perceive yourself negatively.

Negative self-perception has effects that lead to a *self-fulfilling prophecy*, which is something that comes true because you have convinced yourself it will. First you believe you are incapable of being or doing something, then you neglect to try, and finally you probably don't do or become what you had already decided was impossible.

Imagine that you think you can't pass a certain course. Because you feel you don't have a chance, you don't put as much effort into the work for that course. Sure enough, at the end of the semester, you don't pass. The worst part is that you may see your failure as proof of your incapability instead of realizing that you didn't allow yourself to try. This chain of events can occur in many situations. When it happens in the workplace, people lose jobs. When it happens in personal life, people lose relationships.

A negative self-image comes from one or more different sources. Accepting a negative self-image from such sources often reveals one or more thinking errors (see Chapter 3). Here are some possibilities:

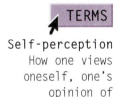

TERMS

Self-perception
How one views
oneself, one's
opinion of
oneself.

- *Critical parents or guardians.* All children hear some criticism. If you heard repeated negative comments and received little positive reinforcement, though, you can easily believe what you heard.
- *Instructors or other authority figures.* Critical authority figures who focus on the negative can influence your self-perception. As with parents, accepting the judgment of authority figures—"I'm no good because they say so"—reflects a false-cause thinking error. Other peoples' judgments may or may not have anything to do with your true abilities.
- *Magazines, television, and other media.* The media set a standard for the "right" way to look, behave, and work. If you and your life don't seem to match this standard, you might take that as a negative reflection on yourself. This reflects an overgeneralization thinking error. You might believe, based on what the media conveys, that only thin people—or beautiful people, or young people, or people who work in the computer industry—have what it takes to succeed.
- *Unrealistic expectations.* Many people expect too much of themselves. When they don't live up to these expectations, they often are their own worst critics, labeling efforts as "failures" and playing a constant inner tape of negative self-talk.

Refine your self-image so that it reflects more of your true self. The following strategies might help.

1. *Believe in yourself.* If you don't believe in yourself, others may have a harder time believing in you. Work to eliminate negative self-talk. Take action that helps to build your faith in your abilities. When you set your goals, stick to them. Look carefully at the cause-and-effect pattern of your actions instead of making hasty assumptions.
2. *Talk to people you trust.* People who know you well often have a more realistic perception of you than you do of yourself. Ask them to help you think critically about what they see happening with you and why.
3. *Take personal time.* Stress makes having perspective on your life more difficult. Take time out to clear your mind and think realistically about who you are and who you want to be.
4. *Look at all of the evidence.* Mistakes can loom large in your mind, leading you to commit the thinking error of leaving out information by refusing to look at what you have done well. Consider your successes and accomplishments as carefully as you consider your stumbles.

Building a positive self-perception is a lifelong challenge. If you maintain a bright but realistic vision of yourself, it will take you far along the road toward achieving your goals.

Interests

Taking some time now to explore your interests will help you later when you select a major and a career. Maybe you are aware of many of your general interests already. Ask yourself these questions:

- What areas of study do I like?
- What activities make me happy?
- What careers seem interesting to me?
- What kind of daily schedule do I like to keep (early riser or night owl)?
- What type of home and work environment do I prefer?

Interests play an important role in the workplace. Despite this, many people do not take their interests seriously when choosing a career. Some make salary or stability their first priority. Some take the first job that comes along. Some do not realize they can do better. Not considering what you are interested in can lead to an area of study or a job that leaves you unhappy, uninterested, or unfulfilled.

Here are three positive effects of focusing on your interests:

1. You will have more energy. Think about how you feel when you are looking forward to seeing a special person, participating in a favorite sports activity, or enjoying some entertainment. When you're doing something you like, time seems to pass quickly. Contrast this with how you feel about disagreeable activities. The difference in your energy level is immense. You will be able to get much more done in a subject or career area that you enjoy.

2. You will perform better. When you were in high school, you probably got your best grades in your favorite classes and excelled in your favorite activities. That doesn't change as you get older. You usually will find the most success in work you like to do. The more you like something, the harder you work at it—and the harder you work, the more you will improve.

3. You will have a more positive attitude. On the one hand, a positive attitude creates a positive environment and might even make up for areas in which you lack ability or experience. On the other hand, even if you perform well, a negative attitude can sour the atmosphere for your coworkers and ultimately can cost you your job. This is especially important when working in a team. Because businesses currently emphasize teamwork to such a great extent, your ability to maintain a positive attitude might mean the difference between success and failure.

Choosing to consider your interests and happiness takes courage but brings benefits. Think about your life. You spend hours attending classes and studying outside of class. You probably will spend at least eight hours a day, five or more days a week, up to fifty or more weeks a year as a working contributor to the world. Although your studies and work won't always make you deliriously happy, it is possible to spend your school and work time in a manner that suits you.

Habits

A preference for a given action that you do a certain way, and often regularly or at certain times, is a habit. You might have a habit of showering in the morning, channel surfing with the TV remote control, talking for hours on

TERMS

Attitude
A state of mind or feeling toward something.

"The greatest discovery of any generation is that human beings can alter their lives by altering their attitudes of mind."

ALBERT SCHWEITZER

the phone, or studying late at night. Your habits reveal a lot about you. You consider some habits to be good habits, and some may be bad habits.

Bad habits earn that title because they can prevent you from reaching important goals. Some bad habits, such as chronic lateness, have obvious negative effects. Other habits, such as renting movies three times a week, may not seem bad until you realize that you needed to spend those hours studying. People maintain bad habits because they offer immediate, enjoyable rewards, even if later effects are negative. Going out to eat frequently may drain your budget, but at first it seems easier than shopping for food, cooking, and washing dishes.

Good habits are those that have positive effects on your life. You often have to wait longer and work harder to see a reward for good habits, which makes them harder to maintain. If you cut out fattening foods, you won't lose weight in two days. If you reduce your nights out to gain study time, your grades won't improve in a week. When you strive to maintain good habits, trust that the rewards are somewhere down the road. Changing a habit can be a long process.

Take time to evaluate your habits. Look at the positive and negative effects of each, and decide which are helpful and which are harmful to you. Following are steps you can take to change a habit that has more negative effects than positive ones.

1. *Be honest about your habits.* Admitting negative or destructive habits can be hard to do. You can't change a habit until you admit that it is a habit.

2. *Recognize the habit as troublesome.* Sometimes the trouble may not seem to come directly from the habit. For example, spending every weekend working on the house may seem important, but you might be overdoing it and ignoring friends and family members.

3. *Decide to change.* You might realize what your bad habits are but do not yet care about their effects on your life. Until you are convinced that you will receive something positive and useful from changing, your efforts will not get you far.

4. *Start today.* Don't put it off until after this week, after the family reunion, or after the semester. Each day lost is a day you haven't had the chance to benefit from a new lifestyle. Use your decision-making skills to evaluate the situation and make a choice that will have more positive effects.

5. *Change one habit at a time.* Changing and breaking habits is difficult to do. Attempting to be perfect overnight will only frustrate you. Trying to spend more time with your family, increase studying, and save more money all at once can bring on a fit of deprivation, sending you scurrying back to all your old habits. Easy does it.

"To fall into a habit is to begin to cease to be."

MIGUEL UNAMUNO

6. *Reward yourself appropriately for positive steps taken.* If you earn a good grade, don't slack off on your studies the following week. If you've lost weight, avoid celebrating in an ice-cream parlor. Choose a reward that will not encourage you to stray from your target.

7. *Keep it up.* To have the best chance at changing a habit, be consistent for at least three weeks. Your brain needs time to become accustomed to the new habit. If you go back to the old habit during that time, you might feel like you're starting all over again.

8. *Don't get too discouraged.* Rarely does someone make the decision to change and do so without a setback or two. Being too hard on yourself might cause frustration that tempts you to give up and go back to the habit.

Abilities

Everyone's abilities include both strengths and limitations. Both are part of you. Examining both strengths and limitations is part of establishing the kind of clear vision of yourself that will help you maximize your potential.

Strengths

As you think about your preferences, your strengths will come to mind because you often like best the things you can do well. Some strengths seem to be natural—things you learned to do without ever having to work too hard. Others you struggled to develop and continue to work hard to maintain. Asking yourself these questions may help you define more clearly what your abilities are:

- What have I always been able to do well?
- What have others often praised about me?
- What do I like most about myself, and why?
- What is my learning-style profile?
- What are my accomplishments—at home, at school, and at work?

As with your preferences, knowing your abilities will help you find a job that makes the most of them. When your job requires you to do work you like, you are more likely to perform to the best of your ability. Keep that in mind as you explore career areas. Assessments and inventories that will help you further assess your abilities may be available at your school's career center or library. Once you know yourself, you will be more able to set appropriate goals.

Limitations

Nobody is perfect, and no one is good at everything. Everyone has limitations. That doesn't mean they are any easier to take. Limitations can make you frustrated, stressed, or angry. You may feel as though no one else has the limitations you have or that no one else has as many.

You can deal with your limitations in at least three ways. The first two—ignoring them or dwelling on them—are the most common. Both are natural, but neither is wise. The third way is to face them and to work to improve them while keeping the strongest focus on your abilities.

1. Ignoring your limitations can cause you to be unable to accomplish your goals. Say you are an active, global learner with a well-developed interpersonal intelligence. You have limitations in logical-mathematical intelligence and in linear thought. Ignoring that fact, you decide that you can make good money in computer programming, and you sign up for math and programming courses. You certainly won't fail automatically, but if you ignore your limited ability in these courses and don't seek extra help, you may have more than a few stumbles.

2. Dwelling on your limitations can make you forget you have any strengths at all. This results in negative self-talk and a poor self-perception. Continuing the example, if you were to dwell on your limitations in math, you could stop trying altogether.

3. Facing limitations and working to improve them is the best response. A healthy understanding of your limitations can help you avoid troublesome situations. In the example, you could face your limitations in math and explore other career areas that use your more well-developed abilities and intelligences. If you were to decide to stick with computer technology, you could study an area of the field that focuses on management and interpersonal relationships. Or you could continue to aim for a career as a programmer, seeking special help in areas that give you trouble.

The better you know yourself, the more able you will be to make educational choices that make the most of who you are. In your selection of a major and a curriculum, you exercise your freedom and power of choice.

HOW CAN YOU START THINKING ABOUT CHOOSING A MAJOR?

Although many students come to college knowing what they want to study, many do not. That's completely normal. College is an ideal time to begin exploring your various interests. In the process, you might discover talents and strengths you never realized you had. For instance, taking an environmental class might teach you that you have a passion for finding solutions to pollution problems. You might discover a talent for public speaking and decide to explore on-camera journalism.

Some of your explorations might take you down paths that don't resonate with your personality and interests. Even so, each experience will help to clarify who you really are and what you want to do with your life. Thinking about choosing a major involves exploring potential majors, linking majors to career areas, planning your curriculum, and being open to changing majors.

Exploring Potential Majors

Here are some steps to help you explore majors that may interest you.

Take a variety of classes. Although you will have core requirements to fulfill, you can use your electives to branch out. Try to take at least one class in each area that sparks your interest.

Don't rule out subject areas that aren't classified as "safe." Friends or parents may have warned you against certain careers, encouraging you to stay with "safe" careers that pay well. Even though financial stability is important, following your dreams is equally important. Choosing between the "safe" path and the path of the heart can be challenging. Only you can decide which is the best for you.

Know yourself, your interests, and your abilities. Pay close attention to which areas inspire you to greater heights and which areas seem to deaden your initiative.

Work closely with your advisor. Begin discussing your major with your advisor early on, even if you don't intend to declare a major right away. For any given major, your advisor may be able to tell you about both the corresponding department at your school and the possibilities in related career areas. You also may discuss with your advisor the possibility of a double major (completing the requirements for two different majors) or designing your own major, if your school offers an opportunity to do so.

Take advantage of other resources. Seek opinions from instructors, friends, and family members. Talk to students who have declared majors that interest you. Explore the course materials your college gives you to see what majors your college offers.

Develop your critical-thinking skills. Working toward any major will help you develop your most important skill—knowing how to use your mind. Critical thinking is the most crucial ingredient in any recipe for success in school and career. More than anything, your future career and employer will depend on your ability to think clearly, effectively, creatively, and wisely, and to truly contribute to the workplace.

The point of declaring and pursuing a major is to help you reach a significant level of knowledge in one subject, often in preparation for a certain career area. Thinking ahead about what kind of career you are aiming for will help you determine a suitable major.

Linking Majors to Career Areas

When looking at any major, considering where it may be able to take you in the working world might open doors that you never knew existed. Each major offers career options that aren't obvious right away. For example, a student working toward a teaching certification doesn't have to teach public school. This student could develop curricula, act as a consultant for businesses, develop an online education service, teach overseas for the Peace Corps, or create a public television program.

Explore the educational requirements of any career that interests you. Your choice of major can be more or less crucial, depending on the career area. For example, pursuing a career in medicine almost always requires a major in some area of the biological sciences, whereas lawyers have majored in anything from political science to philosophy. Many employers are more interested in your ability to think than your specific knowledge and therefore might not pay as much attention to your major as they do to your critical thinking skills. Ask advisors or people in your areas of interest what educational background is necessary or helpful to someone pursuing a career in a particular area.

Even though your major eventually becomes your primary focus, you take other courses as well. You do have some control in planning your coursework, although certain courses may be required.

Planning Your Curriculum

Although you won't necessarily want to plan your entire college course load at the beginning of your first semester, thinking through your choices ahead of time has advantages. Planning ahead can give you a clearer idea of where you are headed so you will feel in control of your path. It also can help you avoid pitfalls, such as not being able to secure a space in a course that you need to complete your major. Often, when students wait until the last minute to register, some courses they want have been filled already, and they might have to take courses they would not necessarily have chosen.

When working to plan your college **curriculum,** take advantage of the following ideas and strategies.

TERMS

Curriculum
The specific set
of courses
required for any
degree.

Consult your college catalog. You will get the most general idea of your possibilities by exploring everything your college offers. In addition, what is available to you may go beyond your college's doors. Check into "study abroad" programs (spending a semester or a year at an affiliated college in a different country) and opportunities to take courses at other schools nearby.

Look at the majors that interest you. Each major your college offers has a list of required courses, which you can find in your catalog or get from an academic advisor. Sometimes the list indicates a recommended order in which you should take the courses—certain ones your first year, certain ones your second, and so on. The list will help you to see if you would like what you would be doing over the next few semesters if you choose a given major.

Branch out. Even if you already have a fairly clear idea of your primary area of study, look into courses in other interesting areas that don't necessarily connect to your major. Enlarging the scope of your knowledge will help to improve your critical thinking, broaden your perspectives, and perhaps introduce you to career possibilities you had not even considered.

Get creative. Do you have an idea about what you want to major in but don't see it listed in your college catalog? Don't immediately assume it's impossible. Talk with your academic advisor. Some schools allow certain students to design their own majors, with help and approval from their advisors. In such a case, you and your advisor would come up with a unique list of courses.

Sometimes a decision of what to major in turns out to be not quite right. Other times, the changes that life brings introduce new possibilities. Either way, changing majors is an option.

Changing Majors

Some people change their mind several times before finding a major that fits. Although this can add to the time you spend in college, being happy with your decision is important. An education major might begin student teaching only to discover that he really didn't feel comfortable in front of students. Or a student might declare English as a major only to realize that her passion is in religion.

If this happens to you, don't be discouraged. You're certainly not alone. Changing a major is much like changing a job. Skills and experiences from one job will assist you in your next position, and some of the courses from your first major might apply—or even transfer as credits—to your next major. Talk with your academic advisor about any desire to change majors. Sometimes an advisor can speak to department heads and get the maximum number of credits transferred to your new major.

Whatever you decide, realize that you do have the right to change your mind. Continual self-discovery is part of the journey. No matter how many detours you make, each interesting class you take along the way helps to point you toward a major that feels like home.

Sabiduría

In Spanish, the term *sabiduría* represents the two sides of learning: knowledge and wisdom. Knowledge—building what you know about how the world works—is the first part. Wisdom—deriving meaning and significance from knowledge and deciding how to use it—is the second. As you continually learn and experience new things, the *sabiduría* you build will help you make knowledgeable and wise choices about how to lead your life.

Think of this concept as you discover more about how you learn and gain knowledge in all facets of your life—school, work, and personal situations. As you learn how your unique mind works and how to use it, you can assert yourself more confidently. As you expand your ability to use your mind in different ways, you can create lifelong advantages for yourself.

Chapter 6 Building Thinking Skills

Name _____ Date _____

▣ LIFE THINKING: Applying What You Learn

6.1 *How Do You Learn Best?*

Write your four strongest intelligences here.

_____

_____

_____

_____

Describe the effects of these strengths on your interests, abilities, and experiences. Be specific. For example, describe a specific school or work experience that you can attribute to these strengths.

_____

_____

_____

_____

Name your four least developed intelligences.

_____

_____

_____

_____

As you did with your stronger intelligences, describe the effects of these less developed ones. Do you face specific challenges resulting from your least developed intelligences?

_____

_____

_____

_____

Choose one of the less developed intelligences that you want to improve, and briefly state why (what positive effects this improvement would have for you). Thinking critically, name one step you can take that might help you improve.

_____

_____

_____

_____

6.2 *Your Habits*

You have the power to change your habits. List here three habits that you want to change. Make brief notes about the effects of each and how those effects keep you from reaching your goals.

1. _____

_____

_____

2. _____

_____

_____

3. _____

_____

_____

Out of these three, put a star by the habit you want to change first. Write down a step you can take today toward overcoming that habit.

_____

_____

What helpful habit do you want to develop in its place? For example, if your problem habit were a failure to express yourself when you are angry, a replacement habit might be to talk calmly about situations that upset you as soon as they arise. If you have a habit of cramming for tests at the last minute, you could replace it with a regular study schedule that allows you to cover your material bit by bit over a longer time.

_____

_____

One way to help yourself abandon your old habit is to think about how your new habit will improve your life. List two benefits of your new habit.

1. _____

2. _____

Give yourself one month to complete your shift in habit. Set a specific deadline. Keep track of your progress by indicating on a chart or a calendar how well you did each day. If you avoided the old habit, write an X below the day. If you used the new one, write an N. Therefore, a day when you only avoided the old habit will have an X; a day when you did both will have both letters; a day when you did neither will be blank. You can use the chart below or mark your own calendar. Try pairing up with another student to check on each other's progress.

SUNDAY	MONDAY	TUESDAY	WEDNESDAY	THURSDAY	FRIDAY	SATURDAY

Reward yourself for your hard work. Write here what your reward will be when you feel you are on the road to a new and beneficial habit.

_____

_____

_____

_____

_____

TEAM THINKING: Working Together

6.3 *Thinking About Intelligences*

Divide into groups according to four of the multiple intelligences (high scorers in bodily-kinesthetic in one group, high scorers in verbal-linguistic in another, high scorers in visual-spatial in a third, and high scorers in logical-mathematical in the fourth). If you scored the same in more than one of these intelligences, join whatever group is smaller. With your group, brainstorm four lists for your intelligence: the *strengths* or positive effects of having this intelligence, the *struggles* or negative effects it brings, the situations that cause *stress* for your intelligence, and *career* ideas that tend to suit this intelligence.

STRENGTHS

_____

_____

STRUGGLES

_____

_____

And so on

STRESSORS

_____

_____

CAREERS

_____

_____

And so on

If time allows, each group can present this information to the class to enable everyone to have a better understanding and acceptance of one another's intelligences. You also might brainstorm strategies for dealing with the struggles and stressors related to your intelligences and present those ideas to the class.

 WORK THINKING: Career Portfolio

6.4 *Self-Portrait*

A self-portrait is an important step in your career exploration because self-knowledge will allow you to make the best choices about what to study and what career to pursue. Use this exercise to synthesize everything you have been exploring about yourself into one comprehensive "self-portrait."

You will design your portrait in *think-link* style, using words and visual shapes to describe your self-perception, learning style, attitudes, habits, preferences, and abilities. A think link is a visual construction of related ideas, similar to a map or web, that represents your thought process. Ideas are written inside geometric shapes, often boxes or circles, and related ideas and facts are attached to those ideas by lines that connect the shapes. You will learn more about think links in the note-taking section in Chapter 7.

Use the style shown in the example in Figure 6.2, or create your own. For example, in this exercise you might want to create a "wheel" of ideas coming off your central shape, entitled "Me." Then, spreading out from each of these ideas (abilities, learning style, etc.), you would draw lines connecting all of the thoughts that go along with that idea. Connected to "Abilities," for example, might be "Singing," "Good memory," "Get along with people," and "Math skills." You don't have to use the wheel image. You might want to design a treelike think link or a line of boxes with connecting thoughts written below the boxes, or anything else you like. Let your design reflect who you are, just as does the think link itself.

FIGURE 6.2 Sample self-portrait think link.

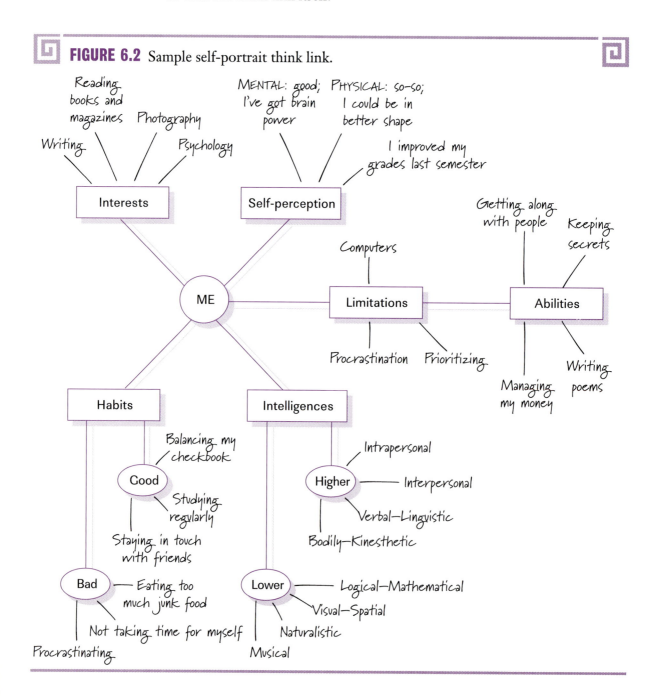

QUESTIONING YOUR WORLD:
Information Literacy Journal

To record your thoughts, use a separate journal or the lined pages at the end of the chapter.

6.5 *Media Perception of Your Learning Style*

Think about how your strengths and weaknesses are portrayed in the information that comes your way. Name any labels that have been put on you, examples of careers to which your "type" is perceived as being suited, or categories in which you have been placed. How does the media's view of you make you feel? How do you think you do or do not fit this view?

Journal

Name _____   Date _____

Thinking in the Classroom

Reading, Note Taking, Memory, and Test Taking

I n school, reading and note taking are the two primary ways you take in information. When you read, you absorb what the writer has to say. When you take notes, either in class or on something you are reading, you record the information that you think you should remember. Memory skills then help you retain this information that you have absorbed. Finally, having good test-preparation and test-taking skills will help you to show what you have retained.

Critical thinking flows through all of these activities, because as you read, take notes, remember, and record information on tests, you evaluate what is important about the information, relate it to other similar or different information, use it to create new ideas, and explain it using examples. This chapter will lead you through some practical, critical-thinking–based ways to approach how you take in, remember, and express information on tests.

In this chapter, you will explore answers to the following questions:

- How can you respond critically to what you read?
- How can you make the most of your notes?
- What note-taking system should you use?
- What will help you improve your memory?
- How can you prepare for tests?
- What can help you succeed on tests?

HOW CAN YOU RESPOND CRITICALLY TO WHAT YOU READ?

The fundamental purpose of all college reading is to understand the material. Reading critically allows you to reach the highest possible level of understanding. Think of your reading process as an archaeological dig. The first step is to excavate a site and uncover the artifacts—which corresponds to your initial survey and reading of the material. As important as the excavation is, the process would be incomplete if you were to stop there and take home a bunch of items covered in dirt. The second half of the process is to investigate each item critically, evaluate what the items mean, and derive new knowledge and ideas from what you discover.

A critical reader can:

- Discern the central idea of a piece of reading material, as well as identify what in that piece is true or useful, such as when using material as a source for an essay.
- Compare two pieces of material and evaluate which makes more sense, which proves its thesis more successfully, and which is more useful for the reader's purposes.
- Select important ideas, identify examples that support them, and ask questions about the text without the aid of any special features.

You can respond critically to what you read by using SQ3R to form an initial idea of the material, asking questions based on critical thinking processes, and being an information literate reader.

Use SQ3R to "Taste" Reading Material

SQ3R is a technique, developed more than 55 years ago by Francis Robinson, that will help you "own" what you read (learn it well enough to apply it to what you do).[1] The symbols S-Q-3-R stand for *survey, question, read, recite,* and *review*—all steps in the studying process. Actively reading SQ3R will help you form an initial idea of what a piece of reading material is about and more effectively learn and remember what you read.

Moving through the stages of SQ3R requires that you know how to skim and scan. **Skimming** involves rapid reading of chapter elements, including introductions, conclusions, and summaries; the first and last lines of paragraphs; boldface and italicized terms; pictures, charts, and diagrams. The goal of skimming is to quickly construct the main ideas. In contrast, **scanning** involves the search for specific facts and examples. You might use scanning during the review phase of SQ3R, when you need to locate specific information.

Survey

Surveying is the process of previewing, or prereading, a book before you actually study it, and is encouraged when reading textbooks. Most textbooks include devices that give students an overview of the text as a whole, as well as of the contents of individual chapters. As you look at Figure 7.1, think about how many of these devices you use already.

When you survey, ask yourself why you are reading the material. Establishing a reading purpose in this way gives you direction. Common purposes of reading are:

- Reading for understanding (comprehension of general ideas and specific examples)

▲ TERMS

Skimming
Rapid, superficial reading of material to determine central ideas and main elements.

Scanning
Reading material in an investigative way, searching for specific information.

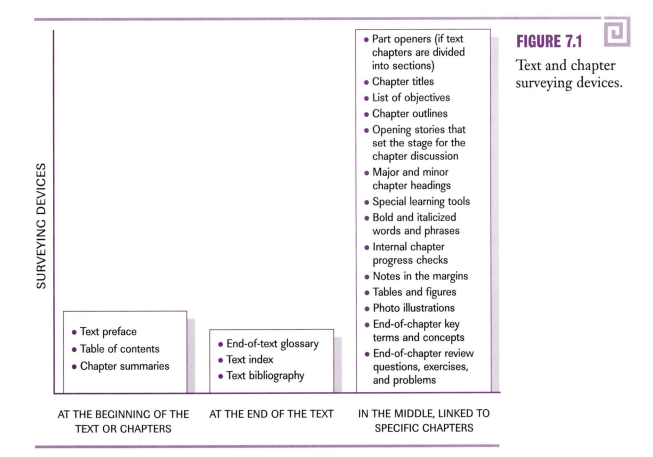

SURVEYING DEVICES

- Part openers (if text chapters are divided into sections)
- Chapter titles
- List of objectives
- Chapter outlines
- Opening stories that set the stage for the chapter discussion
- Major and minor chapter headings
- Special learning tools
- Bold and italicized words and phrases
- Internal chapter progress checks
- Notes in the margins
- Tables and figures
- Photo illustrations
- End-of-chapter key terms and concepts
- End-of-chapter review questions, exercises, and problems

- Text preface
- Table of contents
- Chapter summaries

- End-of-text glossary
- Text index
- Text bibliography

AT THE BEGINNING OF THE TEXT OR CHAPTERS

AT THE END OF THE TEXT

IN THE MIDDLE, LINKED TO SPECIFIC CHAPTERS

FIGURE 7.1

Text and chapter surveying devices.

- Reading for critical evaluation (an understanding that goes beyond basic recall)
- Reading for practical application (gathering information to apply to a specific goal)

Question

Your next step is to examine the material (and chapter headings, if any) and, on your own paper, write *questions* arising from them. These questions focus your attention and increase your interest, helping you comprehend and relate new ideas to what you know already. When you survey, you can take questions from the textbook or from your notes or come up with them on your own, based on what ideas you think are most important.

There is no "correct" set of questions, although the more useful kinds of questions engage critical-thinking mind actions and processes.

Read

Your questions give you a starting point for *reading*, the first R in SQ3R. Read the material with the purpose of answering each question you raised. As you read, record key words, phrases, and concepts in a notebook.

If you own the textbook, mark it up in a way that helps you to make sense of the material. You may want to write notes in the margins, circle key ideas, or highlight key sections. Be careful, though, not to mistake highlighting for learning. You will not learn what you highlight unless you review it carefully. Here are some tips on how to strike a balance.

- Mark the text *after* you read the material through once.
- Highlight key ideas and the examples that explain and support them. Try highlighting ideas in one color and examples in another.
- Avoid overmarking. A phrase or two is enough in most paragraphs. Set off long passages with brackets rather than marking every line.
- Write notes in the margins that will help you find key sections later on.

One critical step in the reading phase is to divide your reading into digestible segments. Pace your reading so you understand as you go.

Recite

Once you finish reading a topic, stop and answer the questions you raised in the Q stage of SQ3R. You might decide to *recite* each answer aloud, silently speak the answers to yourself, tell the answers to another person as if you were teaching him or her, or write your ideas and answers in brief notes. Writing is often the most effective way to solidify what you have read, because writing from memory checks your understanding. Use whatever techniques best suit your learning style (see Chapter 6).

Repeat the question-read-recite cycle until you complete the entire chapter. If, during this process, you find yourself fumbling for thoughts, you might not "own" the ideas yet. Reread the section that's giving you trouble until you master its content. Understanding each section as you go is crucial because the material in one section often forms a foundation for the next.

Review

Review soon after you finish a chapter. Here are some techniques for reviewing.

- *Skim and reread.* Focus on the preface, headings, tables and figures, and sections you have highlighted.
- *Summarize in writing.* To construct a **summary,** focus on central ideas of the piece and the main examples that support them. A summary does not contain your own ideas or evaluation of the material. It simply condenses the material, making it easier to focus on the most important information. Rewriting the sections and phrases you have highlighted or bracketed may help.
- *Answer questions.* You can use the text's end of chapter questions or the questions you raised in the Q stage. If you don't know the answers right away, scan the material.
- *Use visual review techniques.* Create a summary in outline or think-link form (see the section on note taking later in this chapter). Construct a think link that shows how important concepts relate to one another or how ideas are supported by examples. Test yourself using flashcards.
- *Recite and use audio review aids.* Recite important concepts to yourself, or record important information on a cassette tape and play it on a portable tape player or in your car.
- *Study with others.* Study group members can benefit from one another's differing perspectives and abilities. See Chapter 10 for more on teamwork and studying.

TERMS

Summary
A concise restatement of the material, in your own words, that covers the main points.

Repeating the review process renews and solidifies your knowledge. Try to review once a week. Refreshing your knowledge is easier and faster than learning it the first time. Review that uses critical thinking increases the likelihood of retention.

Ask Questions Based On Critical Thinking Processes

The essence of critical reading, as with critical thinking, is asking questions. Instead of simply accepting what you read, seek understanding by questioning the material as you go along. Using the mind actions to formulate your questions will help you understand the material.

What parts of the material you focus on will depend on your purpose for reading. For example, if you are writing a paper on the causes of World War II, you might look at how certain causes fit your thesis. If you are comparing two pieces of writing that contain opposing arguments, you could pick out their central ideas and evaluate how well the writers use examples to support them.

Following are some ways to question reading material critically. Replace the words *it* and *this* with what you are questioning (the entire piece, a specific fact or idea, or the examples provided as support for an idea).

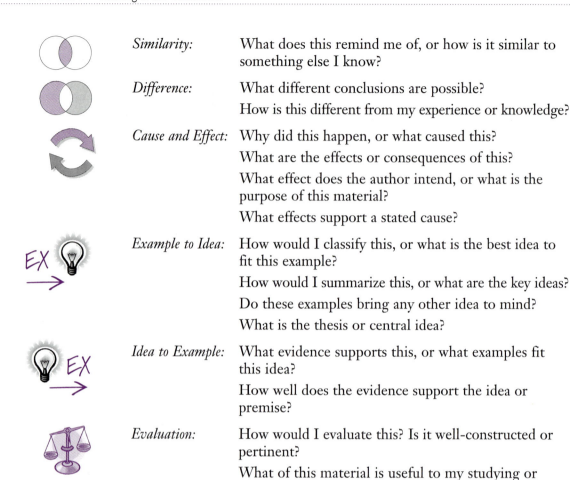

	Similarity:	What does this remind me of, or how is it similar to something else I know?
	Difference:	What different conclusions are possible?
		How is this different from my experience or knowledge?
	Cause and Effect:	Why did this happen, or what caused this?
		What are the effects or consequences of this?
		What effect does the author intend, or what is the purpose of this material?
		What effects support a stated cause?
	Example to Idea:	How would I classify this, or what is the best idea to fit this example?
		How would I summarize this, or what are the key ideas?
		Do these examples bring any other idea to mind?
		What is the thesis or central idea?
	Idea to Example:	What evidence supports this, or what examples fit this idea?
		How well does the evidence support the idea or premise?
	Evaluation:	How would I evaluate this? Is it well-constructed or pertinent?
		What of this material is useful to my studying or writing?

Certain thinking processes can deepen your analysis and evaluation of what you read. Within these processes you will ask questions that use the mind actions.

Evaluating Fact and Opinion

With what you know from Chapter 3, you can evaluate statements, central ideas, or entire pieces of reading material. Examine whether it is fact or opinion, using fact and opinion indicators. Evaluate how it is supported with examples. Identify and challenge assumptions. Use questions such as these:

- What facts or examples are given as evidence that this is true?
- How could I test the validity of this? Are there other facts that contradict it?
- What assumptions underlie this? What examples do or do not fit the assumption?
- What else do I know that is similar to this?
- Are the stated effects of this information the real effects?
- How reliable are the sources of information?

Imagine that a piece of writing states, "The dissolving of the family unit is the main cause of society's ills." You might question this statement by looking at what facts and examples support it. You might question the writer's sources. You might investigate by reading other materials. You could discern that this statement hides an assumption of what a family is or what constitutes "society's ills." You also could find examples that do not fit this assumption, such as successful families that don't fit the definition of "family" used by the writer.

Evaluating an Argument

When your reading material contains one or more arguments, evaluate whether the writer has constructed his or her argument effectively. Ask questions like these:

- What are the topic, issue, and premise? What evidence is used to support the premise?
- What persuasive techniques is the writer using?
- Do the effects flow logically from the causes?
- Is the evidence fact or opinion, and are its sources reliable?
- Do the examples adequately support the central idea of the argument?
- What different and perhaps opposing arguments seem just as valid?

Don't rule out the possibility that you might agree with an argument. Use critical thinking, however, to make an informed decision, rather than accepting the argument outright.

Recognizing Perspective

Reading materials are written from a certain perspective. For example, if a recording artist and a music censorship advocate were each to write a piece about a controversial song created by that artist, their different perspectives would result in two very different pieces of writing.

To analyze perspective, ask questions like the following:

- *What perspective is guiding this?* What underlying ideas influence this material? What examples, evidence, or reasons are given in support of this perspective?
- *What do the title and author tell about the perspective and intent of the material?* For example, promotional materials for a new drug written by the manufacturer may intend to sell the drug, and a doctor's evaluation of the drug might intend to communicate research information (and perhaps persuade some patients to use or not use the drug).
- *What positive and negative effects could come from taking this perspective?* Are the effects different on different people and different situations? How might the perspective have value even if it has negative effects for some people?
- *How is this perspective similar to or different from mine?* Examine your reaction to the perspective, and think about what you may be able to learn from it.

"No barrier of the senses shuts me out from the sweet, gracious discourse of my book friends. They talk to me without embarrassment or awkwardness."

HELEN KELLER

Be Information Literate

What you know about information literacy applies to your college reading material. The authors of even seemingly objective textbooks have particular perspectives which may influence the information they include or how they include it. For example, the growing awareness of the multicultural heritage of the United States has prompted revision of many history texts that previously ignored or shortchanged such topics as Native-American history. In all your reading, especially primary sources, keep the following in mind:

- Your reading materials are created by people who have perspectives unique to them.
- Authors sometimes use certain wording or tone to create an effect on a reader.
- Different readers may have different interpretations of a piece of reading material, depending on individual perspective and experience.
- Users of media may intend to market a product to you.
- Any written material carries the values of the people who created it and is influenced, to varying degrees, by the authors' perspectives and intents.

As an information-literate reader, you have the ability to stay aware of these realities and to sift through your materials critically so you gain from them what is most useful to you.

Reading is a deliberate, purposeful process of meaning construction. Effective note taking will help you to master the concepts and skills presented to you in class and in your texts.

HOW CAN YOU MAKE THE MOST OF YOUR NOTES?

Note taking, by its very nature, involves critical thinking. Because it is virtually impossible to write down everything you hear or read, the act of note taking means continually evaluating what is most important to remember.

Your class notes have two purposes: First, they should reflect what you heard in class. Second, they should be a resource for studying, writing, or comparing with your text material.

What to Do During Class

Here is a list of note-taking ideas to try as you explore what works best for you. Experiment with these strategies until you think you have found a successful combination.

- Identify each page using a date and number or letter—for example, 11/27A, 11/27B.
- Record whatever your instructor emphasizes. Figure 7.2 provides more details about how an instructor might call attention to certain information.

- Continue to take notes during class discussions and question-and-answer periods. What your fellow students ask about may help you as well.

- Leave one or more blank spaces between points. This white space will help you review your notes because information will be in self-contained segments.

- Draw pictures and diagrams that help illustrate ideas.

- Write quickly but legibly. When you can, use abbreviations and symbols, or shorten words that appear often in your notes.

- Indicate material that is especially important with a star, underlining, a highlighter pen, a different-color pen, or capital letters.

- If you don't understand something, leave space and place a question mark in the margin. Then consult your instructor, a classmate, or your textbook after class, and fill in the blank when the idea is clear.

- Make your notes as legible and organized as possible. You can't learn from notes that you can't read or understand. You can always rewrite and improve your notes.

- Use your text to add to your notes after class to make a superior, "deeper and wider" set of information to study.

Review and Revise Your Notes

Class notes are a valuable study tool when you review them regularly. Begin your review within a day of the lecture, if possible. Read your notes to learn the information, clarify points, write out abbreviations, fill in missing information, and underline or highlight key ideas. Try to review each week's notes

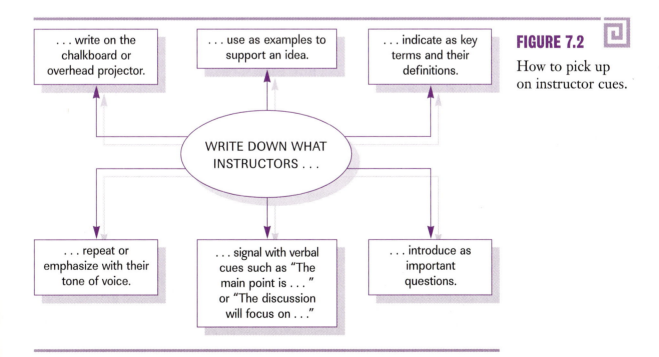

FIGURE 7.2

How to pick up on instructor cues.

at the end of that week. Think critically about the material, in writing, study-group discussions, or quiet reflective thought, using the following questions.

- Can I easily recall the facts I have written?
- What do these ideas mean? What examples support or negate them?
- Are these ideas important, and if so, why? How fully do I understand them?
- What similar facts or ideas does this information call to mind?
- How does this information differ from what I know already?
- What new ideas can I form from learning this information?
- How do these ideas, facts, and statements relate to one another? Do any of them have cause-and-effect relationships?

Writing a summary of your notes is another important review technique. Evaluate which ideas and examples are most important, and then rewrite the material in a shortened form, emphasizing those important ideas and examples. You may prefer to summarize as you review, although you also might try summarizing your notes from memory after you review them.

Study groups can be a useful way to review notes. For example, if you happened to focus well on one particular part of the lecture and lost concentration during another, a fellow student may have been taking good notes on the part you missed.

Whether you are taking notes in class or while reading, there are different note-taking systems from which you can choose.

WHAT NOTE-TAKING SYSTEM SHOULD YOU USE?

You will benefit most from the system that feels most comfortable to you and makes the most sense for the type of content covered in any given course. For example, you might take notes in a different style for a history class than for a foreign language class. When choosing a system, consider your intelligences. Your learning style might help you see what works best for you. The most common note-taking systems are outlines, the Cornell system, and think links.

Taking Notes in Outline Form

When a reading assignment or a lecture seems well organized, you might choose to take notes in outline form. When you use an outline, you construct a line-by-line representation, with certain phrases set off by varying indentations, showing how ideas relate to one another and are supported by facts and examples.

Formal outlines indicate ideas and examples using Roman numerals, capital and lower-case letters, and numbers. When you are pressed for time, such as during class, you can use an informal system of consistent indenting and dashes instead. Formal outlines also require at least two headings on the same level—that is, if you have a IIA, you must also have a IIB. Figure 7.3 shows an outline on civil rights legislation.

> Civil Rights Legislation: 1860–1968
>
> I. Post–Civil War Era
>   A. Fourteenth Amendment, 1868: equal protection of
>   the law for all citizens
>   B. Fifteenth Amendment, 1870: constitutional rights of
>   citizens regardless of race, color, or previous servitude
> II. Civil Rights Movement of the 1960s
>   A. National Association for the Advancement of Colored
>   People (NAACP)
>   1. Established in 1910 by W.E.B. DuBois and others
>   2. Legal Defense and Education fund fought school
>   segregation
>   B. Martin Luther King Jr., champion of nonviolent civil
>   rights action
>   1. Led bus boycott 1955–1956
>   2. Marched on Washington D.C.: 1963
>   3. Awarded NOBEL PEACE PRIZE: 1964
>   4. Led voter registration drive in Selma, Alabama:
>   1965
>   C. Civil Rights Act of 1964: prohibited discrimination
>   in voting, education, employment, and public facilities
>   D. Voting Rights Act of 1965: gave the government
>   power to enforce desegregation
>   E. Civil Rights Act of 1968: prohibited discrimination
>   in the sale or rental of housing

FIGURE 7.3

Notes in outline form.

Using the Cornell Note-Taking System

The Cornell note-taking system, also known as the T-note system, was developed by Walter Pauk at Cornell University.[2] It consists of three sections on ordinary notepaper:

- *Section 1*, the largest section, is on the right. Record your notes here in informal outline form.
- *Section 2*, to the left of your notes, is the *cue column*. Leave it blank while you read or listen. When you review, fill it with comments that highlight main ideas, clarify meaning, suggest examples, or link ideas and examples. You can even draw diagrams.
- *Section 3*, at the bottom of the page, is known as the *summary area*. Here you use a sentence or two to summarize the notes on the page. Use this section during the review process to reinforce concepts and provide an overview of what the notes say.

When you use the Cornell system, create the note-taking structure before class begins. Picture an upside-down letter T and use Figure 7.4 as your guide. Make the cue column about 2½ inches wide and the summary area 2 inches tall. Figure 7.4 shows how a student used the Cornell system to take notes in an introduction-to-business course.

FIGURE 7.4

Notes taken using the Cornell System.

October 3, 199x, p. 1

Why do some workers have a better attitude toward their work than others?

Some managers view workers as lazy; others view them as motivated and productive.

Maslow's Hierarchy

self-actualization needs (challenging job)

esteem needs (job title)

social needs (friends at work)

security needs (health plan)

physiological needs (pay)

<u>Understanding Employee Motivation</u>

Purpose of motivational theories
—To explain role of human relations in motivating employee performance
—Theories translate into how managers actually treat workers

2 specific theories
—<u>Human resources model</u>, developed by Douglas McGregor, shows that managers have radically different beliefs about motivation.
  —Theory X holds that people are naturally irresponsible and uncooperative
  —Theory Y holds that people are naturally responsible and self-motivated

<u>Maslow's Hierarchy of Needs</u> says that people have needs in 5 different areas, which they attempt to satisfy in their work
  —Physiological need: need for survival, including food and shelter
  —Security need: need for stability and protection
  —Social need: need for friendship and companionship
  —Esteem need: need for status and recognition
  —Self-actualization need: need for self-fulfillment

Needs at lower levels must be met before a person tries to satisfy needs at higher levels.

—Developed by psychologist Abraham Maslow

Two motivational theories try to explain worker motivation. The human resources model includes Theory X and Theory Y. Maslow's Hierarchy of Needs suggests that people have needs in 5 different areas: physiological, security, social, esteem, and self-actualization.

Creating a Think Link

A think link, also known as a mind map, is a visual form of note taking. When you draw a think link, you diagram ideas by using shapes and lines that tie together ideas and supporting details and examples. The visual design makes the connections easy to see, and the use of shapes and pictures extends the material beyond just words. Many learners respond well to the power of visualization. You can use think links to brainstorm ideas for paper topics as well.

One way to create a think link is to start by circling your topic in the middle of a sheet of paper. Next, draw a line from the circled topic and write the name of one major idea at the end of the line. Circle that idea also. Then jot down specific facts related to the idea, linking them to the idea with lines. Continue the process, connecting thoughts to one another by using circles, lines, and words.

Figure 7.5 shows a think link on social stratification (a sociology concept) that follows this structure. This is only one of many think link styles. Other examples include stair steps (showing connecting ideas that build to a conclusion) and a tree shape (roots as causes and branches as effects). You can design any think link that makes sense to you.

A think link could be difficult to construct in class, especially if your instructor talks quickly. You might want to use another system during class and make a think link when you review.

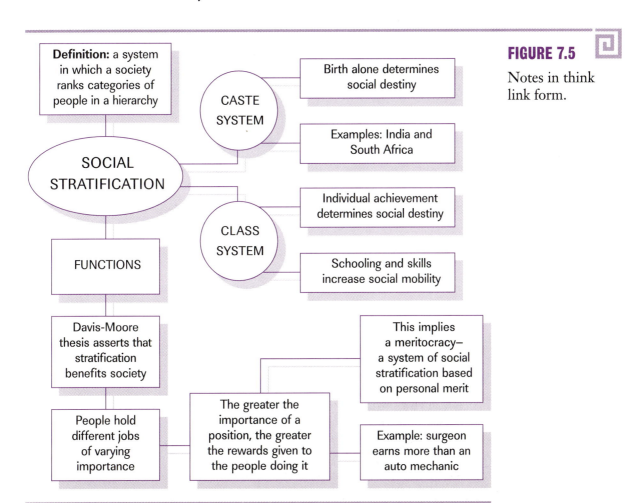

FIGURE 7.5

Notes in think link form.

Once you choose a note-taking system, your success will depend on how well it serves you. The best system for you is the one that most helps you retain information. Following are some more ideas about how to remember what you learn.

WHAT WILL HELP YOU IMPROVE YOUR MEMORY?

You need an effective memory to use the knowledge you gain throughout your life. Human memory works like a computer—both memory and computers encode, store, and retrieve information.

Memories are stored in three different "banks." The first, *sensory memory*, is an exact copy of what you see and hear and lasts for a second or less. Certain information then is selected from sensory memory and moves into *short-term memory*, a temporary storehouse that lasts no more than ten to twenty seconds. Unimportant information then is dumped, and important information is transferred to *long-term memory*—the mind's more permanent information storehouse.

Suppose your instructor is lecturing on the Civil War. As you listen, the incoming information immediately goes into sensory memory, and the five major causes of the war are transferred to short-term memory. Realizing that you probably will be tested on this information, you decide that it is important enough to remember. It then becomes part of long-term memory.

Having information in long-term memory does not necessarily mean you will be able to recall it when you need it. Some techniques can help you improve your recall.

Memory-Improvement Strategies

As a student, your job is to understand, learn, and remember information—everything from general concepts to specific details. The following suggestions will help improve your recall.

Understand What You Memorize

Make sure that everything you want to remember makes sense to you. Something that has meaning is easier to recall than something that is gibberish. This basic principle applies to everything you study. If something you need to memorize makes no sense, consult textbooks, fellow students, or an instructor.

Recite, Rehearse, and Write

When you *recite* material, you repeat it aloud to remember it. Reciting helps you retrieve information as you learn it. Frequently stopping to summarize aloud as you read can maximize your textbook studying. *Rehearsing* is similar to reciting, but is done silently. It is the process of mentally repeating, summarizing, and associating information with other information. *Writing* is rehearsing on paper. The act of writing solidifies the information in your memory.

"Learning means keeping the mind open and active to receive all kinds of experience."

GILBERT HIGHET

Separate Main Points from Unimportant Details

Use critical-thinking skills to select and focus on the most important information. Highlight only the most important information in your texts, and write notes in the margins about central ideas. When you review your lecture notes, highlight or rewrite the most important information to remember. Figure 7.6 shows how this is done on a section of text that introduces the concept of social groups. This excerpt is from the sixth edition of a sociology text.[3]

 FIGURE 7.6   Highlighting.

SOCIAL GROUPS

Virtually everyone moves through life with a sense of belonging; this is the experience of group life. A **social group** refers to *two or more people who identify and interact with one another.* Human beings continually come together to form couples, families, circles of friends, neighborhoods, churches, businesses, clubs, and numerous large organizations. Whatever the form, groups encompass people with shared experiences, loyalties, and interests. In short, while maintaining their individuality, the members of social groups also think of themselves as a special "we."

Groups, Categories, and Crowds

People often use the term "group" imprecisely. We now distinguish the group from the similar concepts of category and crowd.

Category

A *category* refers to people who have some status in common. Women, single fathers, military recruits, homeowners, and Roman Catholics are all examples of categories.

Why are categories not considered groups? Simply because, while the individuals involved are aware that they are not the only ones to hold that particular status, the vast majority are strangers to one another.

Crowd

A *crowd* refers to a temporary cluster of individuals who may or may not interact at all. Students sitting in a lecture hall do engage one another and share some common identity as college classmates; thus, such a crowd might be called a loosely formed group. By contrast, riders hurtling along on a subway train or bathers enjoying a summer day at the beach pay little attention to one another and amount to an anonymous aggregate of people. In general, then, crowds are too transitory and impersonal to qualify as social groups.

The right circumstances, however, could turn a crowd into a group. People riding in a subway train that crashes under the city streets generally become keenly aware of their common plight and begin to help one another. Sometimes such extraordinary experiences become the basis for lasting relationships.

Primary and Secondary Groups

Acquaintances commonly greet one another with a smile and the simple phrase, "Hi! How are you?" The response is usually a well scripted "Just fine, thanks. How about you?" This answer, of course, is often more formal than truthful. In most cases, providing a detailed account of how you are *really* doing would prompt the other person to beat a hasty and awkward exit.

Sociologists classify social groups by measuring them against two ideal types based on members' genuine level of personal concern. This variation is the key to distinguishing *primary* from *secondary* groups.

According to Charles Horton Cooley (1864–1929), who is introduced in the box, a **primary group** is *a small social group whose members share personal and enduring relationships.* Bound together by primary relationships, individuals in primary groups typically spend a great deal of time together, engage in a wide range of common activities, and feel that they know one another well. Although not without periodic conflict, members of primary groups display sincere concern for each other's welfare. The family is every society's most important primary group.

Cooley characterized these personal and tightly integrated groups as *primary* because they are among the first groups we experience in life. In addition, the family and early play groups also hold primary importance in the socialization process, shaping attitudes, behavior, and social identity.

Source: Sociology, 6/E by John J. Macionis, © 1997. Reprinted by permission of Prentice-Hall, Inc., Upper Saddle River, NJ.

Study During Short but Frequent Sessions

Research has shown that you can improve your chances of remembering material if you learn it more than once. Study in short sessions followed by brief periods of rest rather than studying continually with little or no rest. Try studying between classes or during other breaks in your schedule.

Separate Material Into Manageable Sections

Generally, when material is short and easy to understand, studying it all at once improves recall. With longer material, however, you might benefit from dividing it into logical sections, mastering each, putting the sections together, and then testing your memory of all the material.

Use Visual Aids

A visual representation of study material can help you remember. Try converting material into a think link or an outline. Use any visual that helps you recall it and link it to other information.

Flash cards can give you short, repeated review sessions that provide immediate feedback. Make your cards from 3 × 5-inch index cards. Use the front of the card to write a word, an idea, or a phrase you want to remember. Use the back side for a definition, an explanation, and other key facts. Figure 7.7 shows two flash cards used to study for a psychology exam. Here are some suggestions for making the most of your flash cards:

- Carry the cards with you and review them frequently
- Shuffle the cards and learn the information in various orders
- Test yourself in both directions (first, look at the terms and provide the definitions or explanations; then turn the cards over and reverse the process)

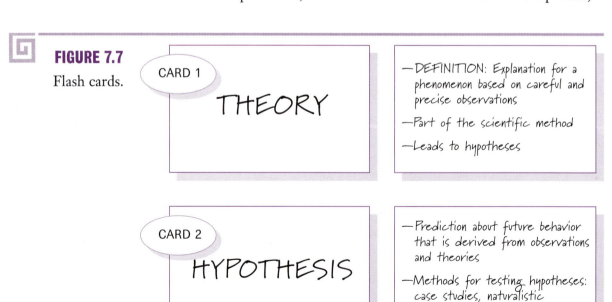

FIGURE 7.7
Flash cards.

CARD 1

THEORY

—DEFINITION: Explanation for a phenomenon based on careful and precise observations

—Part of the scientific method

—Leads to hypotheses

CARD 2

HYPOTHESIS

—Prediction about future behavior that is derived from observations and theories

—Methods for testing hypotheses: case studies, naturalistic observations, and experiments

Use Critical Thinking

Your knowledge of the critical-thinking mind actions can help you remember information. Many of the mind actions use the principle of *association*—considering new information in relation to information you already know. The more you can associate a piece of new information with your current knowledge, the more likely you are to remember it.

Say you have to remember information about a specific historical event—for instance, the signing of the Treaty of Versailles, the agreement that ended World War II. You might put the mind actions to work in the following ways:

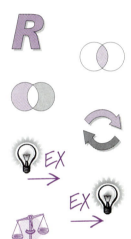

- *Recall* everything you know about the topic.
- Think about how this event is *similar* to other events in history, recent or long ago.
- Consider what is *different* and unique about this treaty in comparison to other treaties.
- Explore the *causes* that led up to this event, and look at the event's *effects*.
- From the general *idea* of treaties that ended wars, explore other *examples* of such treaties.
- Think about *examples* of what happened during the treaty signing, and from those examples come up with *ideas* about the tone of the event.
- Looking at the facts of the event, *evaluate* how successful you think the treaty was.

You don't have to use every mind action in every memory situation. Choose the ones that will help you most. The more information and ideas you can associate with the new item you're trying to remember, the more successful you will be.

Mnemonic Devices

Mnemonic devices (pronounced neh MAHN ick) work by connecting information you are trying to learn with simpler information or information that is familiar. Instead of learning new facts by rote (repetitive practice), associations give you a hook on which to hang these facts and to retrieve them. Mnemonic devices make information familiar and meaningful through unusual, unforgettable mental associations and visual pictures.

Suppose you want to remember the names of the first six presidents of the United States. The first letters of their last names—Washington, Adams, Jefferson, Madison, Monroe, and Adams—together read W A J M M A. To remember them, first you might add an e after the J and create a short nonsense word: *wajemma*. Then, to make sure you don't forget the nonsense word, picture the six presidents sitting in a row and wearing pajamas.

There are different kinds of mnemonic devices, including visual images and associations and acronyms. Study how these devices work, then apply them to your own memory challenges.

TERMS

Mnemonic devices
Memory technique that involves associating new information with simpler information or information you already know.

Create Visual Images and Associations

Visual images are easier to remember than images that rely on words alone. The best mental images often involve bright colors, three dimensions, action scenes, inanimate objects with human traits, ridiculousness, and humor.

Turning information into mental pictures helps improve memory, especially for visual learners. To remember that the Spanish artist Picasso painted *The Three Women*, you might imagine the women in a circle dancing to a Spanish song with a pig and a donkey (pig-asso). Don't reject outlandish images—as long as they help you.

Create Acronyms

Acronym
A word formed from the first letters of a series of words, created to shorten the term and thereby help you remember the series.

Another helpful association method involves the use of the **acronym.** For example, the acronym "Roy G. Biv" can help students remember the colors of the spectrum. Roy G. Biv stands for R(ed), O(range), Y(ellow), G(reen), B(lue), I(ndigo), and V(iolet).

When you can't create a name like Roy G. Biv, create an acronym from an entire sentence in which the first letter of each word in each sentence stands for the first letter of the memorized term. When science students want to remember the list of planets in order of their distance from the sun, they learn the sentence: My very elegant mother just served us nine pickles (Mercury, Venus, Earth, Mars, Jupiter, Saturn, Uranus, Neptune, and Pluto).

Improving your memory requires energy, time, and work. By using the specific memory techniques described in this chapter, you will be able to learn more in less time—and remember what you learn for exams and beyond.

HOW CAN YOU PREPARE FOR TESTS?

Like a runner who prepares for a marathon by exercising, eating right, taking practice runs, and getting rest, you can take steps to master your exams. Important preparation strategies are discussed next.

Identify Type of Test and Material Covered

Before you begin studying, find out what you can about the test. Try to identify:

- The type of questions on the test (short-answer, essay, or a combination)
- What the test will cover (class lectures and readings)
- Whether the test deals with material from the whole semester or a more limited topic

Your instructors might answer these questions. Beyond the information they give you, here are a few other strategies for predicting what could be on a test.

- *Use SQ3R to identify important ideas and facts.* The questions you write and ask when you read assigned materials may be part of the test. Textbook study questions also are good candidates.

- *Talk to people who took the course before.* Ask how difficult the tests are, what materials are covered (readings, lectures, or both), and what types of questions are used.
- *Examine old tests if instructors make them available in class or on reserve in the library.* Old tests will help you determine what the instructor emphasizes and whether the test requires straight memorization or critical thinking.

If you can't get copies of old tests and your instructor doesn't give too many details about the test, use clues from the class to predict test questions. After taking the first exam in the course, you will have more information about what to expect in the future.

Choose Study Materials

Once you have identified as much as you can about the subject matter of the test, choose the materials that contain the information you need to study. Save time by making sure you don't study anything you don't need to. Go through your notes, your texts, related primary-source materials, and any handouts from your instructor. Then set aside any materials you don't need.

Set a Study Schedule and Plan

Use your time-management skills to set a schedule that will help you feel as prepared as you can be. Consider all the relevant factors: the materials you need to study, how many days or weeks until the test date, and how much time you can study each day. If you establish your schedule ahead of time and write it in your date book, you will be much more likely to follow it.

Schedules vary widely according to situation. For example, if you have three days before the test and no other obligations during that time, you might set two 2-hour study sessions during each day. On the other hand, if you have two weeks before a test, classes during the day, and work three nights a week, you might spread out your study sessions over the nights you have off during those two weeks. A form like the one in Figure 7-8 will help you get organized and stay on track as you prepare for each test.

Prepare Through Critical Thinking

Approach your test preparation as an active, critical thinker, working to understand material rather than just to repeat facts. As you study, try to connect ideas to examples, analyze causes and effects, establish truths, and view issues from different perspectives.

Instructors often look for evidence that you can link seemingly unrelated ideas into logical patterns. As you study, try to explore concepts from different perspectives and connect ideas and examples that on the surface appear to be unrelated. Although you'll probably find answers to these questions in your text or class notes, you may have to work at putting together different ideas. Critical thinking takes work but may promote more understanding of the subject—and probably a higher grade on the exam.

FIGURE 7.8

Pretest checklist.

Course: _____ Teacher: _____

Date, time, and place of test: _____

Type of test (e.g., Is it a midterm or a minor quiz?): _____

What the instructor has told you about the test, including the types of test questions, the length of the test, and how much the test counts in your final grade:

_____

_____

_____

Topics to be covered on the test in order of importance:

1. _____
2. _____
3. _____
4. _____
5. _____

Study schedule, including materials you plan to study (e.g., texts and class notes) and date you plan to complete each source:

Source   *Date of Completion*

1. _____
2. _____
3. _____
4. _____
5. _____

Materials you are expected to bring to the test (e.g., your textbook, a sourcebook, a calculator):

_____

Special study arrangements (e.g., study-group meetings, meeting with instructor, tutoring):

_____

_____

Life management issues (e.g., make child-care arrangements, rearrange work hours):

_____

_____

_____

Source: Adapted from Ron Fry, *"Ace" Any Test,* 3d ed. (Franklin Lakes, NJ: Career Press, 1996), 123–124.

Critical thinking is especially important for essay tests that ask you to develop and support a thesis. Prepare by identifying three or four potential essay questions and writing out your responses.

Work Through Test Anxiety

A certain amount of stress can be a good thing. Your body is alert, and your energy motivates you to do your best. For some students, however, the time before and during an exam can be miserable. Many students have had some level of test anxiety at some time during their studies. A bad case of nerves that makes it hard to think or remember, test anxiety also can cause physical symptoms such as sweating, nausea, dizziness, headaches, and extreme fatigue. Work through test anxiety by dealing with its two primary antidotes: preparation and attitude.

Preparation

Preparation is the basic defense against anxiety. The more confident you feel about your knowledge of the material, the more you'll feel able to perform on test day. In this way, you can consider all of the preparation and study information in this chapter as test anxiety assistance. Also, finding out what to expect on the exam—the material covered, the question format, the length of the exam, and so on—will help you feel more in control.

Making and following a detailed study plan will help you build the kind of knowledge that can help you fight off anxiety. Divide the plan into a series of small tasks. As you finish each one, you will build your sense of accomplishment, confidence, and control. Prepare physically as well. Get some sleep (avoid all-nighters if possible), and eat a light, well-balanced meal before the test. If time is short, grab a quick-energy, low-sugar snack.

Preparation is all about action. Instead of sitting and worrying about the test, put your energy toward concrete, active steps that will help you succeed.

"Fear is nature's warning sign to get busy."
HENRY C. LINK

Attitude

Although good preparation will help build your confidence, maintaining a positive *attitude* is as important as studying. Here are some key ways to maintain an attitude that will help you.

- *Think of the test as an opportunity*. Know that a test is an opportunity to show what you have learned, as well as to learn something new about the material and about test taking itself.
- *See the test as a signpost*. It's easy to see a test as a contest. If you pass, or "win" the contest, you might feel no need to retain what you've learned. If you fail, or "lose" the contest, you might feel no need to try again. But if you see the test as a signpost along the way to a greater goal, you probably will be more likely to try your best and learn from the experience.
- *Give your instructor a positive role*. Your instructors test you to give you an opportunity to grow and to demonstrate what you have accomplished. They test you so that, in rising to this challenge, you will become better prepared for the challenges that lie ahead, outside of school.

- *Put the test in perspective.* A test is a small part of your education and an even smaller part of your life. Your test grade does not reflect the kind of person you are.

- *Seek study partners who challenge you.* Your anxiety may get worse if you study with someone who feels just as unprepared as you do. Find someone who can inspire you to do your best.

- *Set yourself up for success.* Try not to expect failure before you even start. Create a setting for success through your preparation. Know that you are ultimately responsible for the outcome.

- *Practice relaxation.* When you feel test anxiety coming on, take some deep breaths, close your eyes, and visualize positive mental images related to the test, such as getting a good grade and finishing confidently, with time to spare. Ease muscle tension by tightening and then releasing muscles, or by doing a few stretches.

When you have prepared by using the strategies that work for you, you are ready to take your exam. Now you can focus on methods to help you succeed when the test begins.

WHAT CAN HELP YOU SUCCEED ON TESTS?

Even though every test is different, using general test strategies and thinking critically will help you handle almost any test.

Use General Test Strategies

General test strategies include the following:

- *Write down key facts.* Before you even look at the test, write down any key information—including formulas, rules, and definitions—that you studied recently. Recording this information at the start will make forgetting less likely.

- *Begin with an overview of the exam.* Spend a few minutes at the start to get a sense of the kinds of questions you'll be answering, what mind actions they require, the number of questions in each section, and their point values. Use this information to schedule your time. For example, if a two-hour test is divided into two sections of equal point value—an essay section with four questions and a short-answer section with sixty—you can spend an hour on the essays (15 minutes per question) and an hour on the short-answer section (one minute per question).

- *Read test directions.* Reading directions carefully can save you trouble. For example, although a test of 100 true-or-false questions and one essay question might look straightforward, the directions may tell you to answer 80 of the 100 questions or that the essay is an optional bonus. Directions might also indicate that some questions or sections are weighted more heavily than others, in which case it's smart to spend more time on the parts that are worth more.

- *Work from easy to hard.* Begin with the parts or questions that seem easiest to you. You generally will take less time to answer questions you know well, leaving more time for questions that require more effort. If you like to work through questions in order, mark difficult questions as you reach them and come back to them later. Answering easier questions first also can boost your confidence, helping you to believe in yourself when you work on more difficult sections.

- *Watch the clock.* Keep track of your progress and how much time is left. Wear a watch or bring a small clock with you to the test room (in case it has no clock). Some students are so concerned about time that they rush through the test, have time left over, and are tempted to leave early. The best move is to take your time. Use any extra time to refine and check your work. It couldn't hurt—and it might help.

Think Critically

Critical thinking can help you work through each question thoroughly and avoid errors. Following are some critical-thinking strategies to use during a test.

- *Recall facts, procedures, rules, and formulas.* Base your answers on the information you recall. Think carefully to make sure you recall it accurately.

- *Think about similarities.* If you don't know how to attack a question or problem, consider any similar questions or problems that you have worked on in class or while studying.

- *Notice differences.* Especially with objective questions, items that seem different from the material you have studied might indicate answers you can eliminate.

- *Think through causes and effects.* For a numerical problem, think about how you plan to solve it and see if the answer—the effect of your plan—makes sense. For an essay question that asks you to analyze a condition or a situation, consider both what caused it and what effects it has.

- *Find the best idea to match the example or examples given.* For a numerical problem, decide what formula (idea) best applies to the example or examples (the data of the problem). For an essay question, decide what idea applies to, or links, the examples given.

- *Support ideas with examples.* When you put forth an idea in an answer to an essay question, be sure to back up your idea with an adequate number of examples that fit.

- *Evaluate each test question.* In your initial approach to any question, decide what kinds of thinking will best help you solve it. For example, essay questions often require cause-and-effect and idea-to-example thinking, whereas objective questions often benefit from thinking about similarities and differences.

These general strategies also can help you address specific types of test questions.

Master Different Types of Test Questions

Objective
questions
Short-answer
questions that
test your ability
to recall, com-
pare and contrast
information, and
link ideas to
examples.

Subjective
questions
Questions that
require you to
express your
answer in terms
of your own per-
sonal knowledge
and perspective.

Every type of question has a different way of finding out what you know about a subject. The strategy changes according to whether the question is objective or subjective.

For **objective questions,** you choose or write a short answer you believe is correct, often making a selection from a limited number of choices. Multiple-choice, fill-in-the-blank, and true-or-false questions fall into this category. **Subjective questions** demand the same information recall but also require you to plan, organize, draft, and refine a written response. They may also require more extensive critical thinking and evaluation. All essay questions are subjective.

Figure 7.9 shows some examples of objective and subjective questions you might encounter in an Introduction to Psychology course.

Multiple-Choice Questions

Multiple-choice questions are the most popular type of question on standardized tests. The following strategies can help you answer them:

- *Read the directions.* Directions can be deceptive. For example, whereas most test items ask for a single correct answer, some give you the option of marking several choices that are correct.

FIGURE 7.9

Examples of test questions.

MULTIPLE CHOICE

1. Arnold is at a company party and has had too much to drink. He releases all of his pent-up aggression by yelling at his boss, who promptly fires him. Arnold normally would not have yelled at his boss, but after drinking heavily he yelled because

   a. parties are places where employees are supposed to be able to "loosen up"

   b. alcohol is a stimulant

   c. alcohol makes people less concerned with the negative consequences of their behavior

   d. alcohol inhibits brain centers that control the perception of loudness

TRUE OR FALSE

1. Alcohol use is clearly related to increases in hostility, aggression, violence, and abusive behavior. T or F

FILL-IN-THE-BLANK

One probable influence in the development of alcoholism in our society is _____.

ESSAY

1. Summarize the theories and research on the causes and effects of daydreaming.

2. Discuss the possible uses for daydreaming in a healthy individual.

Source: Gary W. Piggrem, Test Item File for Charles G. Morris, *Understanding Psychology,* 3d ed. (Upper Saddle River, NJ: Prentice Hall, 1996).

- *Read each question and its choices thoroughly.* Then try to answer the question. This strategy will reduce the possibility that the choices will confuse you.

- *Underline key words and phrases in the question.* If the question is complicated, try to break it down into small parts that are easy to understand.

- *Pay special attention to words that could throw you off.* For example, it is easy to overlook negatives in a question ("Which of the following is *not* . . . ").

- *If you don't know the answer, eliminate answers that you know or suspect are wrong.* Your goal is to leave yourself with two possible answers, which would give you a fifty-fifty chance of making the right choice. The following are questions you can ask as you eliminate choices:

  - Is the choice accurate in its own terms? If there's an error in the choice—for example, a term that is defined incorrectly—the answer is wrong.

  - Is the choice relevant? An answer could be accurate but not related to the question.

  - Are there any qualifiers? Absolute qualifiers like *always, never, all, none,* or *every* often signal an exception that makes a choice incorrect. For example, the statement "normal children always begin talking before the age of two" is false; although most children begin talking before age two, some start later. Choices containing conservative qualifiers (*often, most, rarely,* or *may sometimes be*) are often correct.

- *Look for patterns that may lead to the right answer, then make an educated guess.* The ideal is to know the material so well that you don't have to guess, but that isn't always possible. Test-taking experts have found patterns in multiple-choice questions that might help you. Here is their advice:

  - Consider that a more *general* choice than the others could be the right answer.

  - Consider the possibility that a choice that is *longer* than the others is the right answer.

  - Look for two choices that have *similar* meanings. One of them may be correct.

When questions are keyed to a long reading passage, read the questions first. This will help you, when you read the passage, to focus on the information you need to answer the questions.

True-or-False Questions

True-or-false questions test your knowledge of facts and concepts. Read them carefully to evaluate what they say. Look for qualifiers—such as *all, only,* and *always* (the absolutes that often make a statement false) and *generally, often, usually,* and *sometimes* (the conservatives that often make a statement true)—that can turn a statement that otherwise would be true into one that is false, or vice versa. For example, "The grammar rule 'I before E except after C' is *always* true" is false, whereas "The grammar rule 'I before E except after C' is *usually* true" is true.

Essay Questions

An essay question allows you to express your knowledge and views on a topic in a much more extensive manner than any short-answer question can. With the freedom to express your views, though, comes the challenge to both exhibit knowledge and show you have command of how to organize and express that knowledge clearly.

1. *Start by reading the essay questions.* Decide which to tackle (if there's a choice). Then focus on what each question is asking and the mind actions you will need to use. Read directions carefully. Some essay questions contain more than one part.

2. *Watch for action verbs.* Certain verbs can help you figure out how to think. Figure 7.10 explains some words commonly used in essay questions. Underline these words as you read the question, clarify what they mean, and use them to guide your writing.

FIGURE 7.10

Common action verbs on essay tests.

Analyze   Break into parts and discuss each part separately.

Compare   Explain similarities and differences.

Contrast   Distinguish between items being compared by focusing on differences.

Criticize   Evaluate the positive and negative effects of what is being discussed.

Define   State the essential quality or meaning. Give the common idea.

Describe   Visualize and give information that paints a complete picture.

Discuss   Examine in a complete and detailed way, usually by connecting ideas to examples.

Enumerate/List/Identify   Recall and specify items in the form of a list.

Explain   Make the meaning of something clear, often by making analogies or giving examples.

Evaluate   Give your opinion about the value or worth of something, usually by weighing positive and negative effects, and justify your conclusion.

Illustrate   Supply examples.

Interpret   Explain your personal view of facts and ideas and how they relate to one another.

Outline   Organize and present the sub-ideas or main examples of an idea.

Prove   Use evidence and argument to show that something is true, usually by showing cause and effect or giving examples that fit the idea to be proven.

Review   Provide an overview of ideas, and establish their merits and features.

State   Explain clearly, simply, and concisely, being sure that each word gives the image you want.

Summarize   Give the important ideas in brief.

Trace   Present a history of the way something developed, often by showing cause and effect.

3. *Budget your time and begin to plan.* Create an informal outline or think link to map your ideas, and indicate examples you plan to cite in support. Avoid spending too much time on introductions or flowery prose.

4. *Write your essay.* Start with an idea that states your topic and premise. In the first paragraph, introduce the essay's key points (sub-ideas, causes, effects, or even examples). Use simple, clear language. Carefully establish your ideas and support them with examples. Then look back at your outline to make sure you are covering everything. Wrap it up with a conclusion that is short and to the point. Write legibly; if your instructor can't read your ideas, it doesn't matter how good they are.

5. *Reread and revise your essay.* Look for ideas you left out, ideas you didn't support with enough examples, and sentences that might confuse the reader. Check for mistakes in grammar, spelling, punctuation, and usage. No matter what you are writing about, having a command of these factors will make your work more complete and impressive.

One final note on test taking: The purpose of a test is to see how much you know, not merely to achieve a grade. Making mistakes, or even failing a test, is human. Instead of ignoring your test mistakes when you get your tests back, take the time to examine them. Critically evaluate what went wrong, and come up with ideas about how you can improve the next time. Working through your mistakes will help you avoid repeating them again on another test—or outside of school life.

читать

Although this word may look unfamiliar, anyone who can read the Russian language and alphabet will know that it means "read." People who read languages such as Russian, Japanese, or Greek learn to process their language characters as easily as you process the letters of your native alphabet. Your mind learns to process individually each letter or character you see. This ability enables you to move to the next level of understanding: making sense of the letters or characters when they are grouped to form words, phrases, and sentences.

Think of this concept when you read, take notes, and take tests. Your mind processes immeasurable amounts of information so you can understand the concepts on the page. Give it the best opportunity to succeed by reading as often as you can and by focusing on all of the elements that help you read to the best of your ability.

Chapter 7 Building Thinking Skills

Name _____ Date _____

LIFE THINKING: Applying What You Learn

7.1 *Focusing on Your Purpose for Reading*

Read the paragraphs on kinetic and potential energy (p. 191) and the first law of thermodynamics.[4] When you have finished, answer the questions that follow.

1. *Reading for critical evaluation.* Evaluate the material by answering these questions:

   a. Were the ideas clearly supported by examples? If you think one or more were not supported, give an example.

   _____

   _____

   _____

   b. Did the author make any assumptions that weren't examined? If so, name one or more.

   _____

   _____

   _____

   c. Do you disagree with any part of the material? If so, which part, and why?

   _____

   _____

   _____

2. *Reading for practical application.* Imagine you have to give a presentation on this material the next time the class meets. On a separate sheet of paper, create an outline or think link that maps out the key elements you would discuss.

3. *Reading for comprehension.* Answer the following questions to determine the level of your comprehension.

   a. Name the two types of energy.

   _____

   _____

Among the fundamental characteristics of all living organisms is the ability to guide chemical reactions within their bodies along certain pathways. The chemical reactions serve many functions, depending on the nature of the organism: to synthesize the molecules that make up the organism's body, to reproduce, to move, even to think. Chemical reactions either require or release **energy**, which can be defined simply as *the capacity to do work*, including synthesizing molecules, moving things around, and generating heat and light. In this chapter we discuss the physical laws that govern energy flow in the universe, how energy flow in turn governs chemical reactions, and how the chemical reactions within living cells are controlled by the molecules of the cell itself. Chapters 7 and 8 focus on photosynthesis, the chief "port of entry" for energy into the biosphere, and glycolysis and cellular respiration, the most important sequences of chemical reactions that release energy.

Energy and the Ability to Do Work

As you learned in Chapter 2, there are two types of energy: **kinetic energy** and **potential energy**. Both types of energy may exist in many different forms. Kinetic energy, or *energy of movement*, includes light (movement of photons), heat (movement of molecules), electricity (movement of electrically charged particles), and movement of large objects. Potential energy, or *stored energy*, includes chemical energy stored in the bonds that hold atoms together in molecules, electrical energy stored in a battery, and positional energy stored in a diver poised to spring (Fig. 4-1). Under the right conditions, kinetic energy can be transformed into potential energy, and vice versa. For example, the diver converted kinetic energy of movement into potential energy of position when she climbed the ladder up to the platform; when she jumps off, the potential energy will be converted back into kinetic energy.

To understand how energy flow governs interactions among pieces of matter, we need to know two things: (1) the quantity of available energy and (2) the usefulness of the energy. These are the subjects of the laws of thermodynamics, which we will now examine.

The Laws of Thermodynamics Describe the Basic Properties of Energy

All interactions among pieces of matter are governed by the two **laws of thermodynamics**, physical principles that define the basic properties and behavior of energy. The laws of thermodynamics deal with "isolated systems," which are any parts of the universe that cannot exchange either matter or energy with any other parts. Probably no part of the universe is completely isolated from all possible exchange with every other part, but the concept of an isolated system is useful in thinking about energy flow.

The First Law of Thermodynamics States That Energy Can Neither Be Created nor Destroyed

The **first law of thermodynamics** states that within any isolated system, energy can neither be created nor destroyed, although it can be changed in form (for example, from chemical energy to heat energy). In other words, within an isolated system *the total quantity of energy remains constant*. The first law is therefore often called the **law of conservation of energy**. To use a familiar example, let's see how the first law applies to driving your car (Fig. 4-2). We can consider that your car (with a full tank of gas), the road, and the surrounding air roughly constitute an isolated system. When you drive your car, you convert the potential chemical energy of gasoline into kinetic energy of movement and heat energy. The total amount of energy that was in the gasoline before it was burned is the same as the total amount of this kinetic energy and heat.

An important rule of energy conversions is this: Energy always flows "downhill," from places with a high concentration of energy to places with a low concentration of energy. This is the principle behind engines. As we described in Chapter 2, temperature is a measure of how fast molecules move. The burning gasoline in your car's engine consists of molecules moving at extremely high speeds: a high concentration of energy. The cooler air outside the engine consists of molecules moving at much lower speeds: a low concentration of energy. The molecules in the engine hit the piston harder than the air molecules outside the engine do, so the piston moves upward, driving the gears that move the car. Work is done. When the engine is turned off, it cools down as heat is transferred from the warm engine to its cooler surroundings. The molecules on both sides of the piston move at the same speed, so the piston stays still. No work is done.

b. Which one "stores" energy? _____

c. Can kinetic energy be turned into potential energy? _____

d. What term describes the basic properties and behaviors of energy?

_____

e. Mark the following statements as true (T) or false (F).

_____ Within any isolated system, energy can be neither created nor destroyed.

_____ Energy always flows downhill, from high concentration levels to low.

_____ All interactions among pieces of matter are governed by two laws of thermodynamics.

_____ Some parts of the universe are isolated from other parts.

7.2 *Improving Your Notes*

Look back at a set of notes that you recently took in one of your courses. Evaluate your level of success using the following questions.

TRUE OR FALSE

I kept up with the lecture.	T	F
My handwriting is clear and legible.	T	F
I wrote supporting facts and examples for ideas.	T	F
This set of notes makes sense to me.	T	F
This set of notes reflects my normal habits.	T	F
I would be comfortable studying from these notes.	T	F

FILL IN THE BLANK

What note-taking system did you use?

_____

If your notes aren't as clear as you'd like them to be, name the reason(s) why (fatigue, distraction, dislike of class material, etc.).

_____

_____

Now, looking at your answers, evaluate your note-taking skills:

What about your note-taking skills has positive effects on your learning and studying?

_____

_____

_____

What has negative effects, and why do you think this happens?

_____

_____

_____

Identify two primary goals for improving your note-taking ability.

First goal:

_____

_____

Second goal:

_____

_____

Choose the goal that you think is most important. Using your decision-making skills, come up with three potential choices of how to attain this goal.

1. _____
2. _____
3. _____

7.3 Creating a Mnemonic Device

Choose a set of information from this book. It could be the mind actions, a list of reading techniques, the five core concepts of media literacy, or anything that you want to be able to remember easily.

Create a mnemonic device to help you remember this set of information. It can be a visual image or association, an acronym, or any combination of the two. Write or describe it here. If it is a visual, you might want to draw it on a separate piece of paper.

_____

_____

_____

Wait a day, then use the mnemonic to remember the information. How did you do?

_____

_____

_____

TEAM THINKING: Working Together

7.4 Note-Taking Comparison

This teamwork exercise will show you how your note-taking techniques compare with those of other students. It also will help you analyze what makes one set of notes more useful than another.

- Start by choosing a two-to three-page excerpt from this book or any other text you are all reading. The excerpt should contain a lot of "meaty" information but should have no tables or figures. Don't read the excerpt before you start the exercise.

- Form groups of four students each. Within each group, one student will play the role of instructor and the other three will be students. Assign different note-taking strategies to each student. One will use outlining, one the Cornell system, and one think links. The "instructor" will read the excerpt as if he or she were delivering a classroom lecture. The "students" will take notes on the material. You then will have three different sets of notes on the same material.

- Now come together with all four groups' participants to review and compare all three versions. Read each version carefully and answer the following questions:

  1. Did all three note takers record the important information? If there are differences, why do you think these differences occurred? (You can ask the note takers to explain why they chose to include some information and omit other information.)

  _____

  _____

  _____

  _____

  2. How did each student feel about his or her note-taking strategy? Who felt comfortable and who didn't, and why?

  _____

  _____

  _____

  3. Evaluate the different sets of notes. For this material and situation, which set of notes is likely to be the most helpful study tool for you?

  _____

  _____

  _____

  _____

WORK THINKING: Career Portfolio

7.5 *Test Taking and Career Investigation*

Depending on what careers you are considering, you might encounter one or more tests—for entry into the field (such as the medical boards), on equipment (such as a proficiency test on Microsoft Word), or that move you to the next level of employment (such as a technical certification test). This portfolio exercise has two parts. If for any reason no potential career of yours involves tests, complete part two only.

Part One

Choose one career you are thinking about and investigate what tests are involved in entering this field. Be sure to look for tests in any of the areas described above. On a separate piece of paper, write down everything you find out about each test involved:

- What it tests you on
- When, in the course of pursuing this career, you would need to take the test
- What preparation is necessary for the test (including coursework)
- Whether the test will have to be retaken at any time (e.g., airline pilots usually need to be recertified every few years)

Once you have recorded your information, see if you can look at, or even take for practice, any of the tests you will face if you pursue this career. For example, if you will be tested on a computer program, your career or computer center might have the test available.

Part Two

Your school's career center will have one or more "tests" that investigate your interests and abilities and make suggestions about what careers might be suitable for you. Explore the possibilities by taking one or more of these tests at the center. You could end up with results that match what you already want to do—or you may be surprised. Keep an open mind and take time to consider any surprises you encounter. Even if you do not want to follow any of the career areas suggested by the test, think about what the results say about you.

QUESTIONING YOUR WORLD:
Information Literacy Journal

To record your thoughts, use a separate journal or the lined pages at the end of the chapter.

7.6 *Perspectives in Your Reading*

Look no farther than the book you are holding. Your authors write from their own perspectives just as any other authors do. Choose a section in this book and analyze it critically. What is the perspective? What assumptions underlie this perspective? Do you agree or disagree with it, or with part of it? What in the passage seems to be fact, and what opinion? If the passage makes an argument, are you convinced?

Journal

Name _____   Date _____

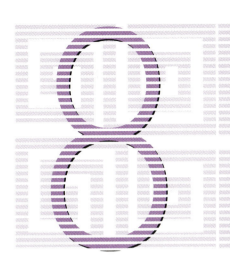

Critical Thinking

Thinking About Expression

Listening, Communication, and Writing

Your school, work, and personal life revolve around the exchange of ideas as people express them to one another. You listen in class as instructors discuss key concepts, and members of your study group listen to you as you exchange thoughts. You accomplish work goals using on-the-job communication and advance personal relationships through your conversations. Through writing, for school assignments or for work, you develop knowledge and state your ideas. Your outlets for self-expression are your tools for growth.

This chapter will help you develop your ability to express yourself and also to take in what others express to you. Through critical thinking, you will learn how to listen more effectively and communicate more clearly. You will explore some tips on speaking in front of a group—a more specialized communication situation. Finally, the chapter will illustrate ways to communicate your ideas in writing, showing how good writing is linked to clear thinking.

In this chapter, you will explore answers to the following questions:

- How can you become a better listener?
- How can you express yourself effectively?
- What are the elements of effective writing?
- What is the writing process?

HOW CAN YOU BECOME A BETTER LISTENER?

The act of hearing isn't quite the same as the act of listening. Whereas *hearing* refers to sensing spoken messages from their source, *listening* involves a complex process of communication. Successful listening results in the speaker's intended message reaching the listener. Whereas poor listening results in communication breakdowns and mistakes, skilled listening promotes progress and success. Listening is a teachable—and learnable—skill.

Listening is also a crucial work skill. If you don't accurately hear what others in your workplace tell you, the quality of your work can suffer, no matter how much effort you put forth. If an order of "twenty thousand" business cards sounds to you like "two thousand," you could have an unhappy customer on your hands. The way in which employees and managers listen to customers and to one another greatly affects their ability to work effectively.

Effective listening depends first of all on knowing how the listening process works.

Know the Stages of Listening

Listening is made up of four stages: sensing, interpreting, evaluating, and reacting. These stages take the message from the speaker to the listener and back to the speaker (see Figure 8.1).

1. During the *sensation* stage (also known as hearing), your ears pick up sound waves and transmit them to the brain. For example, you are sitting in class and hear your instructor say, "The only opportunity to make up last week's test is Tuesday at five o'clock."

2. In the *interpretation* stage, listeners attach meaning to a message. This involves understanding what is being said and relating it to what you know already. For example, you relate this message to your knowledge of the test, whether you need to make it up, and what you are doing on Tuesday at five o'clock.

3. In the *evaluation* stage of listening, you decide how you feel about the message—whether, for example, you like it or agree with it. This involves evaluating the message as it relates to your needs and values. If the message goes against your values or does not fulfill your needs, you might reject it or stop listening. In the example, if you do need to make

FIGURE 8.1 Stages of listening.

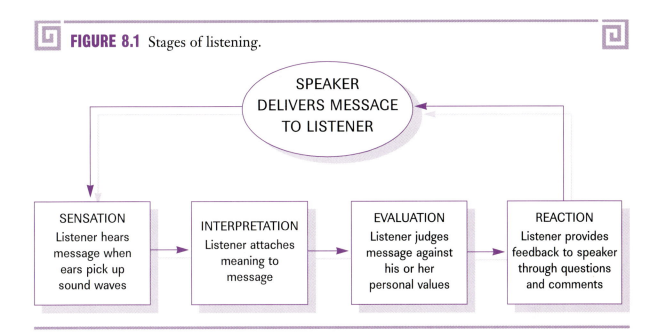

up the test but have to be at work Tuesday by five o'clock, you probably will evaluate the message as less than satisfactory.

4. The final stage of listening is a *reaction* to the message in the form of feedback. In a classroom, feedback often means questions and comments. Your reaction, in the example, might be to ask the instructor if there is any alternative to that particular test time.

Improving your skills also involves managing challenges and becoming an active listener. Although good listening will help in every class, it is crucial in subject areas you find difficult.

Manage Listening Challenges

Classic studies have shown that immediately after listening, students are likely to recall only half of what was said. This is partly because of listening challenges such as divided attention and distractions, the tendency to rush to judgment, and partial hearing loss or learning disabilities.[1] To help create a positive listening environment in both your mind and your surroundings, explore how to manage these challenges.

Divided Attention and Distractions

Imagine you are talking with a friend at a party when you hear your name mentioned across the room. You strain to hear what someone might be saying about you, and you only half-listen to your friend. Chances are that you hear neither person very well. This situation illustrates the consequences of divided attention. Even though you are capable of listening to more than one message at a time, chances are that you will hear neither message completely.

Internal and external distractions often divide your attention. *Internal distractions* include anything from hunger to a headache to personal worries.

Something the speaker says also could trigger a recollection that may cause your mind to drift. In contrast, *external distractions* are outside noises (whispering, say, or sirens) and excessive heat or cold.

Reduce distractions so you can focus. Sitting where you can clearly see and hear will help you listen and be more willing to listen. Dress comfortably, paying attention to the temperature of the classroom, and try not to go to class hungry or thirsty. Concentrate on class when you're in class and try to save worrying about personal problems for later.

Rushing to Judgment

"No one cares to speak to an unwilling listener. An arrow never lodges in a stone; often it recoils upon the sender of it."

ST. JEROME

Instead of paying attention to everything a speaker says, people often immediately judge, or evaluate, what they hear. You tend to stop listening when you hear something you don't like, find too difficult, or consider uninteresting. Judgments also involve reactions to the speakers themselves. If you do not like your instructors or if you have made negative assumptions about their ideas or background, you might decide that their words have little value.

Hasty evaluation can lead you to pay attention to one part of the message and shut out the rest. Remember, though, that listening brings you the information—the input—that is your raw material for thinking. Approaching listening as a critical thinker means taking in as much information as possible up front, without judgment. This will give you the most comprehensive material with which to work when you begin evaluate the information critically.

Recognize and control your judgments. Being aware of what you tend to judge will help you not to reject messages that clash with your perspective. Consider education as a continuing search for evidence, regardless of whether that evidence supports or negates your point of view.

Partial Hearing Loss and Learning Disabilities

Good listening techniques don't solve every listening problem. If you have some hearing loss, seek out special services that can help you listen in class. Maybe you will require special equipment, or you might benefit from tutoring. You might be able to arrange to meet with your instructor outside of class to clarify your notes.

Other disabilities, such as attention deficit disorder (ADD) or a problem with processing heard language, can make it difficult to focus on and understand what is heard. If you have a disability, your counseling center, student health center, advisor, and instructors should be able to assist you in meeting your challenges.

Become an Active Listener

Listening is an active process that involves a positive attitude and the following strategies.

Accept responsibility for listening. Although instructors are responsible for communicating information to you, they cannot force you to listen. You are responsible for taking in that information. If you work to take in the whole message in class, you will be able to read your notes later and think critically about what is most important.

Set purposes for listening. Active listening is possible only if you know (and care) why you are listening. In any situation, establish what you want to achieve through listening, such as better understanding of the material, staying awake in class, or better note taking. Having a goal motivates you to listen.

Ask questions. Willingness to question shows a desire to learn and is the mark of an active listener and critical thinker. Some questions are *informational*—seeking information—such as questions beginning with the phrase, "I don't understand. . . ." *Clarifying* questions state your understanding of what you have just heard and ask if that understanding is correct. Some clarifying questions focus on a key concept ("So, some learning disorders can be improved with treatment?"). Others highlight specific facts ("Is it true that dyslexia can cause people to reverse letters?").

Pay attention to verbal signposts. You can identify important facts and ideas and predict test questions by paying attention to the speaker's specific choice of words. **Verbal signposts** often involve transition words and phrases that help organize information, connect ideas, and indicate what is important and what is not. Let phrases like those in Table 8.1 direct your attention to the material that follows them.

Effective listening will enable you to acquire knowledge. Listening is also a crucial component of communication. If you listen well and take in information accurately, you will be able to process it and communicate about it effectively.

TERMS

Verbal signposts Spoken words or phrases that call your attention to the information that follows.

TABLE 8.1 Paying attention to verbal signposts.

SIGNALS POINTING TO KEY CONCEPTS	SIGNALS OF SUPPORT
There are two reasons for this . . .	For example, . . .
A critical point in the process involves . . .	Specifically, . . .
Most important, . . .	For instance, . . .
The result is . . .	Similarly, . . .
SIGNALS POINTING TO DIFFERENCES	SIGNALS THAT SUMMARIZE
On the contrary, . . .	Finally, . . .
On the other hand, . . .	Recapping this idea, . . .
In contrast, . . .	In conclusion, . . .
However, . . .	As a result, . . .

Source: Adapted from George M. Usova, *Efficient Study Strategies: Skills for Successful Learning* (Pacific Grove, CA: Brooks/Cole, 1989), p. 69.

HOW CAN YOU EXPRESS YOURSELF EFFECTIVELY?

The only way for people to know one another's needs is to communicate as clearly and directly as possible. Successful communication promotes successful school, work, and personal relationships. Addressing communication issues will help you express yourself effectively.

Addressing Communication Issues

Communication is an exchange between two or more people. The speaker's goal is for the listener (or listeners) to receive the message as the speaker intends. This goal is compounded because different people have different styles of communicating. Communication problems may occur when information is not presented clearly or when those who receive information filter it through their own perspectives and interpret it differently. Some of the most common communication issues are described next, along with strategies to help you address them.

Issue: Different styles of communication

Solution: Be aware of the styles of others

It doesn't matter how clearly you think you are communicating if the person you are speaking to doesn't understand your style and can't "translate" your message. Try to take your listener's style into consideration when you communicate. For example, if you were to critique the essay of a fellow student who tends to focus on detail, your saying "You introduced your central idea at the beginning but then didn't really support it until the fourth paragraph" would be far more effective than saying, "Your writing isn't clear."

Conversely, when you are the listener, be aware of the communication style of the person who is speaking to you. Try to translate the speaker's message into one that makes sense to you. For example, if an employee of yours focuses on emotion more than you do, consider his or her messages in that light.

Issue: Communication that goes beyond words

Solution: Become aware of body language

Your actions—gestures, eye movement, facial expression, body positioning and posture, touching behavior, and use of personal space—are the most basic form of communication, called body language. Body language can reinforce or contradict verbal statements. When body language contradicts verbal language, the message conveyed by the body is dominant. Consider, for example, if someone asks you how you feel, and you say "Fine" even though you don't feel fine at all. In such a case, your posture, eye contact, and other body language may convey the real message loud and clear.

To make the most of body language, pay attention to what other people communicate nonverbally. Also, keep an eye on your own body language, and make sure that it reinforces your words and does not confuse anyone to whom you are speaking. Finally, be aware of cultural differences. The United States, for example, values eye contact, whereas in some other cultures, looking an authority figure or superior directly in the eye is considered disrespectful.

Issue: Unclear or incomplete explanation

Solution: Support ideas with examples

When you clarify a general idea with supporting examples that illustrate how it works and what effects it causes, you will help your receiver understand what you mean and thus have a better chance at holding his or her attention.

For example, if you recommend that a friend take a certain class, that person might not take you seriously until you explain why. If you then communicate the positive effects of taking that class (progress toward a major, an excellent instructor, and friendly study sessions), you have a better chance of getting your message across. Work situations, too, benefit from explanation. If you assign a task without explanation, you might get a delayed response or find mistakes in your employees' work. If you explain the possible positive effects of the task, you'll have better results.

Issue: Attacking the receiver

Solution: Send "I" messages

When a conflict arises, often the first instinct is to pinpoint what someone else did wrong: "You didn't lock the door!" "You never called last night!" Making an accusation, especially without proof, puts the other person on the defensive and shuts down the lines of communication.

Using "I" messages will help you communicate your own needs rather than focusing on what you think someone else should do differently: "I felt uneasy when I came to work and the door was unlocked." "I became worried about you when I didn't hear from you last night." "I" statements soften the conflict by highlighting the effects of the other person's actions on you rather than the person or the actions themselves. When you point out your own response and needs, your receiver might feel more free to respond, perhaps offering help and even acknowledging mistakes.

Issue: Passive or aggressive communication styles

Solution: Become assertive

Among the three major communication styles—aggressive, passive, and assertive—the one that conveys a message in the clearest, most productive way is the **assertive** style. The other two, although commonly used, throw communication out of balance. Assertive behavior strikes a balance between aggression and passivity. If you can be an assertive communicator, you will be more likely to get your message across while ensuring that others have a chance to speak as well. Table 8-2 compares some characteristics of each kind of communicator.

Aggressive communicators emphasize their own needs. They sometimes become angry and impatient when those needs are not satisfied immediately. To become more assertive, aggressive communicators might try to take time to think before speaking, avoid ordering people around, use "I" statements, and attempt to listen to what the other person has to say.

By contrast, passive communicators deny themselves the power that aggressive people grab. They focus almost exclusively on others' needs instead of their own needs. In doing so, they experience unexpressed frustration and tension. To become more assertive, passive communicators might try

TERMS

Assertive
Able to declare and affirm one's own opinions while respecting the rights of others to do the same.

TABLE 8.2	AGGRESSIVE	PASSIVE	ASSERTIVE
Aggressive, passive, and assertive styles.	Loud, heated arguing	Concealing one's own feelings	Expressing feelings without being nasty or overbearing
	Physically violent encounters	Denying one's own anger	Acknowledging emotions but staying open to discussion
	Blaming, name-calling, and verbal insults	Feeling that one has no right to express anger	Expressing oneself and giving others the chance to express themselves equally
	Walking out of arguments before they are resolved	Avoiding arguments	Using "I" statements to defuse arguments
	Being demanding: "Do this"	Being noncommittal: "You don't have to do this unless you really want to . . . ."	Asking and giving reasons: "I would appreciate it if you would do this, and here's why . . . ."

to acknowledge anger or hurt more often, speak up when they feel strongly about something, realize that they have a right to make requests, and know that their ideas and feelings are as important as anyone else's.

Speaking/Oral Presentations

Speaking in front of others is a specialized communication situation that requires specific preparation and strategy. Whether you are giving group project results to your class or making a presentation to coworkers, you have to think critically to make your communication as effective as it can be. Use the strategies that follow.

Compare Speaking to Writing

If you think of speaking as a verbal equivalent to writing, you can apply writing strategies to speaking. Here are some strategies that apply to both activities (you will learn more about these later in the chapter):

1. *Think through what you want to say and why.* What is your purpose—to make or refute an argument, present information, entertain? Have a goal for your speech.
2. *Plan.* Get organized beforehand. Brainstorm your topic. Narrow it with pre-writing strategies, determine your central idea or argument, and write an outline. Do research if you need to.
3. *Draft your thoughts.* It's important to get your thoughts organized for both speaking and writing. But you may not want to write out complete sentences for a speech in the same way you would for a paper. That could tempt you to read it verbatim, which can disconnect you from

your audience. Instead, make a draft using "trigger" words or phrases that will remind you of what you want to say.

4. *Use clear thinking.* Example-to-idea and idea-to-example thinking are crucial for expressing yourself clearly to your audience. Illustrate ideas with examples, and show how examples lead to ideas. As in writing, have a clear beginning and end. Begin with an attention-getter, and end with a wrap-up that summarizes your thoughts and leaves your audience with something to remember.

Think Critically About Your Audience

Your speech will be most effective if it takes your audience into consideration. As in writing, take time to think about who will comprise your audience and how you expect your audience to respond. Consider the following about your audience:

- Profile (ages, backgrounds, interests)
- Roles (instructors, students, coworkers, customers)
- Expected knowledge base (experts, beginners, in between)
- Expected response (in agreement, in disagreement, open- or closed-minded)

When you have developed a picture of whom you will be talking to, think about how to tailor your speech to that audience. For example, presenting information to a group of informed coworkers would be quite different from presenting the same information to a group of students who have no prior knowledge of your topic.

Practice Your Performance

The element of performance distinguishes speaking from writing. You communicate in the moment rather than take time to organize the message on paper and finalize it before you give it to someone. The following strategies will help to combat any performance anxiety you might have.

1. *Model after good speakers.* Observe people whom you consider to be successful oral communicators. Watch them live, on TV, or on videotape. Listen to them on the radio. Think about what elements draw you in, keep your attention, and inspire you to consider ideas.
2. *Know the parameters.* How long do you have? What topics do you have to choose from? Make sure you stick to the guidelines your instructor gives you. Where will you be speaking? Be aware of the physical setting—where your audience will be, where you will be, and what you have around you to use (podium, table, chair, chalkboard).
3. *Use index cards or notes.* It's helpful to have notes to refer to. Keep them out of your face, however. It's tempting to hide behind them. Use visuals if you have them and if they help you to illustrate your ideas.
4. *Pay attention to the physical.* Your body positioning, your voice, and what you wear contribute to the impression you make. Look good and sound

good. Walk around if you like to talk that way. Above all, make eye contact with your audience members. You are speaking to them, so be sure to look at them.

5. *Practice ahead of time.* Do a test run or two with friends or alone. If you can, practice in the room where you will speak. Audiotape or videotape yourself practicing, and use the tapes to evaluate yourself.

Be Yourself

When you write, you express your personality through your own style of putting words together. When you speak, you do the same, plus you have the additional element of your presence in person. First, if you have a choice of topic, choose something that moves or interests you. Then don't be afraid to add your own bits of humor or style to the presentation. Finally, take deep breaths. Smile. Know that you can communicate successfully—and that, in most situations, your audience has the same hope for you.

Being yourself in writing is just as important as in speaking. Explore the writing process so that you can express yourself to the best of your ability.

 ## WHAT ARE THE ELEMENTS OF EFFECTIVE WRITING?

Writing means using on-paper communication to achieve a goal, whether educational, professional, or personal. Almost any college course—and many jobs—require you to communicate knowledge and thought processes in writing. You might write papers, essays, answers to essay test questions, job application letters, resumes, business proposals and reports, memos to coworkers, and letters to customers. Instructors, supervisors, and other people who see your writing judge your thinking ability based on what you write and how you write it.

Good writing depends on and reflects clear thinking. Therefore, a clear thought process is the best preparation for a well-written document, and a well-written document shows the reader a clear thought process. Good writing also depends on reading. Critical reading increases your learning and generates new ideas you can use in writing. Reading and writing are interrelated; the skills in one process tend to enhance the skills in the other.

Every writing situation is different, depending on three elements:

- *Your purpose:* What do you want to accomplish with this piece of writing?
- *Your topic:* What is the subject about which you will write?
- *Your audience:* Who will read your writing?

TERMS

Audience
The reader or readers of any piece of written material.

Figure 8.2 shows how these elements depend on one another. Just as a triangle needs three points to be complete, a piece of writing requires these three elements. Consider purpose and **audience** even before you begin to plan. Topic will come into play during the planning stage (the first stage of the writing process).

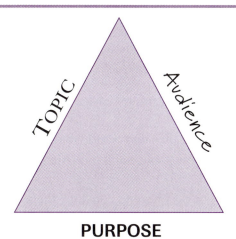

FIGURE 8.2
The three elements of writing.

Writing Purpose

Writing without having set your purpose first is like driving without deciding where you want to go. You'll get somewhere, but chances are it won't be where you needed to be. Therefore, when you write, set a goal for what you want to accomplish. Although writing has many different purposes, the two you will use most commonly are to inform and to persuade.

Informative Writing

The purpose of *informative writing* is to present and explain facts and ideas in an unbiased way, without introducing a point of view. A research paper on how hospitals use donated blood, for example, informs readers without trying to mold opinion. Newspaper articles, except on the opinion and editorial pages, are examples of informative writing.

Persuasive Writing

Persuasive writing tries to convince readers to adopt a point of view. Say, as a member of the student health committee, that you write a newspaper column attempting to persuade readers to give blood. Examples of persuasive writing include newspaper editorials, business proposals, books, and magazine articles with a byline. If you are writing a persuasive paper, keep in mind what you know about constructing an argument (see Chapter 3).

Knowing Your Audience

In almost every case, a writer creates written material so others can read and understand it. The writer and the audience are partners in this process. Knowing who your audience is will help you communicate successfully.

In school, your primary audience consists of your instructors. For many assignments, instructors will want you to assume that they are typical readers. Writing for "typical readers" usually means that you should be as complete as possible in your explanations. At times you might have to write papers that address informed instructors or some other specific reading audience. In those cases, you might ask yourself some or all of the following questions, depending on which apply.

- What are my readers' ages, cultural backgrounds, interests, and experiences?
- What are their roles? Are they instructors, students, employers, customers?
- How much do they know about my topic? Are they experts in the topic or novices?
- Are they interested, or do I have to convince them to read what I write?
- Can I expect my audience to have open or closed minds?

As you write, take into consideration what you discover. In addition, keep in mind the persuasive techniques you read about in Chapter 3. Consider which of these techniques might be most effective with your specific audience.

Effective and successful writing involves following the steps of the writing process.

WHAT IS THE WRITING PROCESS?

The writing process provides an opportunity for you to state and refine your thoughts until you have expressed yourself as clearly as possible. Critical thinking plays an important role in every step along the way. The four main parts of the process are planning, drafting, revising, and editing.

Planning

TERMS

Pre-writing
strategies
Techniques for
generating ideas
about a topic and
finding out how
much you already
know before you
start your
research and
writing.

Planning gives you a chance to gather ideas and information without judging and then begin to think about what you want to do with it. Planning involves brainstorming for ideas, defining and narrowing your topic by using **pre-writing strategies,** writing a thesis statement, and writing a working outline. Although these steps are discussed in sequence, in real life the steps overlap as you plan.

Open Your Mind Through Brainstorming

Brainstorm to develop ideas about what you want to write. Brainstorming is a creative technique that involves generating ideas about a subject without making judgments (see Chapter 2).

First, let your mind wander. Write down anything on the assigned subject that comes to mind, in no particular order. Then organize that list into an outline or think link separating the items on the list into general ideas or categories and sub-ideas or examples and associating them with the ideas they support or fit. Figure 8.3 shows a portion of an outline that a student, Michael, constructed from his brainstorming list. The assignment is a five-paragraph essay on a life-changing event. The subject that Michael chose is shown broken down into different ideas.

FIGURE 8.3

Part of a brainstorming outline.

BOOT CAMP

  —physical conditioning

    • swim tests

    • intensive training

    • ENDLESS pushups!

  —Chief who was our commander

  —mental discipline

    • military lifestyle

    • perfecting our appearance

  —self-confidence

    • walk like you're in control

    • don't blindly accept anything

Narrow Your Topic Through Pre-writing Strategies

When your brainstorming has generated some possibilities, narrow your topic. The sub-ideas and examples from your brainstorming session can point you toward possible topics. Choose one or more that you like, and explore them by using pre-writing strategies such as brainstorming, freewriting, and asking journalists' questions.[1] Pre-writing strategies will help you decide which of your possible topics you would most like to pursue.

Brainstorming. The same process you used to generate ideas will also help you narrow your topic further. Generate thoughts about the possibility you have chosen and write them down. Then, organize them into categories, noticing any patterns that appear. See if any of the sub-ideas or examples seem as if they might make good topics.

Freewriting. When you *freewrite*, you write whatever comes to mind without evaluating ideas or worrying about grammar, spelling, punctuation, or organization. Freewriting helps you think creatively and begin to weave in information you already know. Freewrite on the sub-ideas or examples you have created to see if you want to pursue them. Here is a sample of freewriting:

> Boot camp for the Coast Guard really changed my life. First of all, I really got in shape. We had to get up every morning at 5 A.M., eat breakfast,

and go right into training. We had to do endless military-style push-ups—but we later found out that these have a purpose, to prepare us to hit the deck in the event of enemy fire. We had a lot of aquatic tests. Once we were awakened at 3 A.M. to do one in full uniform! Boot camp also helped me to feel confident about myself and be disciplined. Chief Marzloff was the main person who made that happen. He was tough but there was always a reason. He got angry when I used to nod my head whenever he would speak to me. He said that made it seem like I was blindly accepting whatever he said, which was a weakness. From him I have learned to keep an eye on my body's movements when I communicate. I learned a lot more from him too.

Asking journalists' questions. When journalists work on a story, they ask themselves Who? What? Where? When? Why? How? Use these *journalists' questions* to focus your thinking. Ask these questions about any sub-idea or example to discover what you may want to discuss.

Who?	Who was at boot camp? Who influenced me the most?
What?	What about boot camp changed my life? What did we do?
When?	When in my life did I go to boot camp, and for how long? When did we fulfill our duties?
Where?	Where was camp located? Where did we spend our day-to-day time?
Why?	Why did I decide to go there? Why was it such an important experience?
How?	How did we train in the camp? How were we treated? How did we achieve success?

As you pre-write, keep an eye on length of the paper, assignment due date, and any other requirements (such as topic area or purpose). These requirements influence your choice of a final topic. For example, if you have a month to write an informative twenty-page paper on a learning disability, you might discuss the symptoms, effects, and treatment of attention deficit disorder. If you have a week to write a five-page persuasive essay, you might write about how elementary students with ADD need special training.

Pre-writing will help you develop a topic broad enough to give you something with which to work but narrow enough to be manageable. Pre-writing also helps you see what you know and what you don't know. If your assignment requires more than you already know, you may have to do research. Use the library research strategies from Chapter 4.

Write a Thesis Statement

Your work until this point has prepared you to write a thesis statement, the central message you want to communicate. The thesis statement states your subject and point of view, reflects your writing purpose and audience, and acts as the organizing principle of your paper. It tells your readers what they should expect to read. Here is an example from Michael's paper:

Topic	Coast Guard boot camp
Purpose	To inform and narrate
Audience	Instructor with unknown knowledge about the topic
Thesis statement	Chief Marzloff, our Basic Training Company Commander at the U.S. Coast Guard Basic Training Facility, shaped my life through physical conditioning, developing our self-confidence, and instilling strong mental discipline.

For a persuasive paper, you are essentially constructing an argument. In that case, your thesis statement corresponds to the premise. Here is an example:

Topic	Food and Drug Administration (FDA)
Issue	Whether the FDA should regulate distribution of herbal supplements
Purpose	To persuade
Audience	Instructor with unknown knowledge about the topic
Thesis/premise	The FDA should treat herbal supplements as they do any drug, and should test them before approving them for market.

A thesis statement is just as important in a short document, such as a letter, as it is in a long paper. For example, when you write a job application letter, a clear thesis statement will help you tell the recruiter why you deserve the job.

Write a Working Outline

The final step in the planning process is writing a working outline. Use this outline as a loose guide instead of a final structure. As you draft your paper and get closer and closer to what you really want to say, your ideas and structure probably will change many times. Some students prefer a more formal outline, and others like to use a think link. Choose whatever form suits you best.

Drafting

A *first draft* involves putting ideas down on paper for the first time—but not the last. You likely will write many different versions of the assignment until you do one you like. Each version moves you closer to communicating exactly what you want to say in the way you want to say it. It is as if you were to start with a muddy pond and gradually clear the mud away until your last version became a clear body of water, showing the rocks and the fish beneath the surface. Think of your first draft as a way of establishing the pond before you start clearing it up.

The elements of writing a first draft are freewriting, crafting an introduction, organizing the ideas in the body of the paper, formulating a conclusion, and citing sources.

> "Omit needless words. . . . This requires not that the writer make all his sentences short, or that he avoid all detail and treat his subjects only in outline, but that every word tell."
>
> WILLIAM STRUNK, JR.

Freewriting Your Draft

Take everything you have developed in the planning stages and freewrite a very rough draft. Don't evaluate your work yet. For now, don't consciously think about your introduction, conclusion, or structure within the body of the paper. Concentrate on getting your ideas out of the realm of thought and onto the paper, in whatever form you prefer at the moment.

When you have the beginnings of a paper in your hands, you can start to shape it into something with a more definite form. First, work on how you want to begin.

Writing an Introduction

The introduction tells your readers what the rest of the paper will contain. A thesis statement is essential. Here is a draft of an introduction for Michael's paper about the Coast Guard. The thesis statement is underlined at the end of the paragraph:

> Chief Marzloff took on the task of shaping the lives and careers of the youngest, newest members of the U.S. Coast Guard. During my eight weeks in training, he was my father, my instructor, my leader, and my worst enemy. He took his job very seriously and demanded that we do the same. <u>The Chief was instrumental in conditioning our bodies, developing our self-confidence, and instilling mental discipline within us.</u>

When you write an introduction, you might try to pull the reader in with an anecdote—a story related to the thesis. You can try other **hooks,** such as a relevant quotation, dramatic statistics, or questions that encourage critical thinking. Whatever strategy you choose, link it to your thesis statement.

After you have an introduction that seems to set up the purpose of your paper, make sure that the body fulfills that purpose.

Organizing the Body of a Paper

The body of the paper contains your central ideas and supporting evidence. *Evidence*—proof that informs or persuades—consists of the facts, statistics, examples, sub-ideas, and expert opinions that you know or have gathered during research.

Look at the array of ideas and evidence in your draft in its current state. Think about how you might group certain items of evidence with the ideas each supports. Then try to find a structure that helps you to organize these evidence groups into a clear pattern. Here are some strategies to consider.

- *Arrange ideas by time.* Describe events in order or in reverse order.
- *Arrange ideas according to importance.* You might choose to start with the idea that carries the most weight and move to ideas with less value or influence. Or, you could move from the least important to the most important idea.
- *Focus on cause and effect.* Discuss a series of causes, each with its related effects.

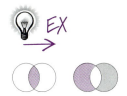

- *Arrange ideas by problem and solution.* Start with a specific problem, then discuss one or more solutions.
- *Classify or compare ideas.* Group similar ideas and discuss their similarities, or set up the paper as a comparison between two different ideas and their respective examples.

Recall from Chapter 3 the different effects that fact and opinion have on an audience. As you write, keep in mind how you want your audience to respond and what combination of fact and opinion will be most likely to generate that response.

Formulating the Conclusion

The conclusion is a statement or paragraph communicating that your paper is complete. Summarize the information that is in the body of your paper and critically evaluate what is important about it. Try one of the following strategies:

- Summarize main points (if material is longer than three pages)
- Relate a story, statistic, quote, or question that makes the reader think
- Call the reader to action
- Look to the future

As you work on your conclusion, try not to introduce new facts or restate what you believe you have proved ("I have successfully proven that violent cartoons are related to increased violence in children"). Let your ideas as they are presented in the body of the paper speak for themselves. Readers should feel that they have reached a natural point of completion.

Citing Sources

When you write a paper using any materials other than your own thoughts and recollections, the ideas you gathered in your research become part of your own writing. This does not mean you can claim these ideas as your own. Using an idea, phrase, or word-for-word paragraph without crediting its author is considered theft and may have unfavorable consequences. Most colleges have stiff penalties for plagiarism as well as for other cheating offenses.

To avoid **plagiarism,** you have to credit authors for their ideas and words. Knowing the difference between a quotation and a paraphrase will help. A *quotation* refers to a source's exact words, set off from the rest of the text by quotation marks. A *paraphrase* is a restatement of the quotation in which you completely rewrite the idea. A paraphrase may not be acceptable if it is too close to the original. Figure 8.4 demonstrates the differences.

Plagiarism often begins by accident when you do research. You might intend to cite or paraphrase but never get around to it. To avoid forgetting, write something like "Quotation; rewrite later" next to quoted material, and note at that time the specifics of the original document (title, author, source, page number, etc.), so you don't spend hours trying to locate it later.

Even an acceptable paraphrase requires citation of the source of the ideas within it. Credit any source that you quote, paraphrase, or use as evidence. To

TERMS

Plagiarism The act of using someone else's exact words, figures, unique approach, or specific reasoning without giving appropriate credit.

FIGURE 8.4

Avoiding plagiarism by paraphrasing.

QUOTATION

"The most common assumption made by persons who are communicating with one another is . . . that the other perceives, judges, thinks, and reasons the way he does. Identical twins communicate with ease. Persons from the same culture but with a different education, age, background, and experience often find communication difficult. American managers communicating with managers from other cultures experience greater difficulties in communication than with managers from their own culture."

Source: Philip R. Harris and Robert T. Moran, *Managing Cultural Differences,* 3d ed. (Houston, TX: Gulf Publishing, 1991), p. 59.

UNACCEPTABLE PARAPHRASE

(The underlined words are taken directly from the quoted source.)

When we communicate, we assume that the person to whom we are speaking <u>perceives, judges, thinks, and reasons the way</u> we do. This is not always the case. Although <u>identical twins communicate with ease, persons from the same culture but with a different education, age, background, and experience often</u> encounter communication problems. Communication problems are common among American managers as they attempt to <u>communicate with managers from other cultures.</u> They experience greater communication problems than when they communicate <u>with managers from their own culture.</u>

ACCEPTABLE PARAPHRASE

Many people fall into the trap of believing that everyone sees the world exactly as they do and that all people communicate according to the same assumptions. This belief is difficult to support even within our own culture as African Americans, Hispanic Americans, Asian Americans, and others often attempt unsuccessfully to find common ground. When intercultural differences are thrown into the mix, such as when American managers working abroad attempt to communicate with managers from other cultures, clear communication becomes even harder.

---

credit a source, write a footnote or endnote that describes it. Use the format that your instructor prefers. Handbooks such as the *Modern Language Association* (MLA) *Handbook* contain acceptable formats.

Revising

When you revise, you critically evaluate the word choice, paragraph structure, and style of your first draft. Any draft, no matter how good, can be improved. You might want to make notes and corrections on hard copy before you make changes on a typewritten or computer printed version. Figure 8.5 shows a paragraph from Michael's first draft with revision comments.

Revision is where your critical thinking skills go into high gear. You can improve your draft by asking questions, evaluating paragraph structure, and checking for clarity and conciseness.

FIGURE 8.5

Revision notes.

> *military recruits*
> *undergo*
>
> Of the changes that ~~happened to us,~~ the physical
>
> *most evident*
> transformation is the ~~biggest. When we arrived at the~~
>
> *Too much ↗*
> ~~training facility, it was January, cold and cloudy. At the~~
>
> *Maybe— upon my January arrival at the*
> ~~time,~~ I was a little thin, but I had been working out and
>
> *training facility,*
> thought that I could physically do anything. Oh boy, was
>
> I wrong! The Chief said to us right away: "Get down,
>
> *↙ his trademark phrase*   *were*
> maggots!" Upon this command, we ˄ all to drop to the
>
> *endless*
> ground and do ˄ military-style push-ups. Water survival
>
> tactics were also part of the training ~~that we had to~~
> *unnecessary*
> ~~complete.~~ Occasionally, my dreams of home were
>
> interrupted at 3 a.m. when we had a surprise aquatic
>
> *resented*
> test. Although we ~~didn't feel too happy about~~ this
>   *mention how*
>   *chief was*
> sub-human treatment at the time, we learned to ── *involved*
>
> appreciate how the conditioning was turning our bodies
>
> *say more about*
> into fine-tuned machines. *this (swimming in*
>   *uniform incident?)*

Asking Questions About Your Writing

Thinking critically when writing will help you move beyond restating what you have researched and read. Although the information you cite is a crucial part of your writing, what will make your work even more important and unique is how you construct your own new ideas and knowledge from what you have learned.

The key to constructing new ideas and knowledge in your writing is asking the question, "So what?" For example, if you were writing a paper on nutrition, you might discuss a variety of good eating habits. Asking "So what?" could lead into a discussion of what positive effects these habits have. If you were writing a paper on the novel *All the King's Men* by Robert Penn Warren, you might first list examples of egg imagery. Then, asking "So what?" could lead you to evaluate why that imagery is so strong and what idea you think those examples convey.

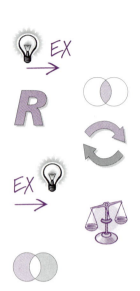

As you revise, ask yourself questions that can help you think through ideas and examples, come up with your own original insights about the material, and be as complete and clear as possible. Use the mind actions to guide you. Here are some examples of questions you might ask:

- Are these examples connected clearly to the idea?
- Do I know of any similar concepts or facts that can add to how I support this?
- What else can I recall that can help to support this idea?
- In evaluating any event or situation, have I clearly indicated the causes and effects?
- What new idea comes to mind when I think about these examples or facts?
- How do I evaluate any effect, fact, or situation? Is it good or bad, useful or not?
- What different arguments might a reader think of that I should address here?

Finally, critical thinking can help you evaluate the content and form of your paper. As you start your revision, ask yourself the following questions.

- Will my audience understand my thesis and how I've supported it?
- Does the introduction prepare the reader and capture attention?
- Is the body of the paper organized effectively?
- Is each idea fully developed, explained, and supported by examples?
- Are my ideas connected to one another through logical **transitions?**
- Do I have a clear, concise, simple writing style?
- Does the paper fulfill the requirements of the assignment?
- Does the conclusion provide a natural ending to the paper?

Evaluating Paragraph Structure

Think of your paragraphs as mini-versions of your paper, each with an introduction, a body, and a conclusion. Make sure that each paragraph has a *topic sentence* stating the paragraph's main idea (a topic sentence does for a paragraph what a thesis statement does for an entire paper). The rest of the paragraph should support the idea with examples and other evidence. Although some topic sentences are placed just after the first sentence of a paragraph, or even at the end, most occur at the beginning. An example is:

> <u>Chief Marzloff played an integral role in the development of our self-confidence.</u> He taught us that anything less than direct eye contact was disrespectful to both him and ourselves. He encouraged us to be confident about our own beliefs and to think about what was said to us before we decided whether to accept it. Furthermore, the Chief reinforced self-confidence through his own example. He walked with his

TERMS

Transitions
Words and phrases that build bridges between ideas, leading the reader from one idea to the next.

chin up and chest out, like the proud parent of a newborn baby. He always gave the appearance that he had something to do and that he was in complete control.

Examine how your paragraphs flow into one another by evaluating your use of transitions. Words such as *also*, *in addition*, and *next* indicate that another idea is coming. Similarly, *finally*, *as a result*, and *in conclusion* tell readers a summary is on its way.

Checking for Clarity and Conciseness

Use critical thinking to write more clearly by questioning the effects of the words and sentences you choose. Examine whether they are communicating what you want to say. Do they get to the point, or do they distract from your ideas? Eliminate extra words and rewrite wordy phrases in a way that more clearly communicates your ideas. For example, you can write "if" instead of "in the event that," or "now" instead of "at this point in time."

In addition to revising on your own, ask another student to read your work and offer suggestions. A peer reviewer can provide enlightening feedback, telling you what comes across well and what seems confusing.

Editing

Editing involves correcting technical mistakes in spelling, grammar, and punctuation, as well as checking style consistency for elements such as abbreviations and capitalizations. Editing comes last, after you are satisfied with your ideas, organization, and style of writing. Computer users often use the grammar-check and spell-check functions to find mistakes. Although a spell-checker helps, you still need to check your work on your own. A spell-checker won't pick up the mistake in the following sentence, but someone who is reading for sense will:

They are not hear on Tuesdays.

Proofreading—reading every word and sentence to check for accuracy—is the last editing stage and happens after your paper is in its final form. This is the time to correct technical mistakes and word usage problems. Rewrite run-on sentences and sentence fragments. Explain unclear references. If possible, have someone look over your work as you edit and proofread. Another pair of eyes might spot errors that you didn't notice on your own.

Your final paper reflects all the hard work you put in during the writing process. Figure 8.6 shows the final version of Michael's paper.

> "See revision as 'envisioning again.' If there are areas in your work where there is a blur or vagueness, you can simply see the picture again and add the details that will bring your work closer to your mind's picture."
> NATALIE GOLDBERG

FIGURE 8.6

One student's completed essay.

March 19, 1999
Michael B. Jackson

BOYS TO MEN

His stature was one of confidence, often misinterpreted by others as cockiness. His small frame was lean and agile, yet stiff and upright, as though every move were a calculated formula. For the longest eight weeks of my life, he was my father, my instructor, my leader, and my worst enemy. His name is Chief Marzloff, and he had the task of shaping the lives and careers of the youngest, newest members of the U. S. Coast Guard. As our Basic Training Company Commander, he took his job very seriously and demanded that we do the same. Within a limited time span, he conditioned our bodies, developed our self-confidence, and instilled within us a strong mental discipline.

Of the changes that recruits in military basic training undergo, the physical transformation is the most immediately evident. Upon my January arrival at the training facility, I was a little thin, but I had been working out and thought that I could physically do anything. Oh boy, was I wrong! The Chief wasted no time in introducing me to one of his trademark phrases: "Get down, maggots!" Upon this command, we were all to drop to the ground and produce endless counts of military-style push-ups. Later, we found out that exercise prepared us for hitting the deck in the event of enemy fire. Water survival tactics were also part of the training. Occasionally, my dreams of home were interrupted at about 3 a.m. when our company was selected for a surprise aquatic test. I recall one such test that required us to swim laps around the perimeter of a pool while in full uniform. I felt like a salmon swimming upstream, fueled only by natural instinct. Although we resented this sub-human treatment at the time, we learned to appreciate how the strict guidance of the Chief was turning our bodies into fine-tuned machines.

Beyond physical ability, Chief Marzloff also played an integral role in the development of our self-confidence. He would often declare in his raspy voice, "Look me in the eyes when you speak to me! Show me that you believe what you're saying!" He taught us that anything less was an expression of disrespect. Furthermore, he appeared to attack a personal habit of my own. It seemed that whenever he would speak to me individually, I would nervously nod my head in response. I was trying to demonstrate that I understood, but to him, I was blindly accepting anything that he said. He would roar, "That is a sign of weakness!" Needless to say, I am now conscious of all bodily motions when communicating with others. The Chief also reinforced self-confidence through his own example. He walked with his square chin up and chest out, like the proud parent of a newborn baby. He always gave the appearance that he had something to do, and that he was in complete control. Collectively, all of the methods that the Chief used were successful in developing our self-confidence.

(continued)

FIGURE 8.6

Continued.

> Perhaps the Chief's greatest contribution was the mental discipline that he instilled in his recruits. He taught us that physical ability and self-confidence were nothing without the mental discipline required to obtain any worthwhile goal. For us, this discipline began with adapting to the military lifestyle. Our day began promptly at 0500 hours, early enough to awaken the oversleeping roosters. By 0515 hours, we had to have showered, shaved, and perfectly donned our uniforms. At that point, we were marched to the galley for chow, where we learned to take only what is necessary, rather than indulging. Before each meal, the Chief would warn, "Get what you want, but you will eat all that you get!" After making good on his threat a few times, we all got the point. Throughout our stay, the Chief repeatedly stressed the significance of self-discipline. He would calmly utter, "Give a little now, get a lot later." I guess that meant different things to all of us. For me, it was a simple phrase that would later become my personal philosophy on life. The Chief went to great lengths to ensure that everyone under his direction possessed the mental discipline required to be successful in boot camp or in any of life's challenges.
>
> Chief Marzloff was a remarkable role model and a positive influence on many lives. I never saw him smile, but it was evident that he genuinely cared a great deal about his job and all the lives that he touched. This man single-handedly conditioned our bodies, developed our self-confidence, and instilled a strong mental discipline that remains in me to this day. I have not seen the Chief since March 28, 1992, graduation day. Over the years, however, I have incorporated many of his ideals into my life. Above all, he taught us the true meaning of the U.S. Coast Guard slogan, "Semper Peratus" (Always Ready).

Suà

Suà is a Shoshone Indian word, derived from the Uto-Aztecan language, meaning "think." Whereas much of the American Indian tradition in the Americas emphasizes oral communication, written languages have allowed American Indian perspectives and ideas to be understood by readers outside the American Indian tribal cultures. The writings of Leslie Marmon Silko, J. Scott Momaday, and Sherman Alexis have expressed important insights that all readers can consider.

Every time you listen, speak, and write, think of *suà*, and of how you can communicate your thinking to others. The power of expression allows you to share your insights so others can consider them and perhaps benefit from knowing them. Explore your perspectives, sharpen your ideas, and remember the incredible power of the clearly communicated thought.

Chapter 8   Building Thinking Skills

Name _____   Date _____

 LIFE THINKING: Applying What You Learn

8.1 *Pre-Writing*

Choose a topic you are interested in and know something about—for instance, college sports, handling stress, the emphasis of U.S. society on youth, or child rearing. Narrow your topic, then use the following pre-writing strategies to discover what you already know and what you would need to learn if you ever have to write an essay about the subject for one of your classes (if necessary, use a separate sheet of paper).

Brainstorm your ideas:

_____

_____

_____

_____

_____

_____

Freewrite:

_____

_____

_____

_____

_____

_____

_____

Ask journalists' questions:

_____

_____

_____

_____

_____

_____

_____

8.2 *Writing a Thesis Statement*

Write two thesis statements for each of the following topics. The first statement should try to inform the reader, and the second should try to persuade. In each case, writing a thesis statement will require that you narrow the topic:

• The rising cost of a college education

Thesis with an informative purpose:

_____

_____

Thesis with a persuasive purpose:

_____

_____

• Choosing a major that prepares you for a career

Thesis with an informative purpose:

_____

_____

Thesis with a persuasive purpose:

_____

_____

8.3 *Drafting an Introduction and Conclusion*

Imagine that one of the topics you explored in the last two exercises is the basis for a short paper in one of your courses. Use what you learned in the chapter to write an introduction and conclusion to that paper (if necessary, use a separate sheet of paper):

Introduction:

_____

_____

_____

_____

_____

_____

Conclusion:

_____

_____

_____

_____

_____

_____

_____

 TEAM THINKING: Working Together

8.4 *Hone Your Listening Skills*

Improve listening through teamwork. Divide into groups of five to nine to play a game called Celebrity. Each group will have two or three teams, each with two or three people (for example, a group of seven will have two teams of two and one of three). Using small slips of paper, each person writes down the names of five well-known people, one on each slip. The people may be living or dead and can have achieved celebrity status in any field—sports, entertainment, politics, arts and literature, science and medicine, and so on. Each scrap of paper should be folded to conceal the name written on it. Put all of the scraps together in one container. The only other equipment you need is a watch with a secondhand.

Within each team of two is a giver and a receiver (team members switch roles every time they have a new turn). Teams take turns guessing. While a member of a non-guessing team times the pair for one minute, the giver of the guessing team picks a piece of paper and describes the named celebrity to the receiver without saying any part of the person's name. The giver can use words, sounds, motion, singing, or anything that will help the receiver. (For Jackie Robinson: "Famous baseball player, first Black man on a pro team, first name is the same as President Kennedy's wife," etc.) If and when the receiver guesses correctly, the giver keeps that scrap and chooses another, continuing to go through as many names as possible before the minute is up. When time is called, the container of names (minus the names guessed) moves to the next team. (If a name remains unguessed when time is called, that paper has to go back into the container without the giver revealing the name.) When all the names have been guessed, teams count their papers to learn their scores. Everyone then comes together as a class and takes some time to exchange views about your experience.

How did the time limit, teamwork atmosphere, or noise affect your ability to listen? Which names were you more able to guess? Which gave you trouble, and why? Evaluate your skills. Your ability to "think on your feet" in this way is valuable in all kinds of workplace and personal situations.

WORK THINKING: Career Portfolio

8.5 *Writing Sample: A Job Interview Letter*

To secure a job interview, you likely will have to write a letter describing your background and value to the company. To include in your portfolio, write a one-page, three-paragraph cover letter to a prospective employer. (The letter will accompany your resume.) Be creative—you may use fictitious names, but select a career and industry that interest you. Use the format shown in the sample letter below.

                                        First name Last name
                                        1234 Your Street
                                        Your, ST 12345

January 1, 2000

Ms. Prospective Employer
Prospective Company
5432 Their Street
Them, ST 54321

Dear Ms. Employer:

On the advice of Mr. X, career center advisor at Y College, I am writing to inquire about the open position of production assistant at KKKK Radio. I read the description of the job and the company as it was listed on the career center board, and I wish to offer myself as a candidate for the position.

I am a senior at Y College and will graduate this spring with a degree in communications. Ever since my junior year, when I declared my major, I have wanted to pursue a career in radio. For the last year I have worked as a production intern at KCOL Radio, the college's station, and have occasionally filled in as a disk jockey on the evening news show. I enjoyed being on the air, but my primary interest is production and programming. My enclosed resume will tell you more about my background and experience.

I would be pleased to talk with you in person about the position. You can reach me any time at 555/555-5555 or by e-mail at xxxx@xx.com. Thank you for your consideration, and I look forward to meeting you.

Sincerely,

Sign Your Name

First name Last name

Enclosure   [*use this notation if you have included a resume
             or other item with your letter*]

Introductory paragraph: Start with an attention getter—a statement that convinces the employer to read on. For example, name a person the employer knows who told you to write, or refer to something positive about the company that you read in the paper. Identify the position for which you are applying, and tell the employer that you are interested in working for the company.

Middle paragraph: Sell your value. Try to convince the employer that hiring you will help the company in some way. Highlight your "sales effort"—your experience in school and the workplace. If possible, tie your qualifications to the company's needs. Refer indirectly to your enclosed resume.

Final paragraph: Close with a call to action. Ask the employer to call you, or tell the employer to expect your call to arrange an interview.

Exchange first drafts with a classmate. Read each other's letters and make notes in the margins. Discuss each letter, and make whatever corrections are necessary to produce a well-written, persuasive letter. Create a final draft for your portfolio.

QUESTIONING YOUR WORLD: Information Literacy Journal

To record your thoughts, use a separate journal or the lined pages at the end of the chapter.

8.6 *Information Communication*

Think of some kind of information that has come your way recently—a newspaper or magazine article, a TV news report or show, something on the radio—that you think did not communicate well. Describe it. What communication problem did you see—a mismatch of communication styles, lack of body language awareness, unclear or incomplete explanation, attacking the receiver, passive or aggressive styles? In your own communication, which problem do you think you experience most often?

Journal

Name _____   Date _____

Journal

Name _____   Date _____

Critical Thinking

9

Thinking Quantitatively

Math, Science, and Computers

When asked about math or science, many students reply by saying, "I hate math" or "I was never any good at math and science." In today's world, however, basic knowledge of *quantitative thinking,* or thinking in terms of measurable quantities—including math, science, and computer technology—is as necessary as the ability to read and write.

This chapter will look at the need for quantitative thinking in today's highly competitive and technologically changing world. You will explore two of the most common problem areas in mathematics—word problems and math anxiety—and you will examine several quantitative problem-solving strategies. You will discover that thinking critically about math problems is tied to your ability to think through problem-solving situations in the sciences as well as other aspects of your coursework, job, and life. Finally, the chapter will briefly discuss the increasing role of computers in your personal and academic life, as well as in the business world.

In this chapter, you will explore answers to the following questions:

- Why do you need to be able to think quantitatively?
- How can critical thinking help you master math basics?
- How can you overcome math anxiety?
- What do learning math and learning science have in common?
- What basics should you know about computers?

WHY DO YOU NEED TO BE ABLE TO THINK QUANTITATIVELY?

TERMS

Quantitative
Of, relating to,
or involving the
measurement of
amount or number.

Quantitative thinking goes far beyond a math course or two that you take in school and then put aside. Working with numbers is a crucial skill in the modern world. Consider the following examples of problems requiring quantitative thinking that you might encounter:

- You make $2,000 per month in your job. How do you determine how you allocate your money to pay your bills?
- You want to carpet your house, but many of the rooms and hallways are not regularly shaped. How do you determine how much carpet you need to buy?
- You are trying to schedule your classes for next semester. Each of your classes is offered at only certain times. How do you go about making the best possible schedule?

Some common misconceptions about quantitative thinking include the following:

- Quantitative thinking relies completely on logic, disregarding intuition.
- People are born with or without an ability to think quantitatively.
- Natural quantitative thinkers are able to solve problems quickly, in their heads.
- Few people are any good at quantitative thinking.
- There is always only one best way of solving a problem.[1]

Upon examination, *none* of these statements is universally true.

Quantitative Thinking Is Critical Thinking

The single most important skill that math develops and reinforces is the ability to think critically. Math is, at heart, a problem-solving discipline. The ability to think though problems critically is crucial in everyday life. You think critically about how to plan your day, where to eat, what to eat, how you will drive your car, and so on. Quantitative thinking primarily involves two types of reasoning you studied in Chapter 1: *inductive reasoning* and *deductive reasoning*. Although mathematics seems to develop skill primarily in deductive reasoning, it actually is created through a process of both deductive and inductive reasoning.

Inductive reasoning, or induction, means determining a generalization from a list of specific events. For example, if you see 30 men in a row wearing red shirts, you might conclude that all men wear red shirts. In mathematics, induction often is used in determining what a statement or theorem might be, but it requires a proof of some sort before an induction is considered valid. In the instance above, you would need proof before concluding that all men wear red shirts.

Deductive reasoning means applying a general statement to a specific instance. For example, if you were told that all fish were goldfish and you had a fish in a tank, you could conclude it must be a goldfish. Using deduction requires caution, because when applying any generalization, you need to know whether the generalization is in fact true (which, in the above instance, it is not).

Critical thinking is also involved in the ability to **estimate** when working with quantities, measurement, computation, and problem solving. Estimation requires both inductive and deductive thinking. You might estimate a specific quantitative result to a problem based on what you know of a general principle (deduction), or you might estimate a general quantitative principle based on examples, or results from other problems, that you have seen before (induction). Another important ability is to recognize when estimation is important or useful (involving evaluation).[2]

TERMS

Estimate
To calculate
the approximate
amount of; to
make a rough
or preliminary
calculation.

Math Skills in Daily Life

Math is becoming more and more important in this world of increasingly complicated technology. Although the level of competency needed will vary depending on your specific career goals and objectives, everyone will need some minimum amount of skill. These skills can be broken down broadly into arithmetic, algebra, geometry, probability and statistics, and calculus.

Arithmetic

Many everyday tasks require arithmetic. Arithmetic consists of numerical computations such as addition, subtraction, multiplication, and division. It also encompasses handling decimals, fractions, ratios, and proportions. Examples of where these skills are used are:

- paying the correct amount on a bill and seeing that you receive the correct change
- calculating tips in restaurants
- balancing your checkbook
- comparison shopping at grocery stores, clothing stores, and other stores

Algebra

Knowledge of **algebra** is needed almost as frequently as arithmetic. Many times you figure out problems without consciously realizing that you are using algebra. Some places where algebra shows up are:

- figuring out interest in credit cards, loans, and the like
- figuring your GPA
- solving problems in areas such as geology, biology, anthropology, chemistry, nursing, physics, and astronomy
- determining efficient travel plans

Algebra involves determining an unknown value using known values. For example, if you want to make 100 cookies and have enough flour for only three batches, you might use algebra to figure out how many cookies would have to be in each batch: $3(X) = 100$, where 3 is the number of batches, X is how many cookies, and 100 is the number of cookies. Through algebra, you can find that X = 100 divided by 3, or approximately 33. Therefore, you need a cookie recipe that makes about three dozen cookies.

Geometry

The most important uses of geometry occur in determining areas and volumes, although geometric ideas occur in many other forms, too. Examples of geometry in everyday life are:

- determining the amount of paint needed to paint a room or a house
- determining how closely you can pass a car
- buying and arranging furniture and appliances
- packing luggage

For instance, when you pack a suitcase for a trip, you are calculating in your head the size of the items you will put in the suitcase, adding them up, and determining whether they will fit inside the space determined by the size of the suitcase.

Probability and Statistics

Knowledge of basic **probability** and **statistics** is needed for understanding the relevance and importance (or lack thereof) of the overwhelming amount of statistical data you encounter. Without some knowledge in these areas, you cannot critically evaluate the usefulness of the information. For example, if a woman reads breast cancer statistics, her statistical and probability knowledge can help her determine her chances of contracting breast cancer, and how taking certain precautions can improve those chances.

For some careers, such as actuarial or genetic science, a strong background in probability and statistics is vital. Some areas of business, economics, and engineering also require these skills. Even journalism majors are required to take courses in statistics.

TERMS

Algebra
A generalization of arithmetic in which letters representing numbers are combined, often with other numbers, into equations according to the rules of arithmetic.

TERMS

Probability
The chance that a given event will occur (also, a branch of mathematics concerned with the study of probabilities).

Statistics
A branch of mathematics dealing with the collection, analysis, interpretation, and presentation of numerical data.

Calculus and Differential Equations

Calculus and differential equations are required for most engineering fields, business and economics, physics, and astronomy. Any problem in which a rate of change is needed involves calculus and differential equations. Many problems that involve work, water pressure, areas and volumes also use calculus.

Certainly not every student will need to master calculus. The basics, however, will be of use to everyone.

HOW CAN CRITICAL THINKING HELP YOU MASTER MATH BASICS?

Certain thinking strategies will improve your ability to think quantitatively. Mastering math basics involves taking a critical approach to the classroom, the textbook, studying and homework, and word problems.

The Classroom

When taking a math class, as with any other class, the two most important factors are being in class and being prepared. If you build your base of declarative and procedural knowledge before class by reading about the topic to be covered that day, you will have a context in which to ask questions about the material. Asking questions will allow you to think critically about the important aspects of the material and help you retain and apply it. When you take notes, focus on the central ideas and connect supporting examples to those ideas.

The Textbook

Instead of just reading through math material, interact with it critically as you go. Keep a pad of paper nearby and take note of the examples as you read. If steps are left out, as they often are, work them out on your pad. Draw sketches as you read to help visualize the material. Try not to move on until you understand the example and how it relates to the central ideas. Write down questions you want to ask your instructor or fellow students.

Also, note what formulas are given. Evaluate whether these formulas are important, and recall whether the instructor emphasized them. Be aware that in some classes you are responsible for all formulas, whereas in others the instructors will give them to you. Read the assigned material to prepare you for any homework assigned to you.

Studying and Homework

After class, review your notes as soon as possible. Fill in missing steps in the instructor's examples before you forget them. When reviewing notes, have the book alongside and look for similarities and differences between the lecture information and the book. Then do the homework.

Because math focuses on problem solving, doing a lot of problems is critical. Do not expect to complete every problem without effort. To fight frustration, stay flexible. If you are stuck on a problem, go on to another one. Sometimes you need to take a break to clear your head.

If you have done the assigned homework but still aren't sure about the method, do some other problems. Doing a lot of problems will give you a base of examples that will help to clarify ideas (math concepts and formulas) for you. Also, doing a group of problems similar to one another will help you apply the ideas to similar problems on other assignments and on tests.

Study groups can facilitate quantitative thinking. Other people's perspectives often can help you break through a mental block. Even if your math classes have smaller lab sessions, try to set up study groups outside of class. Do as much of your homework as you can, and then meet to discuss the homework and work through additional problems. Be open to the perspectives of other people, and don't hesitate to ask them to explain their thought processes in detail.

"The word impossible is not in my dictionary."
NAPOLEON I

Word Problems

Because the word problem is the most common way you will encounter mathematics throughout your life, the ability to solve word problems is a necessary skill. Word problems can be tough because they force you to translate between two languages—English and mathematics. Whereas math is a precise language, English and other living languages are not. This difference in precision makes the process of translating more difficult.

Steps in Solving Word Problems

Translating English or any other language to math takes a lot of practice. In his 1945 classic, *How To Solve It*, George Polya devised a four-step method for attacking word problems.[3] The basic steps reflect the general problem-solving process you explored in Chapter 2.

1. *Understand the individual elements of the problem.* Read the problem carefully. Understand what it is asking. Know what information you have. Know what information is missing. Draw a picture, if possible. Take the given information and translate it from words into mathematical language (numbers, symbols, formulas).

2. *Name and explore potential solution paths.* Think about similar problems that you understand and how those were solved. Consider whether this problem is an example of a mathematical idea that you know. In your head, try out different ways to solve the problem to see which may work best.

3. *Carry out your plan.* Choose a solution path and solve the problem. Check each of your steps.

4. *Review your result.* Check your answer, if possible. Make sure you've answered the question the problem is asking. Does your result seem logical in the context of the problem? Are there other ways to do the problem?

Different problem-solving strategies will be useful to you when solving word problems. You use your critical thinking skills both by evaluating which strategy will work best on a given problem and by applying the strategy itself. The following section lays out several problem-solving strategies by working through different types of word problem examples.[4]

Problem-Solving Strategies

Strategy 1: Look for a Pattern. G. H. Hardy (1877–1947), an eminent British mathematician, described mathematicians as makers of patterns and ideas. The search for patterns is one of the best strategies in problem solving. When you look for a pattern, you think inductively, observing a series of examples and determining the general idea that links the examples together.

EXAMPLE: Determine the next three entries in the following:

a. 1, 2, 4, ___, ___, ___
b. O, T, T, F, F, S, S, ___, ___, ___

SOLUTIONS TO EXAMPLE:

a. When trying to identify patterns, you might find a different pattern than someone else does. This doesn't mean yours is wrong. Example 1a actually has several possible answers. Here are two:

  1. Each succeeding term of the sequence is twice the previous term. In that case, the next three values would be 8, 16, 32.

  2. The second term is 1 more than the first term, and the third term is 2 more than the second. This might lead you to guess the fourth term is 3 more than the third term, the fifth term is 4 more than the fourth term, and so on. In that case, the next three terms are 7, 11, 16.

b. Example b is a famous pattern that often appears in puzzle magazines. The key to it is that "O" is the first letter of <u>o</u>ne, "T" is the first letter of <u>t</u>wo, and so on. Therefore, the next three terms would be E, N, and T for <u>e</u>ight, <u>n</u>ine, and <u>t</u>en.

Strategy 2: Make a Table. A table can be used to help organize and summarize information. This may enable you to see how examples form a pattern that leads you to an idea and a solution.

EXAMPLE: How many ways can you make change for a half dollar using only quarters, dimes, nickels, and pennies?

SOLUTION TO EXAMPLE: You might construct several tables and go through every possible case. You could start by seeing how many ways you can make change for a half dollar without using a quarter, which would produce Parts A and B of Table 9.1, below.

There are 36 ways to make change for a half dollar without using a quarter. Using one quarter results in Part C of Table 9.1.

TABLE 9.1   Ways to make change for a half dollar

PART A

Quarters	0	0	0	0	0	0	0	0	0	0	0	0	0	0	0	0	0	0
Dimes	0	0	0	0	0	0	0	0	0	0	0	1	1	1	1	1	1	1
Nickels	0	1	2	3	4	5	6	7	8	9	10	0	1	2	3	4	5	6
Pennies	50	45	40	35	30	25	20	15	10	5	0	40	35	30	25	20	15	10

PART B

Quarters	0	0	0	0	0	0	0	0	0	0	0	0	0	0	0	0	0	0
Dimes	1	1	2	2	2	2	2	2	2	3	3	3	3	3	4	4	4	5
Nickels	7	8	0	1	2	3	4	5	6	0	1	2	3	4	0	1	2	0
Pennies	5	0	30	25	20	15	10	5	0	20	15	10	5	0	10	5	0	0

PART C

Quarters	1	1	1	1	1	1	1	1	1	1	1	1
Dimes	0	0	0	0	0	0	1	1	1	1	2	2
Nickels	0	1	2	3	4	5	0	1	2	3	0	1
Pennies	25	20	15	10	5	0	15	10	5	0	5	0

Using one quarter, you get twelve different ways to make change for a half dollar. Last, using two quarters, there's only one way to make change for a half dollar. Therefore, the solution to the problem is that there are 36 + 12 + 1 = 49 ways to make change for a half dollar using only quarters, dimes, nickels, and pennies.

Strategy 3: Identify a Sub-goal.   Breaking the original problem into smaller and possibly easier problems can lead to a solution to the original problem. This often is the case in writing a computer program.

EXAMPLE: Arrange the nine numbers 1, 2, 3, . . . , 9 into a square subdivided into nine sections in such a way that the sum of every row, column, and main diagonals is the same. This is what is called a magic square.

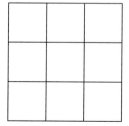

SOLUTION TO EXAMPLE: As each number will go into one of the squares, the sum of all the numbers will end up being three times the sum of any given row, column, or main diagonal. The sum of $1 + 2 + 3 + 4 + 5 + 6 + 7 + 8 + 9 = 45$. Therefore, each row, column, and main diagonal has to sum to $45 \div 3 = 15$. Now you need to see how many ways you can add three of the numbers from 1 to 9 and get 15. In doing this, you should get:

$9 + 1 + 5 = 15$	$8 + 3 + 4 = 15$
$9 + 2 + 4 = 15$	$7 + 2 + 6 = 15$
$8 + 1 + 6 = 15$	$7 + 3 + 5 = 15$
$8 + 2 + 5 = 15$	$6 + 4 + 5 = 15$

Now, looking at your magic square, notice that the center position will be part of four sums (a row, a column, and the two main diagonals). Looking back at your sums, you see that 5 appears in four different sums; therefore, 5 is in the center square.

	5	

Now in each corner, the number there appears in three sums (row, column, and a diagonal). Looking through your sums, you find that 2, 4, 6, and 8 each appear in three sums. Now you have to place them in the corners in such a way that your diagonals add up to 15.

2		6
	5	
4		8

Then, to finish, all you have to do is fill in the remaining squares to get the needed sum of 15 for each row, column, and main diagonal. The completed square is as follows:

2	7	6
9	5	1
4	3	8

Strategy 4: Examine a Similar Problem. Sometimes a problem you are working on has similarities to problems you've already read about or solved. In that case, it is often possible to use a similar approach to solve the new problem.

EXAMPLE: Find a magic square using the numbers 3, 5, 7, 9, 11, 13, 15, 17, and 19.

SOLUTION TO EXAMPLE: This problem is similar to the example for strategy 3. Approaching it in the same fashion, you find that the needed row, column, and main diagonal sum is 33. Writing down all the possible sums of three numbers to get 33, you find that 11 is the number that appears 4 times, so it is in the center.

	11	

The numbers that appear three times in the sums and will go in the corners are 5, 9, 13, and 17. This now gives you:

13		17
	11	
5		9

Finally, completing the magic square gives you:

13	3	17
15	11	7
5	19	9

Strategy 5: Work Backward. You might find it easier with some problems to start with the perceived final result and work backward.

EXAMPLE: In the game of "Life," Carol had to pay $1,500 when she was married. Then she lost half the money she had left. Next she paid half the money she had for a house. Then the game was stopped, and she had $3,000 left. How much money did she start with?

SOLUTION TO EXAMPLE: Carol ended up with $3,000. Just before that, she paid half her money to buy a house. Since her $3,000 was half of what she had before her purchase, she had $2 \times \$3,000 = \$6,000$ before buying the house. Prior to buying the house, Carol lost half her money. This means that the $6,000 is the half she didn't lose. So, before losing half her money, Carol had $2 \times \$6,000 = \$12,000$. Prior to losing half her money, Carol had to pay $1,500 to get married. This means she had $\$12,000 + \$1,500 = \$13,500$ before getting married. Since this was the start of the game, Carol began with $13,500.

Strategy 6: Draw a Diagram. Drawing a picture often aids in solving problems, especially for visual learners. Pictures are especially useful for geometrical problems, but they can be helpful for other types as well.

EXAMPLE: There were 20 people at a round table for dinner. Each person shook hands with the person to his or her immediate right and left. At the end of the dinner, each person got up and shook hands with everybody except the person who sat to his or her immediate right and the one to the left. How many handshakes took place after dinner?

SOLUTION TO EXAMPLE: To solve this with a diagram, it might be a good idea to examine several simpler cases to see if you can determine a pattern of any kind that might help. Starting with two or three people, you can see there are no handshakes after dinner because everyone is adjacent to everyone else.

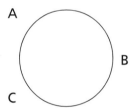

Now, in the case of four people, we get the following diagram, connecting those people who shake hands after dinner:

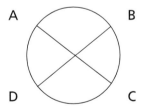

In this situation, you see there are two handshakes after dinner, AC and BD. In the case of five people, you get this picture:

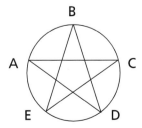

In this case, you have five after-dinner handshakes: AC, AD, BD, BE, and CE. Looking at one further case of six people seated around a circle gives the following diagram:

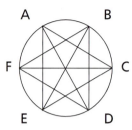

In this diagram, there are now a total of nine after dinner handshakes: AC, AD, AE, BD, BE, BF, CE, CF, and DF. In noticing from the diagrams what is happening, you realize that if there are N people, each person would shake N – 3 people's hands after dinner. (They don't shake their own hands or the hands of the two people adjacent to them). Since there are N people, that would lead to N(N – 3) after dinner handshakes. However, this would double-count every handshake because AD also would be counted as DA. Therefore, this is twice as many actual handshakes. So the correct number of handshakes is [N(N – 3)] /2. So, finally, if there are 20 people, there would be 20(17) /2 = 170 after-dinner handshakes.

Strategy 7: Translate Words Into an Equation. This is often used in algebra.

EXAMPLE: A farmer has to fence a rectangular piece of land. He wants the length of the field to be 80 feet longer than the width. If he has 1,080 feet of fencing available, what should the length and width of the field be?

SOLUTION TO EXAMPLE: The best way to start this problem is to draw a picture of the situation and label the sides.

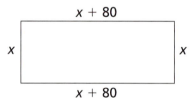

Let x represent the width of the field and x + 80 represent the length of the field. The farmer has 1,080 feet of fencing, and he will need $2x + 2(x + 80)$ feet of fencing to fence his field. This gives you the equation:

$$2x + 2(x + 80) = 1080$$

Multiplying out:	$2x + 2x + 160 = 1080$
Simplifying and subtracting 160:	$4x = 920$
Dividing by 4:	$x = 230$
Therefore,	$x + 80 = 310$
As a check, you find that	$2(230) + 2(310) = 1080.$

Strategy 8: Estimate and Check. Once discouraged in favor of algebraic or other methods, it is now recognized that estimation, or "guess and check," is a way by which many people solve everyday problems. The strategy involves first arriving at an initial estimate through critical thinking, which could involve recalling similar problems or speculating whether the problem is an example of a given mathematical idea. After estimating, you check to see if your guess is correct. If it is not, you use that information to make another guess.

EXAMPLE: Looking out in the backyard one day, Sue saw an assortment of cats and birds. Counting heads, she got a total of 22. Counting the feet, she got a total of 68. How many cats and birds were in the yard?

SOLUTION TO EXAMPLE: Since Sue saw a total of 22 cats and birds (assuming none had more than one head), a good first guess might be that there are 11 cats and 11 birds. Checking the number of legs gives:

$$11(4) + 11(2) = 44 + 22 = 66 \text{ legs.}$$

Since Sue counted 68 legs, this isn't quite correct, but it is close. Since you need more legs, and cats have more legs than birds, there has to be more cats and fewer birds. Suppose, then, there are 12 cats and 10 birds. This would give you

$$12(4) + 10(2) = 48 + 20 = 68 \text{ legs,}$$

which is exactly what you wanted. Therefore, Sue sees 12 cats and 10 birds in the backyard.

These sample problems are designed to boost your ability to think critically through some basic math strategies. If they have made you feel anxious, you will benefit from some information about math anxiety.

HOW CAN YOU OVERCOME MATH ANXIETY?

Math anxiety is a term used to describe any of several high-stress, uncomfortable feelings that arise in relation to quantitative thinking. One of the most common—often caused by failing an exam or failing to learn a topic—is a student's feeling that he or she can't do any math at all. As a result of this feeling, students sometimes just give up, and they often won't ask for help.

Use the questionnaire in Figure 9.1 to get a basic idea of your math anxiety level.

Identifying Math Anxiety

Math anxiety occurs most commonly just before or during an exam. As a student gets ready to take a test or reads a given problem on a test, he or she experiences rising anxiety or even what can be described as "blanking out." This happens on exams for other subjects, too, but seems to occur most often in tests involving quantitative thinking.

FIGURE 9.1

Explore your math anxiety.

Answer the following statements by marking a number from 1 (Disagree) to 5 (Agree).

_____ 1. I don't like math classes, and haven't since high school.

_____ 2. I do okay at the beginning of a math class, but I always feel it will get to the point where it is impossible to understand.

_____ 3. I can't seem to concentrate in math classes. I try, but I get nervous and distracted and think about other things.

_____ 4. I don't like asking questions in math class. I'm afraid that the teachers and/or other students will think I'm stupid.

_____ 5. I stress out when I'm called on in math class. I seem to forget even the easiest answers.

_____ 6. Math exams scare me far more than any of my other exams.

_____ 7. I can't wait to finish my math requirement so that I'll never have to do any math again.

SCORING KEY

28–35: You suffer from full-blown math anxiety.

21–27: You are coping, but you're not happy about mathematics.

14–20: You're doing okay.

7–13: So what's the big deal about math? You have very little problem with anxiety.

Source: Ellen Freedman (March 1997), *Test Your Math Anxiety* [online]. Available: http://fc.whyy.org/CCC/alg1/anxtest.htm (March 1998).

The best way to overcome test-time anxiety is to practice quantitative thinking and thereby increase your confidence. Keeping up with your homework, attending class, preparing well for tests, and doing extra problems will help you feel confident because they increase your familiarity with the material. Figure 9.2 shows additional ways to reduce math anxiety.

FIGURE 9.2

Ten ways to reduce math anxiety.

1. Overcome your negative self-image about math.
2. Ask questions from your teachers, your friends, and seek outside assistance.
3. Math is a foreign language—practice it often.
4. Don't study mathematics by trying to memorize information and formulas.
5. READ your math textbook.
6. Study math according to your personal learning style.
7. Get help the same day you don't understand something.
8. Be relaxed and comfortable while studying math.
9. "TALK" mathematics. Discuss it with people in your class. Form a study group.
10. Develop a sense of responsibility for your own successes and failures.

Source: Ellen Freedman (March 1997), *Ten Ways to Reduce Math Anxiety* [online]. Available: http://fc.whyy.org/CCC/alg1/reduce.htm (March 1998).

Even though math anxiety is a real problem, students must take some responsibility for their responses to quantitative thinking. You can't change the math experiences you have had in the past, but you can make choices about how to respond to quantitative material from here on out. Some of your responsibilities as a quantitative thinker include: [5]

- To attend all classes and do homework
- To seek extra help when necessary, from an instructor, tutor, or fellow student
- To speak up in class when you have questions
- To be realistic about your abilities and to work to improve them
- To approach math with an open mind, avoiding the assumption that it will be a nightmare

Finally, along with being a responsible student, you have rights regarding your mathematical learning. These include:[6]

- The right to learn at your own pace
- The right to ask questions
- The right not to understand
- The right to be treated as a competent person
- The right to believe you are capable of thinking quantitatively

Beyond working to control your math anxiety, several techniques will help you do your very best when you are tested on your math skills.

> "People seldom see the halting and painful steps by which the most insignificant success is achieved."
> ANNIE SULLIVAN

Math Anxiety and Exams

In addition to the general strategies for test taking that you have explored, several techniques that can help you achieve better results on math exams. These are briefly explored.

Read through the exam. When you first get an exam, read through every problem quickly. Make notes on how you might attempt to solve the problem, if something occurs to you immediately. If possible, categorize the problems according to what type of problem they are.

Do "easy" problems first. If you read a problem and know immediately how to do it, do that problem right away. Go through the exam doing all of the problems that come most easily to you. As you do the easier problems, you will gain confidence and tend to relax. In general, following the exam order exactly may not benefit you. Although some tests start with easier problems and increase in difficulty, others list problems in random order.

Use objective exam strategies. If the questions are multiple choice or matching, work out the problem without looking at the answers. Check your work, then look at the choices and see if your answer is one of them. If not, you might be able to eliminate some of the choices immediately. Examine your work and the remaining choices. If possible, put the remaining answers into the problem and see if they work.

Check answers. Look back over your work, especially if you have some problems you're not sure of. This doesn't mean you should automatically begin changing answers, however. Be aware of your own tendencies. For example, if you often lose points for careless mistakes, checking your work can help you catch these.

All the strategies you are learning aren't useful only in your math classes. Many science classes have a mathematical element that require you to use your math knowledge.

WHAT DO LEARNING MATH AND LEARNING SCIENCE HAVE IN COMMON?

Many of the issues you face in mathematics occur also in science. Therefore, many of the strategies discussed about mathematics will be effective in the sciences as well. Sciences such as chemistry, physics, and astronomy are quite often problem-solving courses. Some classes in geology, anthropology, and biology also fall into this category. The math strategies you have explored will be applicable to these sciences.

For example, in beginning chemistry, you usually will have to balance chemical equations. This could involve writing an equation, drawing a diagram, perhaps working backward, or even guess-and-check. In physics, the study of forces involves applying problem-solving strategies developed from vector calculus. In fact, the most common strategy in working force problems involves drawing a diagram called a force diagram. The key thing to remember is that, though these strategies are listed as mathematical strategies, the actual process of applying them is far more wide-ranging, helping you to develop into a critical thinker and problem solver.

Beyond the necessity of gaining problem-solving skills, the change from high school to college science is similar to the change in mathematics courses.

1. *The pace of the courses will be faster.* Quite often, what was done in a year in high school will be done in a semester or less in college.

2. *The assignments will be considered crucial.* Your instructor, however, might not collect them often, if at all. You will be responsible for staying caught up.

3. *The classes might be more focused on theories and ideas.* Your class periods might devote more time to proving and deriving **theorems.** There may be less time spent on examples and problems.

4. *The class size might be considerably larger.* You might be in classes taught in large auditoriums with several hundred people enrolled. Your classes also might be organized differently. You could have a lecture section, a recitation section or discussion section (often led by a teaching assistant), and possibly a lab section.

TERMS

Theorem
A formula or statement in mathematics, accepted or proposed as a demonstrable truth.

5. *Instructors' expectations might be different.* You might be expected to understand and be able to apply the concepts and principles. Skill in manipulating symbols or memorizing facts might be deemphasized.

6. *You might be expected to be technologically proficient.* This could mean using graphing calculators or software such as Mathematica or Maple (mathematical packages), Minitab or SAS (statistical packages), or course-specific software.

Of course, your science courses will go beyond basic mathematical operations. Many of these courses, however, will hinge on mathematical principles. Thinking mathematically will help you understand specific operations and apply them to the more general scientific knowledge you learn.

WHAT BASICS SHOULD YOU KNOW ABOUT COMPUTERS?

As the world continues to become more technologically complicated, the role of computers will become increasingly large. In almost every job, knowledge of basic computer use is a necessity. Computer basics fall into four general categories: word processing, databases and spreadsheets, the Internet, and e-mail.

Word Processing

The ability to use a computer to write letters, papers, briefs, and so on is now a requirement at most institutes of higher learning. Many businesses also require the use of these skills. There are many word-processing software programs, each with its own quirks. Two of the most commonly used are Microsoft Word and Word Perfect. Features such as a spell-check and a grammar checker are extremely useful.

Databases and Spreadsheets

The ability to organize and store large volumes of information and data has always been important in most businesses. The easiest way to do this is through the use of some type of computer software for managing databases and spreadsheets. Again, many software programs are designed specifically to handle, organize, and analyze large volumes of information. Some of the more common programs are Lotus, Symphony, and Microsoft Excel. Knowledge of one or more of these is becoming increasingly beneficial for most careers in business and science, as well as for maintaining personal finance records on a home computer.

The Internet

The Internet, a large, worldwide network of connected businesses, universities, governments, and people, is expanding continually. The ability to use the Internet allows you to access the world and communicate with others almost

> "The proper and immediate object of science is the acquirement, or communication, of truth."
>
> SAMUEL TAYLOR COLERIDGE

instantaneously. You can now do extensive research on any topic, as well as buy, sell, and market products on the Internet. If you have no Internet experience, you will not be well-prepared for the workforce. Internet providers and browsers, such as Netscape, Microsoft Explorer, America On-Line, and Prodigy, offer various Internet services and options.

Once on the Internet, some type of search engine is used to locate information or web "sites" or "pages" (locations on the web established by businesses, organizations, or individuals). Look in the Internet Research Appendix for a listing of some of the most common search engines.

To put a search engine to work, go to your provider's web access field and type in the address of the search engine you want to use. Use the options the search engine provides to search for your topic. Try to narrow it as much as possible to avoid being overwhelmed with too many possibilities or "hits." If you know the web address of a web site, you can type it in directly using a search engine. If you need help learning about the Internet, don't hesitate to ask a librarian, fellow student, or tutor to show you the ropes.

E-mail

The ability to communicate electronically is rapidly becoming a challenge to the Post Office. The major advantage is the speed by which electronic mail (e-mail) can be sent, received and responded to. If your college has an e-mail system in place, you might be required to communicate with your instructor on e-mail, submit homework via e-mail, and even take exams via e-mail. To learn about e-mail, many schools offer some type of orientation. Every student who has access to e-mail should spend time becoming proficient in electronic communication.

The use of computers in composing letters, desktop publishing, maintaining databases, keeping spreadsheets, working on the Internet, communicating by e-mail, and numerous other tasks makes computer literacy a requirement in the job market. The more capable you are of learning and using various computer systems, the more employable you will be.

al-Khowârizmî

Mohammed ibn Musa al-Khowârizmî was an Arabic astronomer who lived around 825 A.D. An 1857 Latin translation of a book no longer existing in the original begins, "Spoken has Algoritmi . . ." Hence, his name had become Algoritmi, from which was derived the present word *algorithm*. An algorithm is a series of steps used to solve a problem in mathematics or the sciences. Many computer software programs are simply strings of algorithms used to do certain functions.

For those of you who don't know Arabic, this word may seem completely out of your realm of knowledge. Just as if you were to study Arabic or any other language, however, success in math boils down to steady work and concentration. When you put your mind to it, you can become as fluent in math, science, and technology as you are in your native language.

Chapter 9   Building Thinking Skills

Name _____   Date _____

LIFE THINKING: Applying What You Learn

9.1 *You and Math*

Math anxiety seems to afflict many people in today's world. As everyday life, society, and business become more technological, anxiety can become a serious problem. The severity of math anxiety is causing critical shortages of people who are qualified to handle this emerging technology. How do you handle the challenges of mathematics? Respond to the following statements as accurately as possible in light of your own experiences and the information provided in the chapter.

1. When I make an error on a math problem, I

   _____

   _____

2. When I get embarrassed about doing math, I

   _____

   _____

3. When I'm unable to solve a particular problem, I

   _____

   _____

4. If I were able to do mathematics, I would

   _____

   _____

5. When I'm able to solve a problem that was difficult, I feel

   _____

   _____

6. One thing I enjoy about doing math is

   _____

   _____

7. Working on mathematics makes me feel

_____

_____

9.2 *Math/Science Autobiography*

For the following exercise, choose a math and science class you are taking (if you have none, choose one you took as recently as possible). With regard to that class, write a brief autobiography of your experiences in the subject. Examine both where you've come from and where you would like to go. Use the information from the chapter to help you.

1. My major reason for taking this class is

_____

_____

2. Before this class, the last math/science course I took was

_____

_____

3. An early experience I recall from a math/science class was

_____

_____

_____

4. I remember one particular math/science teacher because

_____

_____

_____

5. I think _____ was the most difficult topic to learn, because

_____

_____

6. I think _____ was the easiest topic to learn, because

_____

_____

7. I believe I learned my current attitudes about math/science when

_____

_____

8. To improve my attitudes about math/science, I expect to do the following for myself:

_____

_____

_____

9. To improve my performance in math/science, I expect to do the following:

_____

_____

_____

 TEAM THINKING: Working Together

9.3 *Improve Math Through Teamwork*

Choose one or two people from one of your math/science classes—fellow students with whom you feel comfortable working. Use problems from your assigned text.

1. Choose one problem. Each of you work on the same problem separately. After finishing the problem, come together to exchange your methods of solution. Discuss how each of you approached the problem. What steps did you each take in solving the problem? What strategies did you use? How did you check to see if your procedures were correct?

2. Now pick a different problem on which to work together. After solving this problem, discuss how you went through the problem-solving process. Did you learn more or less by working together, as compared to working separately? Were you able to solve the problem faster by working together than you did with the problem you worked alone? Did you gain a better understanding of the problem by working together?

3. Generalize your experiences to discuss attitudes about math/science. What do each of you do to overcome challenges? What positive steps do you each take in problem solving?

WORK THINKING: Career Portfolio

9.4 *Math, Science, and Your Career*

Consider your possible choice of a major or career. What mathematics/science will you need to achieve your goals? Did your feelings and experiences in math and/or science affect your choice of major or career? If so, in what ways?

Interview several people, including an instructor, in your choice of major/career. Ask them how much math and science are needed for this major/career. Did they choose it based on the level of math or science necessary? Now that they are in this field, is the amount of math/science and problem-solving skills more or less than expected? What types of problem-solving skills are needed? In addition, investigate this major/career by looking at the course catalog to see what math and science are needed, and, if you have access, search out information about your major/career choice on the Internet.

After completing your investigation, write an essay reflecting on the roles that math, science, and problem solving have in your choice of a major/career.

QUESTIONING YOUR WORLD:
Information Literacy Journal

To record your thoughts, use a separate journal or the lined pages at the end of the chapter.

9.5 *Numbers in the Media*

The information you encounter often includes scientific evidence or statistics—statistics on auto accidents, evidence that shows a certain food to be unhealthy, the percentages of workers with college degrees, and so on. What effect do statistics and science have on your reaction to information? Are you more or less likely to accept information that uses numbers as evidence? Do you believe that numbers can be used selectively to convey a certain perspective? If you can think of one, describe a statistic or a scientific study that you encountered and did not trust, and tell why.

Journal

Name _____   Date _____

Journal

Name _____   Date _____

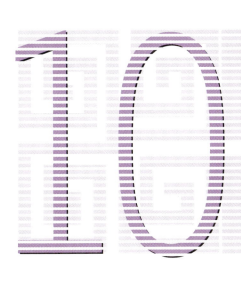

Critical Thinking

10

Thinking for Life

Working Toward Your Personal Best

Your thinking skills will take you far beyond passing your college courses and earning a degree or certificate. Thinking is a skill for life that will allow you to navigate the ups and downs of all facets of your life. If you work to keep an open and active mind, striving to consider information critically and to increase your learning, you will be able to make the most of who you are and what you can do.

This final chapter explores how being a thinker can help you in areas of your life that extend beyond the classroom. You will explore how thinking can help you accept and benefit from diversity, work successfully in teams, and make a strategic plan toward a career. You will learn strategies for adapting to the con-

251

stant change that surrounds you. Finally, the chapter offers ideas about how you can become—and continue to be—a lifelong learner.

In this chapter, you will explore answers to the following questions:

- How can you understand and accept others?
- Why is teamwork important?
- What strategic thinking can help you plan your career?
- How can you live with and adapt to change?
- How can you continue to grow and learn throughout your life?
- How can you live your mission?

HOW CAN YOU UNDERSTAND AND ACCEPT OTHERS?

Human interaction is an essential element of life. In a diverse world, many people are different from that with which you are familiar and perceive as "normal." With an open mind and a willingness to learn, a critical thinker can make the most of differences. Explore diversity in your world, how to overcome barriers to understanding, and the positive effects of accepting diversity.

Diversity in Your World

Diversity is the mosaic of differences that envelops your communities, your nation, and the world. In addition to races and ethnic groups, diversity occurs in traditions, religions, family backgrounds, genders, abilities, economic levels, ages, habits, lifestyles, choices, careers, modes of dress, foods, health conditions, perspectives, opinions, experiences, and more. You encounter diversity every day through images and information—in newspapers and magazines, on television, and on the radio—that tell you about how various people think and live.

Diversity has become more important, partly because the world is becoming more interdependent. As people become more aware of other ways of living, they might be more sensitive to differences. You might encounter examples of diversity like these:

- Communities with people at different stages of life
- Coworkers who represent a variety of ethnic origins
- Classmates who speak a number of different languages
- Social situations featuring people from various cultures, religions, and sexual orientations
- Individuals who marry a person or adopt a child from a different racial or religious background
- Diverse restaurants, services, and businesses in the community
- Neighborhoods with immigrants from a variety of class backgrounds
- Different lifestyles, as reflected in the media and popular culture
- People with any of a variety of disabilities—some more obvious than others

Each person has a choice about how to relate to others—or even whether to relate to them. No one can force you to interact with any other person, or to adopt a certain attitude as being "right." Nevertheless, you do have a responsibility to yourself (to give yourself the time and opportunity to think critically about your ideas) and to others (to treat them with tolerance and respect, acknowledging that they have a right to their opinions).

It's common to let assumptions and perspectives about people block your ability to communicate. Following are some barriers that can hinder your ability to accept and understand others and suggestions for how to overcome them.

Barriers to Understanding

You deserve to feel positive about who you are, where you come from, and what you believe. Problems arise, however, when people use the power of identity to put others down or cut themselves off from others. Table 10.1 shows how an open-minded (critical thinking) approach differs from an approach characterized by quick assumptions.

Stereotypes, prejudice and discrimination all can form barriers to communication.

Stereotypes

A **stereotype** is an assumption about a person or group of people based on one or more characteristics. Why might people develop stereotypes? One reason involves the human desire for order. People often try to make sense of a complex world using the categories that stereotypes provide. Stereotyping is also easy. Making an assumption about a person or group, based on external characteristics, takes less time and energy than exploring individual

TERMS

Stereotype
A standardized mental picture that represents an oversimplified opinion or uncritical judgment.

TABLE 10.1 Approaches to diversity.

YOUR ROLE	SITUATION	CLOSED-MINDED APPROACH	OPEN-MINDED APPROACH
Fellow student	For an assignment, you are paired with a student old enough to be your mother.	You assume that the student will be closed off to the modern world. You think she might preach to you about how to do the assignment.	You get to know the student as an individual. You stay open to what you can learn from her experiences and knowledge.
Friend	You are invited to dinner at a friend's house. When he introduces you to his partner, you realize that he is gay.	You are turned off by the idea of two men in a relationship. You make an excuse to leave early. You avoid your friend after that evening.	You have dinner with the two men and make an effort to get to know more about what their lives are like and who they are individually and as a couple.
Employee	Your new boss is Japanese American, hired from a competing company.	You assume that your new boss is hard-working, has demanding expectations, and doesn't take time to socialize.	You rein in your assumptions, knowing that they are based on stereotypes, and approach your new boss with an open mind.

uniqueness. Furthermore, the media promote stereotypes. The more people see images such as the ditsy blonde or the funny, overweight person, the easier it is to believe that stereotypes like these are universal.

The ease of stereotypes comes at a high price. First and foremost, stereotypes can perpetuate harmful generalizations and falsehoods about others, which promote discrimination. For example, if an employer believes that Iranian people cannot speak English well, he or she might not even bother to interview them. Second, stereotypes communicate disrespect to others, which could encourage others to stereotype in return.

Addressing stereotypes. Recall what you know about assumptions from Chapter 3. Apply these questions to stereotypes:

1. In what cases is this stereotype valid, if ever? What could prove or disprove it?

2. Has stereotyping others benefited me or others? Has it hurt? If so, how?

3. What is the source of this stereotype? Is the source reliable? If someone taught it to me, why might they have done so?

4. What harm could be done by accepting this stereotype as valid?

Using these steps, think about the stereotypes you assume are true. When you hear someone use a stereotype and you know information that disproves it, volunteer that information. Encourage others to think through stereotypes and to reject them if they don't hold up under examination.

Prejudice

TERMS

Prejudice
A preconceived judgment or opinion, formed without just grounds or sufficient knowledge.

Prejudice is revealed when people make a judgment before they have sufficient knowledge on which to base it. People often form prejudiced opinions on the basis of a characteristic—gender, race, sexual orientation, religion, and so on. You probably are familiar with labels for prejudices, such as *racism* (prejudice based on race) or *ageism* (prejudice based on age). Any group can be subjected to prejudice, although certain groups have been victimized more than others. Prejudice can lead people to show disrespect toward, harass, and put down others. In some cases, prejudice leads to unrealistic expectations that aren't necessarily negative, such as if someone were to believe that all Jewish people excel in business.

Common causes of prejudice include the following.

Individual identity. You grow up in a given culture and family and learn their attitudes. When you encounter different ideas, you might react by categorizing them. You also might react with **ethnocentrism.**

TERMS

Ethnocentrism
The condition of thinking that one's ethnic group is superior to others.

Jealousy and fear of personal failure. When people are feeling insecure about their own abilities, they might find it easier to devalue the abilities of others rather than to try harder themselves.

Extending dislike. When people get hurt, they may dislike anyone who seems similar to the person who hurt them. Judging others because of a bad experience is human, especially when a specific characteristic raises strong emotions.

The many faces of prejudice often appear on college campuses. A student might not want to work with students of another race. Campus clubs sometimes limit their membership to a certain group. Religious groups at times devalue the beliefs of other religions. Groups that gather because of a common characteristic might be harassed by others. Students may find that instructors judge their abilities and attitudes according to their gender. Each incident blocks mutual understanding.

Addressing prejudice. Critical thinking is your key to changing prejudicial attitudes. Suppose you find yourself thinking that you don't want to get to know a certain student in your class. Ask yourself: Where did I get this attitude? Am I accepting someone else's judgment? Am I basing my judgments on how this person looks or speaks or behaves? How does having this attitude affect me or others? Have the courage to consider the person with an open, accepting mind.

Another tactic, often an extremely difficult one, is to confront people you know when they display a prejudiced attitude. It can be hard to stand up to someone and risk a relationship or, if the person is your employer, even a job. On the other hand, your silence may imply that you agree. You have choices: You can drop a humorous hint, make a small comment, address the situation directly, or not address it at all. Whatever you do, express your opinion respectfully. Whether the person makes a change or not, you have taken an important stand.

Discrimination

Discrimination is apparent when people deny others opportunities because of their perceived differences. Prejudice often accompanies discrimination. Discrimination can mean being denied jobs or advancement; equal educational opportunities; equal housing opportunities; or access to services, events, people, rights, privileges, or commodities.

Discrimination occurs in all kinds of situations, revolving around gender, language, race, culture, and other factors. For example, a 32-year-old married woman does not get a job because the interviewer assumes that she will become pregnant, or an African-American is passed up by a cab in favor of a person of another race. Even so-called majority populations occasionally experience the power of discrimination. For example, a qualified White man is passed up for a promotion in favor of a female or a minority employee.

Addressing discrimination. U.S. federal law states that it is unlawful for you to be denied an education, work or the chance to apply for work, housing, or basic rights based on your race, creed, color, age, gender, national or ethnic origin, religion, marital status, potential or actual pregnancy, or potential or actual illness or disability (unless the illness or disability prevents you from performing required tasks and unless accommodations for the disability are not possible). Unfortunately, the law is frequently broken, and incidents go unnoticed. Sometimes people don't report violations, fearing trouble from those they accuse. Other times people aren't aware of their discriminatory attitudes.

"I have a dream that one day on the red hills of Georgia the sons of former slaves and the sons of former slave owners will be able to sit down together at the table of brotherhood."

MARTIN LUTHER KING, JR.]

First and foremost, be responsible for your own behavior. Do not knowingly participate in or encourage discrimination. Second, if you witness a discriminatory act or believe you have been discriminated against, decide whether you want to approach an authority. Begin by talking to the person who can most directly affect the situation—an instructor or your supervisor. Don't assume that people know that they have hurt or offended someone. Communicate the situation clearly, and ask for help in resolving the problem.

The Positive Effects of Diversity

More than just "a nice thing to do," accepting diversity has very real benefits. Acceptance and respect form the basis for any successful interaction. As situations bring diverse people together, communication will become more and more dependent on acceptance and mutual understanding. Understanding and communication in your relationships can promote support, achievement, and progress. Conversely, failure to understand and communicate can have negative effects.

Consider, for example, a male Hispanic employee who has a female African-American supervisor. On the one hand, if the employee believes negative stereotypes about women or African-Americans and resists taking directions from the supervisor, he may be viewed as a liability or lose his job. If the supervisor believes negative stereotypes about men or Latinos, she may treat him unfairly and deny the company the benefit of his skills. If both people can respect and communicate with each other, however, their relationship is more likely to become positive and lead to progress for everyone.

Successful interaction with those around you depends on your ability to accept differences. The key is respect—for yourself and for others. Respecting other people's cultures, behaviors, races, religions, appearances, and ideas as you do your own promotes communication and learning. What can you do to accept and deal with differences?

- *Avoid judgments based on external characteristics.* These include skin color, weight, facial features, and gender.
- *Cultivate relationships with people of different cultures, races, perspectives, and ages.* Find out how other people live and think, and see what you can learn from them.
- *Educate yourself and others.* "We can empower ourselves to end racism through massive education," say Tamara Trotter and Joycelyn Allen in *Talking Justice: 602 Ways to Build and Promote Racial Harmony.*[1] "Take advantage of books and people to teach you about other cultures. Empowerment comes through education." Read about other cultures and people.
- *Be sensitive to the needs of others at school and on the job.* Try to put yourself in their place by asking yourself questions about what you would feel and do if you were in a similar situation.
- *Listen to people whose perspectives clash with or challenge your own.* Acknowledge that everyone has a right to his or her opinion, whether you agree with it or not.

- *Look for common ground*—parenting, classes, personal challenges, and interests.
- *Help other people, no matter how different they may be.* Sheryl McCarthy writes about an African American who, in the midst of the 1992 Los Angeles riots, saw a man being beaten and helped him to safety. "When asked why he risked grievous harm to save an Asian man he didn't even know, Williams said, 'Because if I'm not there to help someone else, when the mob comes for me, will there be someone there to save me?'"[2] Continue the cycle of kindness.
- *Explore your own background, beliefs, and identity.* Share what you learn with others.
- *Cultivate your own personal diversity.* Perhaps your father is Navajo Indian and Scottish and your mother is Creole (French, Spanish, and Black). Respect and explore your heritage. Even if you identify with only one group or culture, you have many sides.
- *Take responsibility for making changes instead of pointing the finger at someone else.* Avoid blaming problems in your life on certain groups of people.
- *Learn from the atrocities of history such as slavery and the Holocaust.* Cherish the level of freedom you have, and continually seek improvement at home and elsewhere.
- *Teach your children about other cultures.* Impress on them the importance of appreciating differences while accepting that all people have equal rights.
- *Recognize that people everywhere have the same basic needs.* Everyone loves, thinks, hurts, hopes, fears, and plans. People are united through their essential humanity.

Any team will gain strength from the diversity of its members. Consider a five-person basketball team, made up of a center, a power forward, a small forward, a shooting guard, and a point guard. Each person has a different role and a different style of play, but only by combining their abilities can the players achieve success.

The more diverse the team members, the greater is the chance that new ideas and solutions will find their way to the table, increasing the chances of solving any problem. Keep this in mind as you read about the role of teamwork in your life.

WHY IS TEAMWORK IMPORTANT?

Everything you know and will learn comes from your interaction with the outside world. Often this interaction takes place between you and one or more people. You learn from listening to them, reading what they write, observing them, and trying what they do.

Your success in every aspect of life depends on your ability to cooperate in a team setting—communicating, sharing tasks, and developing a common vision. For example:

- You deal with the challenges of day-to-day life in a family/community team, with the help of parents, siblings, relatives, and friends.
- You achieve work goals in a work team, with supervisors, coworkers, or consultants.
- You learn, complete projects, and pass classes as part of an educational team, with instructors, fellow students, tutors, administrators, and advisors.

Following is some helpful information on working in groups, as well as some specific strategies for teamwork at school.

Working in Groups

Being able to work well together is necessary to accomplish goals. The two major roles in the group experience are those of participant and leader. Any group requires both to function successfully. Become aware of the role you tend to play, and try different roles to help you decide where you can be most effective.[3]

Being an Effective Participant

Like every team member, participants have a responsibility for, and a stake in, the outcome. The following strategies will help a participant to be effective.

- *Get involved.* Let people know your thoughts and ideas. You are as important a team member as anyone else, and your perspective is equally valuable.
- *Be organized.* When you participate, stay focused and organized. The more organized your ideas are, the more people will listen, take them into consideration, and be willing to try them.
- *Be willing to discuss.* Everyone has an equal right to express his or her ideas. Even as you present your opinions enthusiastically, be willing to consider those of others. Avoid attacking the person. Separate the person from the idea, and keep the idea in focus.
- *Keep your word.* Do what you say you're going to do. Bring something to the process so others don't feel as though you weigh them down.
- *Play fairly.* Give everyone a chance to participate. Be respectful of other people's ideas. Don't dominate the discussion or try to control or manipulate others.

Being an Effective Leader

Some people prefer—or have the designated role—to initiate the action, make decisions, express big-picture ideas, and control how things proceed. In any group the following strategies will help a leader succeed.

- *Define and limit projects.* Don't assume that a group will know its purpose on its own. The leader should define the purpose and limit tasks so the group doesn't take on too much.

- *Map out who will do what.* Help different personalities work together by exploring who can do what best. Give people specific responsibilities, and trust that they will do their jobs.

- *Set the agenda.* Establish, and communicate, the goal of the project and how it will proceed. Invite advice from others in this process, write down the agenda, and make copies for everyone.

- *Direct progress.* The leader should do his or her best to keep everyone to the topic at hand. When challenges arise midstream, the leader may have to help the team change direction.

- *Set the tone.* Group members bring different attitudes and mental states to a gathering. Setting a positive tone helps to bring the group together and motivate people to their peak performance.

- *Evaluate results.* The leader should determine whether the team is accomplishing its goals. If the team is not moving ahead, the leader should make changes and decisions.

If you don't believe that you fit into the traditional definition of a leader, there are other ways to lead. You can lead others by setting an honorable example in your actions, choices, or words. You can lead by putting forth an idea that takes a group in a new direction. You can lead by being the kind of person others would like to be.

Achieving a goal takes the participation of all group members. Your contribution is essential. You might even play different roles with different groups. You might be a participator at school and a leader in a self-help group. You could enjoy leading a religious group but prefer to take a back seat at work. Do what feels comfortable. The happier each group member is, the more effectively the group as a whole will function. This goes for study groups as well.

Study Teamwork

Studying with one or more other people can enhance your learning. The way a study group operates depends on the people involved, the subject, and the location and size of the group. No matter what your own group's situation, though, certain general strategies will help.

- *Choose a leader for each meeting, if that is an option.* Rotating the leadership helps all members take ownership of the group. If a leader has to miss class for any reason, choose another leader for that meeting.

- *Set meeting goals.* At the start of each meeting, compile a list of questions you want to address.

- *Adjust to different personalities.* Respect and communicate with members you would not necessarily choose as friends (you won't often be able to choose your coworkers).

- *Share the workload.* Willingness to work is more important than knowledge level.

- *Set general goals.* Determine what the group wants to accomplish over the course of a semester (or other unit of time).

- *Set a regular meeting schedule.* Schedule meetings for every week, every two weeks, or whatever the group can do.
- *Create study materials for one another.* Give each group member the task of finding a piece of information to compile, photocopy, and review for the other group members.
- *Help one another learn.* Have group members teach certain pieces of information; make up quizzes for each other; go through flash cards together.
- *Pool your note-taking resources.* Different group members will have different information in their notes because of differing interests, missed classes, and differing note-taking methods. Compare notes with your group members and fill in any information you don't have.

Benefits of Study Groups

Studying with others isn't "better" than studying alone. Rather, it adds an important dimension to your learning by exposing you to others' knowledge and ideas. Each student has a unique body of knowledge and individual strengths. To have individual students pass on their knowledge to one another in a study group requires less time and energy than for each of the students to learn all of the material alone. Benefits include the following:

- *Solidified knowledge.* When you discuss concepts or teach them to others, you reinforce what you know and strengthen your critical thinking. Part of the benefit comes from simply repeating information aloud and rewriting it on paper, and part comes from how you think through information in your mind before you pass it on to someone else.
- *Increased motivation.* In a study group, you are accountable to group members. Others will see your level of work and preparation, which may increase your motivation.
- *Better teamwork skills.* The more you understand the group dynamics and the more experience you have with groups, the more you will build your ability to work well with others.

Today's workplace emphasizes work done through team effort. Keep your teamwork strategies in mind as you explore how to plan your career.

 ## WHAT STRATEGIC THINKING CAN HELP YOU PLAN YOUR CAREER?

College is an ideal time to investigate careers because so many different resources are available to you. You might not have thought too much about it yet. Or, you might have had a career for years and are looking for a change. You might have been set on a certain career but now are having second thoughts. No matter what is your starting point, now is the time to make progress.

Define a Career Path

Aiming for a job in a given area requires strategically planning the steps that can get you there. Whether these steps take months or years, they help you concentrate your energies on your goal. Defining a career path involves investigating yourself, exploring potential careers, and building knowledge and experience.

Investigate Yourself

Gather everything you know about yourself, from this class or any of your other life experiences, and think critically about the information. What do you know or do best? Reflecting on jobs you've had, what did you like and not like to do? How would you describe your personality? What kinds of careers make the best use of everything you are?

Don't think you should automatically know what you want to do. Most students who have not been in the workplace don't know what career they want to pursue. Students who have been working already often explore other careers. These days, people are changing careers many times in their lives instead of sticking with one. This discovery is a lifelong process.

Explore Potential Careers

Career possibilities extend far beyond what you can imagine. Brainstorm about career areas. Ask instructors, relatives, and fellow students about careers they have or know about. Check your library for books on careers and biographies of people who worked in fields that interest you. Explore careers you discover through newspapers, novels, nonfiction, or even movies.

Your school's *career center* is an important resource in your investigation. The career center offers job listings, occupation lists, assessments of skills and personality types, informational material about different careers, and material about various companies. The people who work at the center can help you sort through the material.

Use your critical-thinking skills to broaden your questions beyond what specific tasks you perform for any given job. Many other factors will be important to you. Look at Table 10.2 for some of the kinds of questions you might ask as you talk to people or investigate materials.

Build Knowledge and Experience

Having knowledge and experience specific to the career you want to pursue will be valuable on the job hunt. Four great ways to build both are courses, internships, jobs, and volunteering.

Courses. When you narrow your career exploration to a couple of areas that interest you, look through your course catalog and take a course or two in those fields. How you react to these courses will give you important clues to how you feel about the area in general.

Internships. Although an **internship** may or may not offer pay, the experience and contacts are worth the work. Companies that offer internships are

TERMS

Internship
A temporary work program in which a student can gain supervised practical experience in a professional field.

TABLE 10.2

Critical-thinking questions for career investigation.

- What can I do in this area that I like/am good at?
- Do I respect the company and/or the industry?
- What are the educational requirements (certificates or degrees, courses)?
- Do companies in this industry generally accommodate special needs (child care, sick days, flextime, or working at home)?
- What skills are necessary?
- Do I have to belong to a union?
- What wage or salary is normal for an entry-level position, and what benefits can I expect?
- Does this industry offer opportunities within a reasonable distance from where I live?
- What kinds of personalities are best suited to this kind of work?
- What other expectations are there beyond the regular workday (travel, overtime, etc.)?
- What are the prospects for moving up to higher-level positions?
- Do I prefer a service or a manufacturing industry?

looking for people who will work hard in exchange for experience you can't get in the classroom. Internships are one of the best ways to show a prospective employer some real-world experience and initiative.

Jobs. No matter how you earn money while you are in college, you might discover career opportunities that appeal to you. Someone who takes a third-shift legal proofreading job to make extra cash might discover an interest in the law. Someone who answers phones for a newspaper might be drawn into journalism. Be aware of the possibilities around you.

Volunteering. Offering your services in the community or at school can introduce you to careers and increase your experience. Some schools have programs that can help you find volunteering opportunities both on and off campus. Be sure to note volunteer activities on your resume; many employers seek candidates who have shown commitment through volunteering.

As you begin to find your path, you can strategize further about how you will follow it.

Map Out Your Strategy

After you've gathered enough information to narrow your career goals, use what you know about strategic planning to achieve them. One idea is to make a career timeline as shown in Figure 10.1. Mark years and half-year points (and months for the first year), and write in the steps when you think they should happen (use this timeline only as a guide, recognizing that your path may change). Set goals that establish the people you will talk to, what courses you will take, what skills you will work on, what jobs or internships you will investigate, and any other research.

The road to a truly satisfying career can be long. Seek support as you work toward your goals. Confide in supportive people, and read inspiring

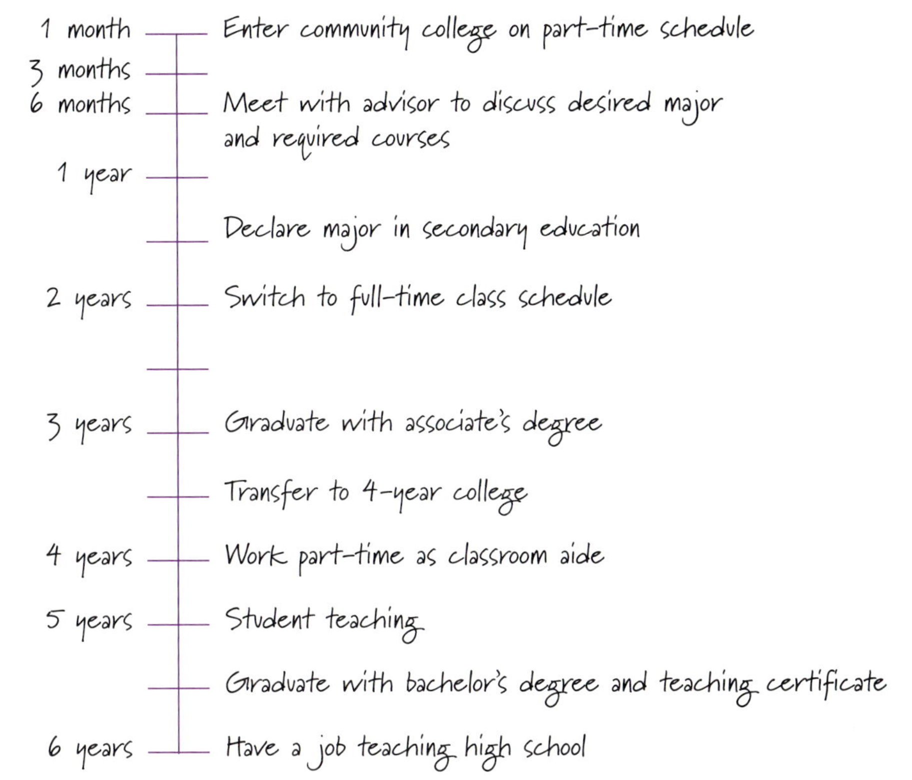

1 month ——	Enter community college on part-time schedule
3 months ——	
6 months ——	Meet with advisor to discuss desired major and required courses
1 year ——	
——	Declare major in secondary education
2 years ——	Switch to full-time class schedule
——	
3 years ——	Graduate with associate's degree
——	Transfer to 4-year college
4 years ——	Work part-time as classroom aide
5 years ——	Student teaching
——	Graduate with bachelor's degree and teaching certificate
6 years ——	Have a job teaching high school

FIGURE 10.1

Career timeline.

books such as *What Color Is Your Parachute?* by Richard Nelson Bolles. More are listed in the bibliography.

Through the process, knowing what employers want will help you to become an excellent job candidate in any career.

Know What Employers Want

Certain skills and qualities signify an efficient and effective employee to a potential employer. You can continue to develop these skills in any job if you always strive to improve.

Communication skills. Being able to listen well and express yourself in writing and speaking is a key to success in the workplace. Much can be accomplished through efficient, open communication. Being able to adjust to different communication styles is important, too.

Problem solving. Any job will present problems that have to be solved. An employee who knows how to assess a situation and apply the problem-solving process will stand out.

Decision making. Decisions, large and small, are made in every workplace every day. Knowing how to think through and make decisions will help you in a job.

Teamwork. The importance of being able to work well with others cannot be overemphasized. If a team has a weak link, the whole company suffers.

Intercultural communication. The workplace is becoming increasingly diverse. The more you can work well with people who are different from yourself, and open your mind to their points of view, the more valuable an employee you will be.

Leadership. The ability to influence others in a positive way will earn you respect and keep you in line for promotions. Taking the lead often commands attention.

Creativity. When you can see the big picture as well as the details and can let your mind come up with unexpected new concepts and plans, you will bring valuable suggestions to your workplace.

Commitment. The ability to continue to work hard in difficult situations is extremely important. In addition, if you introduce a new and creative idea, you can gain support for it if you have a strong commitment to it yourself.

Values and integrity. Your personal values and integrity will guide everything you do. In your actions and decisions, consider what you value and what you believe is right.

Change is becoming a major factor in the modern workplace. Although changing careers used to be a risky and rare practice, people now commonly have as many as five careers over the course of their lives, and this number may well continue to rise. Being able to adapt to change will help you on the job and in all other aspects of your life.

HOW CAN YOU LIVE WITH AND ADAPT TO CHANGE?

Even the most carefully constructed plans can be turned upside down by change. Make change a manageable part of your life by accepting the reality of change, maintaining flexibility, and adjusting your goals.

Accept the Reality of Change

As Russian-born author Isaac Asimov once said, "It is change, continuing change, inevitable change, that is the dominant factor in society today. No sensible decision can be made any longer without taking into account not only the world as it is, but the world as it will be."[4] Change is a sure thing. Two significant causes of change on a global level are technology and the economy.

Technological Growth

Advances in technology come into being daily: Computer companies update programs, new models of cars and machines appear, and scientists discover new possibilities in medicine and other areas. People make changes in the workplace, school, and home to keep up with the new systems and products that technology constantly offers. People and cultures are linked around the world through the Internet and World Wide Web.

The dominance of the media, brought on by technological growth, has increased the likelihood of change. A few hundred years ago, no television or magazines or Internet existed. A village could operate in the same way for years with little change because there would be little or no contact with anyone from the outside who could introduce new ideas, methods, or plans. Now the media constantly present people with new ways of doing things. When people can see the possibilities around them, they are more likely to want to discover new horizons.

Economic Instability

In the unpredictable contemporary economy businesses have had to cut costs to survive, which has affected many people's jobs and careers. Some businesses have discovered the speed and cost-effectiveness of computers and used them to replace workers. Some businesses have merged with others, and people in duplicate jobs were let go. The economy also has affected personal finances. Many people face money problems that force them to make changes in how much they work, how they pursue an education, and how they live.

Maintain Flexibility

The fear of change is as inevitable as change itself. When you are comfortable with something—a schedule, a relationship, a habit—you tend to want it to stay the way it is. Think about your life right now. What do you wish would stay the same? What changes have thrown you off balance?

You have encountered any number of changes in your life, many of them unexpected. You might have experienced ups and downs in relationships, a change in jobs or schools, a change of residence, or shifts in finances or family life. All of these changes, whether perceived as good or bad, cause a certain level of stress. They also cause a shift in your needs, which may lead to new priorities.

Change Brings Different Needs

Your needs can change from day to day, year to year, and situation to situation. Although you know about some changes ahead of time, such as when you plan to move in with a partner, others take you by surprise, such as losing a job. Different times of year bring different needs, such as a need for extra cash around the holidays. Some changes that shift your needs occur within a week or even a day. For example, an instructor might inform you that you have a quiz or an extra assignment at the end of the week. Table 10.3 shows how the effects of certain changes can lead to new priorities.

Flexibility Versus Inflexibility

When change affects your needs, you can react either inflexibly or flexibly, each with its resulting effects.

TABLE 10.3 Change produces new priorities.

CHANGE	EFFECTS AND CHANGED NEEDS	NEW PRIORITIES
Lost job	Loss of income; need for others in your household to contribute more income	Job hunting; reduction in your spending; additional training or education to qualify for a different job
New job	Change in daily/weekly schedule; need for increased contribution of household help from others	Time and energy commitment to new job, maintaining confidence, learning new skills
Started school	Fewer hours for work, family, and personal time; responsibility for classwork; need to plan semesters ahead of time	Careful scheduling; making sure you have time to attend class and study adequately; strategic planning of classes and of career goals
Relationship/marriage	Responsibility toward your partner; merging of your schedules and perhaps your finances and belongings	Time and energy commitment to relationship
Break-up/divorce	Change in responsibility for any children; increased responsibility for your own finances; possibly a need to relocate; increased independence	Making time for yourself, gathering support from friends and family, securing your finances, making sure you have your own income
Bought car	Responsibility for monthly payment; responsibility for upkeep	Regular income so that you can make payments on time; time and money for upkeep
New baby	Increased parenting responsibility; need money to pay for baby's needs or if you had to stop working; need help with other children	Child care, flexible employment, increased commitment from a partner or other supporter
New cultural environment (from new home, job, or school)	Exposure to unfamiliar people and traditions; tendency to keep to yourself	Learning about the culture with which you are now interacting; openness to new relationships

Inflexibility. Not acknowledging a shift in needs can cause trouble. For example, if you lose your job and continue to spend as much money as you did before, you can drive yourself into debt and make the situation worse. Or if you continue to spend little time with a partner who has expressed a need for more contact, you could endanger the relationship.

Flexibility. Being flexible means acknowledging the change, examining your different needs, and addressing them. Discovering what change brings may reveal surprising positive effects. For example, a painful breakup can lead you to discover greater capability and independence. A crisis can spur opportunity, and flexibility will help you to pursue it. Being flexible often means adjusting your goals to suit the changes that occur.

Adjust Your Goals

Your changing life frequently results in the need to adjust goals accordingly. Sometimes goals must change because they weren't appropriate in the first place. Some turn out to be unreachable. Others do not pose enough of a challenge. Still others are unhealthy for the goal-setter or others.

Step One: Reevaluate

Before adjusting in response to change, take time to *reevaluate* the goals themselves as well as your progress toward them.

The goals. First, determine whether your goals still fit the person you have become in the past week or month or year. Circumstances can change quickly. For example, an unexpected pregnancy might cause a female student to rethink her educational goals.

Your progress. If you believe you haven't gotten far, determine whether the goal is out of your range or simply requires more stamina than you had anticipated. As you work toward any goal, you will experience alternating periods of progress and stagnation. Sticking with a tough goal might be the hardest thing you'll ever do, but the payoff may be worth it. You may want to seek the support and perspective of a friend or counselor as you evaluate your progress.

Step Two: Modify

If, after your best efforts, a goal clearly is out of reach, *modifying* your goal may bring success. Perhaps the goal doesn't suit you. For example, an interpersonal learner might become frustrated while pursuing a career that minimizes human contact.

Based on your reevaluation, you can modify a goal in two ways:

> "Whatever you think you can do or believe you can do, begin it. Action has magic, grace, and power in it."
> JOHANN WOLFGANG VON GOETHE

1. *Adjust the existing goal.* To adjust a goal, change one or more aspects that define it—say, the time frame, the due dates, or the specifics of the expectations. For example, a woman with an unexpected pregnancy could adjust her educational due date, taking an extra year or two to complete her coursework. She also could adjust the time frame, taking classes at night if she has to care for her child during the day.

2. *Replace it with a different, more compatible goal.* If you find that you just can't handle a goal, try to find another one that makes more sense at this time. For example, a couple who wants to buy a house but can't afford it can choose to work toward the goal of making improvements to their current living space. Because you and your circumstances never stop changing, your goals should keep up with those changes.

Think about yourself. How has your idea of yourself and your goals changed since you first opened this book? How has your self-image changed? What have you learned about your values and about how you think and learn? No matter what changes come your way, your ability to weather them with an open mind and to adjust will allow you to continue to grow.

HOW CAN YOU CONTINUE TO GROW AND LEARN THROUGHOUT YOUR LIFE?

Learning brings change, and change brings growth. As you change and the world changes, new knowledge and ideas emerge continually. Absorb them so you can propel yourself into the future. Take advantage of your status as a student by making the most of the experiences and information that come your way. Visualize yourself as a student of life who is always learning something new. Here are some lifelong learning strategies that can encourage you to constantly ask questions and explore new ideas.

Investigate new interests. When information catches your attention, explore it further. If you are fascinated by politics on television, find out if your school has political clubs you can explore. If a friend of yours starts to take yoga, try a class. If you really like one portion of a certain course, see if other courses are available that focus on that specific topic.

Read. Reading opens a world of new perspectives. See what's on the bestseller list at your bookstore. Ask your friends about books that have changed their lives. Stay on top of current change in your community, your state, your country, and the world by reading newspapers and magazines. Explore religious literature, family letters, and Internet news groups and Web pages. Challenge what you think and believe by thinking critically about information that presents a perspective, opinion, or set of values different from your own.

Spend time with interesting people. When you meet someone new who inspires you and makes you think, keep in touch. Have a party and invite people from different corners of your life. Start a book club, a home-repair group, a play-reading club, a hiking group, or an investing group. Get to know people of different cultures and perspectives. Learn something new from one another.

Pursue improvement in your studies and in your career. At school, take classes outside of your major. After graduation, stay current in your field by seeking out **continuing education** courses. Some companies offer additional on-the-job training or pay for their employees to take courses that will improve their knowledge and skills.

Nurture a spiritual life. You don't have to attend a house of worship to be spiritual, although that may be important to you. "A spiritual life of some kind is absolutely necessary for psychological 'health,'" says psychologist Thomas Moore in *The Care of the Soul.* "We live in a time of deep division, in which mind is separated from body and spirituality is at odds with materialism."[5] The words *soul* and *spirituality* hold different meanings for each individual. Decide what they mean to you. Whether you discover them in music, organized religion, friendship, nature, cooking, sports, or anything else, making them a priority will help you find greater balance and meaning.

Experience what others create. Art is "an adventure of the mind" (Eugene Ionesco, playwright); "a means of knowing the world" (Angela Carter, author);

TERMS

Continuing
education
Courses that
students can
take without
having to be
part of a
degree program.

something that "does not reproduce the visible; rather, it makes visible" (Paul Klee, painter); a revealer of "our most secret self" (Jean-Luc Godard, film-maker). Explore all kinds of art and focus on what moves you: music, visual arts, theater, photography, dance, domestic arts, film and television, poetry, prose, and more.

Make your own creations. Bring out the creative artist in yourself. Take a class in drawing, in woodworking, or in quilting. Learn to play an instrument. Write poems for your favorite people or stories to read to your children. Invent a recipe. Design and build something for your home. You are a creative being. Express yourself, and learn more about yourself, through art.

Lifelong learning is the master key that unlocks every door you will encounter on your journey. If you keep it firmly in your hand, you will discover worlds of knowledge—and a place for yourself within them. Continuing to learn also can help you live your mission.

HOW CAN YOU LIVE YOUR MISSION?

As you learn and change, so might your life's mission. Whatever the changes, your continued learning will give you a greater sense of security in your choices. Recall your mission statement from Chapter 5. Think about how it is changing as you develop. It will continue to reflect your goals, values, and strength if you live with integrity, observe the role models in your life, expand your vision, and work to achieve your personal best in all that you do.

Live With Integrity

You've spent a lot of time exploring who you are, how you learn, and what you value. **Integrity** is about being true to that picture you have drawn of yourself while also considering the needs of others. Living with integrity will bring you great personal and professional rewards.

Honesty and sincerity are at the heart of integrity. Many of the decisions you make and act on in your life are based on your underlying sense of what is the right thing to do. Having integrity puts that sense into day-to-day action.

The Marks of Integrity

A person of integrity lives by the following principles:

1. *Honest representation of himself or herself and his or her thoughts.* For example, you tell your partner when you are hurt over something that he or she did or didn't do.
2. *Sincerity in word and action.* You do what you say you will do. For example, you tell a coworker that you will finish a project when she has to leave early, and you follow through by completing the work.
3. *Consideration of others' needs.* When making decisions, you take into account your needs and the needs of others. You also avoid hurting

TERMS

Integrity
Adherence to a code of moral values; incorruptibility, honesty.

others for the sake of your personal goals. For example, your sister cares for your elderly father. You spend three nights a week with him so she can take a course toward her degree.

The Benefits of Integrity

When you act with integrity, you earn trust and respect. If people can trust you to be honest, sincere, and considerate of others, they will be more likely to support your goals and reward your work. Think of situations in which integrity has had a positive effect. Have you ever confessed to an instructor that your paper is late without a good excuse, only to find that despite your mistake, you earned the instructor's respect? Have extra efforts in the workplace ever helped you move up? Has your kindness toward a friend or a spouse moved the relationship to a deeper level? When you decide to act with integrity, you can improve your life and the lives of others.

Most important, living with integrity helps you believe in yourself and in your choices. A person of integrity isn't a perfect person but is one who makes the effort to live according to values and principles, continually striving to learn from mistakes and to improve. If you take responsibility for making the right moves, you will follow your mission with strength and conviction.

Learn From Role Models

People often derive the highest level of motivation and inspiration from learning how others have struggled through ups and downs and achieved their goals. Somehow, seeing how someone else went through difficult situations can give you hope for your own struggles. The positive effects of being true to oneself become more real when an actual person has earned them.

TERMS

Role model
A person whose behavior in a role is imitated by others.

Learning about the lives of people who have achieved their own version of success can teach you what you can do in your own life. Bessie and Sadie Delany, sisters and accomplished African-American women born in the late 1800s, are two valuable **role models.** They took risks, becoming professionals in dentistry and teaching at a time when women and minorities often were denied both respect and opportunity. They worked hard to fight racial division and prejudice and taught others what they learned. They believed in their intelligence, beauty, and ability to give, and they lived without regrets. Says Sadie in their *Book of Everyday Wisdom:* "If there's anything I've learned in all these years, it's that life is too good to waste a day. It's up to you to make it sweet."[6]

Expand Your Vision

Every choice you make now will affect what happens to you down the road. Conversely, you will be able to trace everything that happens to you back to a few actions that you took (or should have taken) in the past. The people you meet will affect the courses you take, the courses you take will affect the career you will be able to choose, how you feel about your career will affect your personal life, and so on. Look ahead to see how your school, career, and life paths interconnect and might affect one another.

In addition to looking forward in time, look wide, to the international community of people. In today's media-saturated and information-driven world, people are becoming more and more aware of, and dependent on, each other. What happens to the Japanese economy affects the prices of goods in your neighborhood. A music trend that starts in New York spreads to many European countries. When human rights are violated in one nation, many other nations express their opinions and become involved. You are as important a link as any other person in this worldwide chain of human connection. Together, all people share an interest in making a better world to pass on to future generations. In making the choices that allow you to achieve your potential, you will make the world a better place.

"And life is what we make it, always has been, always will be."

GRANDMA MOSES

Aim for Your Personal Best

Your personal best is simply the best that you can do, in any situation. It may not be the best you have ever done. It will include mistakes, for nothing significant is ever accomplished without making mistakes and taking risks. It might shift from situation to situation. As long as you aim to do your best, though, you are inviting growth and success.

As a critical thinker and lifelong learner, you always will have a new direction in which to grow and a new challenge to face. Seek constant improvement in your personal, educational, and professional life, knowing that you are capable of improvement. Keep your mind alive through your ability to think. Enjoy the richness of life by living each day to the fullest, developing your talents and potential into the achievement of your most valued goals.

Kaizen is the Japanese word for "continual improvement." Striving for excellence, always finding ways to improve on what already exists, and believing that you can effect change are at the heart of the industrious Japanese spirit. The drive to improve who you are and what you do will help to provide the foundation of a successful future.

Think of this concept as you reflect on your mind and your goals. Create excellence and quality by continually asking yourself, "How can I improve?" Living by *kaizen* will help you to be a respected friend and family member, a productive and valued employee, and a truly contributing member of society. You can change the world.

Chapter 10 Building Thinking Skills

Name _____   Date _____

LIFE THINKING: Applying What You Learn

10.1 *Diversity Discovery*

Express your own personal diversity. Describe yourself in response to the following questions.

What ethnic background(s) do you have?

_____

_____

Name one or more facts about you that someone wouldn't know from simply looking at you.

_____

_____

Name two values or beliefs that govern how you live, what you pursue, and/or with whom you associate.

_____

_____

What other characteristics or choices define your uniqueness?

_____

_____

_____

_____

Now, join with a partner in your class. Try to choose someone you don't know well. Your goal is to communicate to your partner what you have written, and for your partner to communicate to you in the same way. Talk with each other for ten minutes and take notes on what the other person says. At the end of that period, join together as a class. Each person will describe his or her partner to the class.

What did you learn about your partner that surprised you?

_____

_____

What did you learn that went against any assumptions you might have made about that person based on his or her appearance, background, or behavior?

_____

_____

Has this exercise changed the way you see this person or other people? Why or why not?

_____

_____

10.2 *Changes in Goals*

As changes occur in your life, your goals change and require reevaluation. Think about what has changed in your school, career, and life goals over the past semester. For each category name an old goal, name the adjusted goal, and discuss briefly why you think the change occurred.

SCHOOL

Old: _____

New: _____

Why the change? _____

CAREER

Old: _____

New: _____

Why the change? _____

LIFE

Old: _____

New: _____

Why the change? _____

TEAM THINKING: Working Together

10.3 *Giving Back*

In your group, research volunteering opportunities in your community. Each group member should choose one possibility to research. Answer questions such as the following: What is the situation or organization? What are its needs? Do any volunteer positions require an application, letters of reference, or background checks? What is the time commitment? Is any special training required? Does this experience have any problematic or difficult elements?

When you have the information, meet with the group again. Each group member should type up an information sheet with a summary of his or her research and make photocopies for the others so everyone will know about each volunteering opportunity. Choose one that you think you will have the time and ability to try next semester. State your choice here, and tell why you selected it.

_____

_____

_____

_____

_____

 WORK THINKING: Career Portfolio

 10.4 *Revised Mission Statement*

Retrieve the mission statement you wrote at the end of Chapter 5. Give yourself a day or so to read it over and think about it. Then revise it according to the changes that have occurred in your life. Add new priorities and goals, and delete those that are no longer valid. Continue to update your mission statement so it reflects your growth and development, helping to guide you through the changes that await you in the future.

 QUESTIONING YOUR WORLD: Information Literacy Journal

To record your thoughts, use a separate journal or the lined pages at the end of the chapter.

 10.5 *New Perspective[7]*

Imagine that you have no choice but to change either your gender or your racial, ethnic, or religious group. Which would you change, and why? What do you anticipate would be the positive and negative effects of the change—in your social life, in your family life, on the job, and at school? Discuss what you think the media image is of the person you would choose to become, and how you think that image might affect your perception of yourself.

Journal

Name _____   Date _____

Journal

Name _____ Date _____

Appendix A
Learning Styles Assessments

Because you are a complex individual, there is more than one way to evaluate your learning style and personality traits. Chapter 6 focuses on an evaluation of your multiple intelligences. This appendix introduces two other assessments that you can use if you have the time and interest. These two assessments, the *Learning Styles Inventory* and the *Personality Spectrum*, give you insights into who you are and how you learn—insights that can reinforce, expand, or even challenge what you already know about yourself.

 ## LEARNING STYLES INVENTORY

One of the first instruments to measure psychological types, the *Myers-Briggs Type Inventory* (MBTI), was designed by Katharine Briggs and her daughter, Isabel Briggs Myers. Later, David Keirsey and Marilyn Bates combined the sixteen Myers-Briggs types into four temperaments. Barbara Soloman, Associate Director of the First Year College at North Carolina State University, has developed the following learning styles inventory based on these theories and on her work with thousands of students.[1]

> "Students learn in many ways," says Professor Soloman. "Mismatches often exist between common learning styles and standard teaching styles. Therefore, students often do poorly and get discouraged. Some students doubt themselves and doubt their ability to succeed in the curriculum of their choice. Some settle for low grades and even leave school. If students understand how they learn most effectively, they can tailor their studying to their own needs."

"Learning effectively" and "tailoring studying to your own needs" means choosing study techniques that help you learn. For example, if a student responds more to visual images than to words, he might want to construct notes in a more visual way. Or, if a student learns better when talking to people than when studying alone, she might want to study primarily in pairs or

FIGURE A.1

Percentages of students with particular learning styles.

Visual   *Verbal*
| 80% | 20% |

Active   Reflective
| 80% | 20% |

FACTUAL   THEORETICAL
| 70% | 30% |

Linear   Holistic
| 85% | 15% |

Source: Barbara Soloman, North Carolina State University.

groups. Figure A.1 provides information on what styles tend to be dominant among students.

This inventory has four dimensions, within each of which are two opposing styles. At the end of the inventory, you will have two scores in each of the four dimensions. The difference between your two scores in any dimension tells you which of the two styles in that dimension is dominant for you. A few people score between the two styles, indicating that they have fairly equal parts of both styles. Following are brief descriptions of the four dimensions. You will learn more about them in the section on study strategies.

1. *Active/Reflective.* Active learners learn best by experiencing knowledge through their own actions. Reflective learners understand information best when they have had time to reflect on it on their own.

2. *Factual/Theoretical.* Factual learners learn best through specific facts, data, and detailed experimentation. Theoretical learners are more comfortable with big-picture ideas, symbols, and new concepts.

3. *Visual/Verbal.* Visual learners remember best what they see: diagrams, flowcharts, timelines, films, and demonstrations. Verbal learners gain the most learning from reading, hearing spoken words, participating in discussions, and explaining things to others.

4. *Linear/Holistic.* Linear learners find it easiest to learn material presented step by step in a logical, ordered progression. Holistic learners progress in fits and starts, perhaps feeling lost for a while but eventually seeing the big picture in a clear and creative way.

LEARNING STYLES INVENTORY

Please complete this inventory by circling "a" or "b" to indicate your answer to each question. Answer every question, and choose only one answer for each question. If both answers seem to apply to you, choose the answer that applies more often.

1. I study best
   a. in a study group.
   b. alone or with a partner.

2. I would rather be considered
   a. realistic.
   b. imaginative.

3. When I recall what I did yesterday, I am most likely to think in terms of
   a. pictures or images.
   b. words or verbal descriptions.

4. I usually think new material is
   a. easier at the beginning and then harder as it becomes more complicated.
   b. often confusing at the beginning but easier as I start to understand what the whole subject is about.

5. When given a new activity to learn, I would rather first
   a. try it out.
   b. think about how I'm going to do it.

6. If I were an instructor, I would rather teach a course
   a. that deals with real-life situations and what to do about them.
   b. that deals with ideas and encourages students to think about them.

7. I prefer to receive new information in the form of
   a. pictures, diagrams, graphs, or maps.
   b. written directions or verbal information.

8. I learn
   a. at a fairly regular pace. If I study hard I'll "get it" and then move on.
   b. in fits and starts. I might be totally confused, and then suddenly it all "clicks."

9. I understand something better after
   a. I attempt to do it myself.
   b. I give myself time to think about how it works.

10. I find it easier
    a. to learn facts.
    b. to learn ideas or concepts.

11. In a book with lots of pictures and charts, I am likely to
    a. look over the pictures and charts carefully.
    b. focus on the written text.

12. It's easier for me to memorize facts from
    a. a list.
    b. a whole story or essay with the facts embedded in it.

13. I will more easily remember
    a. something I have done myself.
    b. something I have thought or read about.

14. I am usually
    a. aware of my surroundings. I remember people and places and usually recall where I put things.
    b. unaware of my surroundings. I forget people and places. I frequently misplace things.

15. I like instructors
    a. who put a lot of diagrams on the board.
    b. who spend a lot of time explaining.

16. Once I understand
    a. all the parts, I understand the whole thing.
    b. the whole thing, I see how the parts fit.

17. When I am learning something new, I would rather
    a. talk about it.
    b. think about it.

18. I am good at
    a. being careful about the details of my work.
    b. having creative ideas about how to do my work.

19. I remember best
    a. what I see.
    b. what I hear.

20. When I solve problems that involve some math, I usually
    a. work my way to the solutions one step at a time.
    b. see the solutions but then have to struggle to figure out the steps to get to them.

21. In a lecture class, I would prefer occasional in-class
    a. discussions or group problem-solving sessions.
    b. pauses that give opportunities to think or write about ideas presented in the lecture.

22. On a multiple-choice test, I am more likely to
    a. run out of time.
    b. lose points because of not reading carefully or making careless errors.

23. When I get directions to a new place, I prefer
    a. a map.
    b. written instructions.

24. When I'm thinking about something I've read
    a. I remember the incidents and try to put them together to figure out the themes.
    b. I just know what the themes are when I finish reading and then I have to back up and find the incidents that demonstrate them.

25. When I get a new computer or VCR, I tend to
    a. plug it in and start punching buttons.
    b. read the manual and follow instructions.

26. In reading for pleasure, I prefer
    a. something that teaches me new facts or tells me how to do something.
    b. something that gives me new ideas to think about.

27. When I see a diagram or a sketch in class, I am most likely to remember
    a. the picture.
    b. what the instructor said about it.

28. It is more important to me that an instructor
    a. lay out the material in clear, sequential steps.
    b. give me an overall picture and relate the material to other subjects.

TABLE A.1   Learning Styles Inventory scores.

Active/Reflective			Factual/Theoretical			Visual/Verbal			Linear/Holistic		
Q#	a	b	Q#	a	b	Q#	a	b	Q#	a	b
1			2			3			4		
5			6			7			8		
9			10			11			12		
13			14			15			16		
17			18			19			20		
21			22			23			24		
25			26			27			28		
Total			Total			Total			Total		

Scoring Sheet: Use Table A.1 to enter your scores.

1. Put 1's in the appropriate boxes in the table (e.g., if you answered **a** to Question 3, put a **1** in the column headed **a** next to the number **3**).

2. Total the 1's in the columns and write the totals in the indicated spaces at the base of the columns.

3. For each of the four dimensions, circle your two scores on the bar scale and then fill in the bar between the scores. For example, if under "ACTV/REFL" you had 2 **a** and 5 **b** responses, you would fill in the bar between those two scores, as this sample shows:

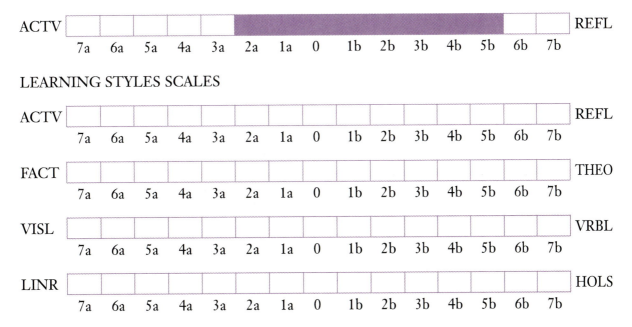

ACTV ▯▯▯▯▮▮▮▮▮▮▮▯▯ REFL
  7a 6a 5a 4a 3a 2a 1a 0 1b 2b 3b 4b 5b 6b 7b

LEARNING STYLES SCALES

ACTV ▯▯▯▯▯▯▯▯▯▯▯▯▯▯ REFL
  7a 6a 5a 4a 3a 2a 1a 0 1b 2b 3b 4b 5b 6b 7b

FACT ▯▯▯▯▯▯▯▯▯▯▯▯▯▯ THEO
  7a 6a 5a 4a 3a 2a 1a 0 1b 2b 3b 4b 5b 6b 7b

VISL ▯▯▯▯▯▯▯▯▯▯▯▯▯▯ VRBL
  7a 6a 5a 4a 3a 2a 1a 0 1b 2b 3b 4b 5b 6b 7b

LINR ▯▯▯▯▯▯▯▯▯▯▯▯▯▯ HOLS
  7a 6a 5a 4a 3a 2a 1a 0 1b 2b 3b 4b 5b 6b 7b

If your filled-in bar has the 0 close to its center, you are well balanced on the two dimensions of that scale. If your bar is drawn mainly to one side, you have a strong preference for that one dimension and may have difficulty learning in the other dimension.

PERSONALITY SPECTRUM

Joyce Bishop developed a system that simplifies learning styles into four personality types. Her work is based on the Myers-Briggs and Keirsey theories. The *Personality Spectrum* will give you a personality perspective on your learning styles. Please complete the following assessment.

PERSONALITY SPECTRUM

Step 1. Rank all four responses to each question from **most** like you (4) to **least** like you (1). Place a 1, 2, 3, or 4 in each box next to the responses, and use each number only once per question.

1. I like instructors who
- ☐ a. tell me exactly what is expected of me.
- ☐ b. make learning active and exciting.
- ☐ c. maintain a safe and supportive classroom.
- ☐ d. challenge me to think at higher levels.

2. I learn best when the material is
- ☐ a. well organized.
- ☐ b. something I can do hands-on.
- ☐ c. about understanding and improving the human condition.
- ☐ d. intellectually challenging.

3. A high priority in my life is to
- ☐ a. keep my commitments.
- ☐ b. experience as much of life as possible.
- ☐ c. make a difference in other's lives.
- ☐ d. understand how things work.

4. Other people think of me as
- ☐ a. dependable and loyal.
- ☐ b. dynamic and creative.
- ☐ c. caring and honest.
- ☐ d. intelligent and inventive.

5. When I experience stress, I am most likely to
- ☐ a. do something to help me feel more in control.
- ☐ b. do something physical and daring.
- ☐ c. talk with a friend.
- ☐ d. go off by myself and think about my situation.

6. I would probably NOT be close friends with someone who is
- ☐ a. irresponsible.
- ☐ b. unwilling to try new things.
- ☐ c. selfish and unkind to others.
- ☐ d. an illogical thinker.

7. My vacations could best be described as
- ☐ a. traditional.
- ☐ b. adventuresome.
- ☐ c. pleasing to others.
- ☐ d. a new learning experience.

8. One word that best describes me is
- ☐ a. sensible.
- ☐ b. spontaneous.
- ☐ c. giving.
- ☐ d. analytical.

Step 2. Add up the total points for each column.

Total for (A)	Total for (B)	Total for (C)	Total for (D)
☐	☐	☐	☐
Organizer	Adventurer	Giver	Thinker

FIGURE A.2   Personality Spectrum—thinking preferences and learning styles.

THINKER

Technical
Scientific
Mathematical
Dispassionate
Rational
Analytical
Logical
Problem Solving
Theoretical
Intellectual
Objective
Quantitative
Explicit
Realistic
Literal
Precise
Formal

GIVER

Interpersonal
Emotional
Caring
Sociable
Giving
Spiritual
Musical
Romantic
Feeling
Peacemaker
Trusting
Adaptable
Passionate
Harmonious
Idealistic
Talkative
Honest

Left Brain   Right Brain

ORGANIZER

Systematic
Administrative   Tactical
Procedural   Planning
Organized   Detailed
Conservative   Practical
Sequential   Confident
Structured   Predictable
Safekeeping   Controlled
Disciplined   Dependable

ADVENTURER

Active   Metaphoric
Visual   Experimental
Risking   Divergent
Original   Fast-paced
Artistic   Simultaneous
Spatial   Competitive
Skillful   Imaginative
Impulsive   Open-minded
            Adventuresome

Source: Understanding Psychology, 3/e, by Morris, © 1996. Adapted by permission of Prentice-Hall, Inc., Upper Saddle River, NJ.

TABLE A.2

Personality Spectrum at school and work.

PERSONALITY	STRENGTHS AT WORK AND SCHOOL	INTERPERSONAL RELATIONSHIPS
Organizer	• Can efficiently manage heavy workloads • Good organizational skills • Natural leadership qualities	• Loyal • Dependable • Traditional
Adventurer	• Adaptable to most changes • Creative and skillful • Dynamic and fast-paced	• Free • Exciting • Intense
Giver	• Always willing to help others • Honest and sincere • Good people skills	• Giving • Romantic • Warm
Thinker	• Good analytical skills • Can develop complex designs • Thorough and exact	• Quiet • Problem solver • Inventive

When you have tallied your scores, plot them on Figure A.2, the brain diagram, to create a visual representation of your spectrum.

Your Personality Spectrum assessment can help you maximize your functioning at school and at work. Each personality type has its own abilities, which improve work and school performance; suitable learning techniques; and ways of relating in interpersonal relationships. Table A.2 explains what suits each type.

Benefits of Different Styles

Following is some information about study strategies that correspond to both the Learning Styles Inventory and the Personality Spectrum dimensions and styles.

1. Active learners and Adventurers like to apply the information to the real world, experience it in their own actions, or discuss or explain to others what they have learned.

   Following are student-suggested strategies for active learners:

   - Study in a group in which members take turns explaining topics to one another and then discussing them.
   - Think of practical uses of the course material.
   - Pace and recite while you learn.
   - Act out material or design games.
   - Use flash cards with other people.
   - Teach the material to someone else.

2. Reflective learners and Thinkers retain and understand information better after they have taken time to think about it.

   Following are student-suggested strategies for reflecticve learners:

   - Study in a quiet setting.
   - When you are reading, stop periodically to think about what you have read.
   - Don't just memorize material; think about why it is important and what it relates to, considering the causes and effects involved.
   - Write short summaries of what the material means to you.

3. Factual learners and Organizers prefer concrete and specific facts, data, and detailed experimentation. They like to use standard methods to solve problems and are patient with details. They don't respond well to surprises and unique complications that upset normal procedure. They are good at memorizing facts.

   Following are student-suggested strategies for factual learners:

   - Ask the instructor how ideas and concepts apply in practice.
   - Ask for specific examples of the ideas and concepts.
   - Brainstorm specific examples with classmates or by yourself.
   - Think about how theories make specific connections with the real world.

4. Theoretical learners prefer innovation and theories. They are good at grasping new concepts and big-picture ideas. They dislike repetition and fact-based learning. They are comfortable with symbols and abstractions, often connecting them with prior knowledge and experience. Most classes are aimed at theoretical learners.

Following are student-suggested strategies for theoretical learners:

- If a class deals primarily with factual information, try to think of concepts, interpretations, or theories that link the facts together.
- Because you become impatient with details, you may be prone to careless mistakes on tests. Read directions and entire questions before answering, and be sure to check your work.
- Look for systems and patterns that arrange facts in a way that makes sense to you.
- Spend time analyzing the material.

5. Visual learners remember best what they see: diagrams, flowcharts, timelines, films, and demonstrations. They tend to forget spoken words and ideas. Classes usually don't include that much visual information. Note that although words written on paper or shown with an overhead projector are something you see, visual learners learn most easily from visual cues that don't involve words.

Following are student-suggested strategies for visual learners:

- Add diagrams to your notes whenever possible. Dates can be drawn on a timeline; math functions can be graphed; percentages can be drawn in a pie chart.
- Organize your notes so you can clearly see main points and supporting facts and how things are connected.
- Connect related facts in your notes by drawing arrows.
- Color-code your notes, using different colored highlighters, so that everything relating to a topic is the same color.

6. Verbal learners remember much of what they hear and more of what they hear and then say. They benefit from discussion, prefer verbal explanation to visual demonstration, and learn effectively by explaining things to others. Because written words are processed as verbal information, verbal learners learn well through reading. The majority of classes, because they present material through the written word, lecture, or discussion, are geared to verbal learners.

Following are student-suggested strategies for verbal learners:

- Talk about what you learn. Work in study groups so you have an opportunity to explain and discuss what you are learning.
- Read the textbook and highlight no more than 10 percent.
- Rewrite your notes.
- Outline chapters.
- Recite information or write scripts and debates.

7. **Linear learners** find it easiest to learn material presented in a logical, ordered progression. They solve problems in a step-by-step manner. They can work with sections of material without yet fully understanding the whole picture. They tend to be stronger when looking at the parts of a whole rather than understanding the whole and then dividing it up into parts. They learn best when taking in material in a progression from easiest to more complex to most difficult. Many courses are taught in a linear fashion.

   Following are student-suggested strategies for linear learners:

   - If you have an instructor who jumps from topic to topic, spend time outside of class with the instructor or a classmate who can help you fill the gaps in your notes.
   - If class notes are random, rewrite the material according to whatever logic helps you understand it best.
   - Outline the material.

8. **Holistic learners** learn in fits and starts. They may feel lost for days or weeks, unable to solve even the simplest problems or show the most basic understanding, until they suddenly "get it." They get discouraged when struggling with material that many other students seem to learn easily. Once they understand, though, they tend to see the big picture to an extent that others do not often achieve. They often are highly creative.

   Following are student-suggested strategies for holistic learners:

   - Recognize that you are not slow or stupid. Don't lose faith in yourself. You will get it.
   - Before reading a chapter, preview it by reading all the subheadings, summaries, and any marginal glossary terms. The chapter also may start with an outline and overview of the entire chapter.
   - Instead of spending a short time on every subject every night, try setting aside evenings for specific subjects and immerse yourself in just one subject at a time.
   - Take difficult subjects in summer school when you are handling fewer courses.
   - Try to relate subjects to other things you already know. Keep asking yourself how you could apply the material.

Appendix B
Researching Information and Student Resources on the Internet

Cynthia B. Leshin

Searching for information is like a treasure hunt. Unless a researcher has knowledge of all the resources and tools available, then the search for useful information may be a time consuming and frustrating process. In this appendix you will learn about resources on the Internet that will facilitate the search for information of interest to you, your career, and your field of study. Careful thought about the desired knowledge sought, where the best place is to begin to look for that knowledge, and extensive exploring and searching in layers of Web links, usually provides the desired reward—the gold nugget Web site.

The tools that you will learn about and use include

- search directories
    Yahoo
    Magellan
    Galaxy
    Snap
- search engines
    Alta Vista
    HotBot
    Northern Light
- image surfers
    Lycos
    Alta Vista
- reference resources.

You will also learn

- how to evaluate information you find on the Internet as to its content validity.

 INTERNET RESEARCH TOOLS

The Internet contains many tools that speed the search for information and resources. Research tools called "search directories" and "search engines" are extremely helpful. Other valuable resources include reference resources and search tools for finding images, sounds, and video.

Search Directories

Search directories are essentially descriptive subject indexes of Web sites. They also have keyword searching options. Directories are excellent places to begin your research.

Search Engines

Search engines are different from search directories in that they search World Wide Web sites, Usenet newsgroups, and other Internet resources to find matches to your descriptor keywords. Many search engines also rank the results according to a degree of relevancy. Most search engines provide options for advanced searching to refine your search.

Image Surfers

Search tools are available from search engines such as Alta Vista and Lycos to help find images, sounds, video, and photographs.

Reference Resources

Reference resources are collections of Internet sites compiled by individuals or organizations. An example of an excellent reference resource is the Reference Desk with links to online dictionaries, library catalogs, and news resources as well as extensive subject collections.

Basic Guidelines for Becoming a Cybersleuth

Search directories and search engines are marvelous tools to help you find information on the Internet. Search directories are often the best places to begin a search, as they frequently yield more relevant returns on a topic than a search engine, which may produce a high proportion of irrelevant information.

Search engines can be frustrating to use and may not be the best Internet resources to begin with, often supplying thousands of links on your keyword search. Although these search tools have advanced options for refining and limiting a search, researchers may discover that finding the desired information is not easy and that search results frequently offer a high percentage of irrelevant and useless information. For example, using a search engine for a search with the keywords business management returned 500,000 occurrences (hits) of the words business and management. Many of the occurrences of these words were in job listings or companies that were advertising their services. This is why search directories are frequently an excellent resource to begin with when starting your research. The search directory may lead you to the goldmine collection of electronic resources you are searching for.

Research Guidelines

When researching information on the Internet, it is essential that you use several search tools. The basic approach to finding information involves the following steps:

1. Begin with a search directory such as
    - Yahoo   http://www.yahoo.com
    - Magellan   http://magellan.mckinley.com
    - Galaxy   http://galaxy.einet.net/galaxy.html
    - Snap   http://www.snap.com

    to search for the information under a related topic or category. Explore the links that seem relevant to your topic, and make bookmarks of the ones you would like to investigate further. Look for one site that has a large collection of links on your topic. This is the resource goldmine that you are looking for.

2. Use reference resources to research your topic. This section provides a listing of some excellent resources that can be used to help you find the information you are looking for. The goal is to find one or two Internet sites that have an extensive collection of resources on your topic.

3. Use search engines to further research your topic by determining one or more descriptive words (keywords) for the subject. Enter your keywords into the search dialog box.

4. Determine how specific you want your search to be. Do you want it to be broad or narrow? Use available options to refine or limit your search. Some search engines permit the use of Boolean operators (AND, OR, NOT) that restrict a search. Always check for Advanced Search options or information provided by the search engine on how to refine and limit your search. Some search engines such as HotBot have pull-down menus or selections to be checked for limiting your search. You will learn more about advanced searching under the "Search Engine" section.

5. Submit your query.

6. Review your list of hits (a search return based on a keyword).

7. Adjust your search based on the information returned. Did you receive too much information and need to narrow your search? Did you receive too little or no information and need to broaden your keywords?

8. If your return provided too many resources, add additional keywords to limit the search.

9. Use several search directories and search engines for your research. No one search tool will provide a complete resource list.

SEARCH DIRECTORIES

Yahoo

http://www.yahoo.com

Yahoo is one of the most popular search tools on the Internet and is an excellent place to begin your search. Although Yahoo is more accurately described as a search directory, this Web site has an excellent database with search options available. There are two ways to find information using Yahoo: search through the subject directory or use the built-in search engine.

Follow these steps to use Yahoo to search for information:

STEP 1

Type in the URL for Yahoo: **http://www.yahoo.com**

NOTE:

If you are using version 4.0 or later of either Netscape Navigator or Internet Explorer you only have to type **yahoo.** The browser enters in the remainder of the URL.

You will be taken to Yahoo's home page.

FIGURE B.1

Yahoo's home page.

Notice the broad subject categories as well as links to help find companies (Yellow Pages), people, maps, news, sports, weather, and stock quotes.

STEP 2

Begin by browsing the subject directory. In this example we will do a search for *comets*. Click on a subject category that this topic would fall under. In this case **Science.**

FIGURE B.2   Subject categories under Science.

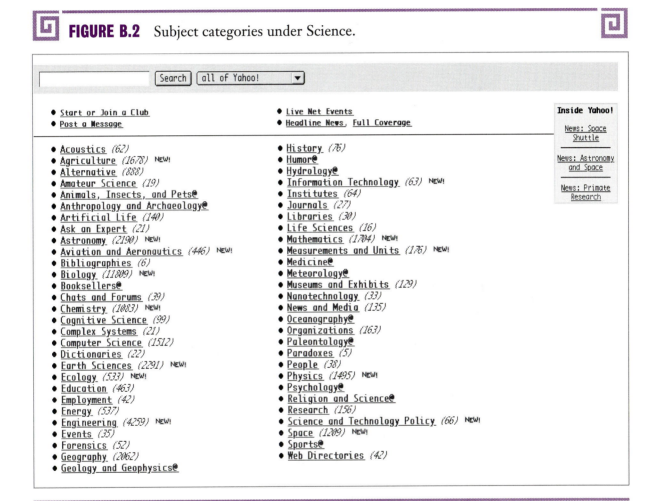

STEP 3

Determine which category would be most appropriate for the topic you are searching for. In this case, we will select **Astronomy.**

Notice the category, **Comets, Meteors, and Asteroids.** Click on that category.

Explore the categories for the information you are searching for.

FIGURE B.3

Yahoo's Astronomy directory

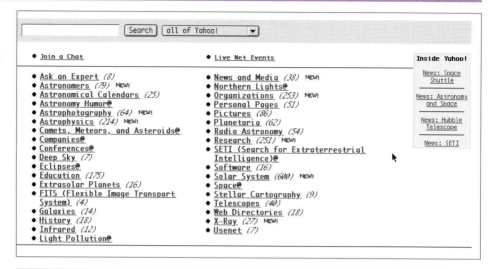

FIGURE B.4

Subject directory for Comets, Meteors, and Asteroids.

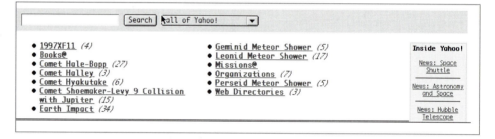

Finding Resources Using Yahoo's Search Tool

Yahoo has a search engine that can be used to find information in its database.

Enter a descriptive keyword(s) for your subject, one that uniquely identifies or describes what you are looking for. It is often helpful to do a broad search first, though results often present the need to change descriptive keywords or to refine your query.

FIGURE B.5

Yahoo's dialog box for a keyword search.

In this example, we will do a search in the **Society & Culture** category for **Egypt.**

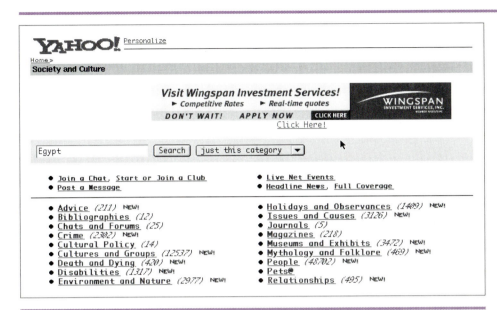

FIGURE B.6

Yahoo page
showing a
keyword search
for Egypt in
the category
Society & Culture.

NOTE:

You can do a search that will look for matches throughout Yahoo or you can
do a search within a category. In this example our search was restricted to only
the Society & Culture category.

Click on the Search button and Yahoo finds matches in its database to the
keywords entered.

Notice that Yahoo found five additional categories under this broad keyword search and 171 Internet sites for *Egypt*.

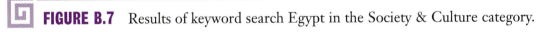

FIGURE B.7   Results of keyword search Egypt in the Society & Culture category.

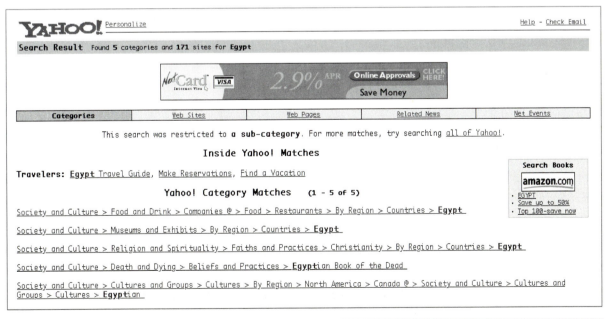

Yahoo Options Limiting a Search

If you are conducting a search using more than one keyword Yahoo's **Options** feature should be used. Search engines work by finding matches to keywords. If more than one keyword is used then the search engine goes out and finds matches to both words. As a researcher you must determine the importance of each keyword and how you want the search engine to use these words in your search.
Click on the **Options** link.

FIGURE B.8

Yahoo's home page showing the Options link.

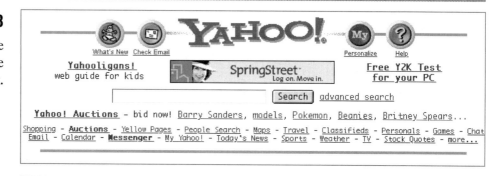

You will be taken to this Yahoo page displaying search options for refining and limiting your search. In this example we will do a search for *pyramids of Egypt*. The advanced searching options allows us to indicate how important the keywords are to the search. In this example we tell the search engine to look for both keywords *pyramids AND Egypt*. Note how the search method, **Matches on all words (AND)** has been selected. This option instructs the search engine to look for only matches that have each of the three keywords. Notice the other search options in Figure B.9 for refining a search.

FIGURE B.9 Yahoo's Options page.

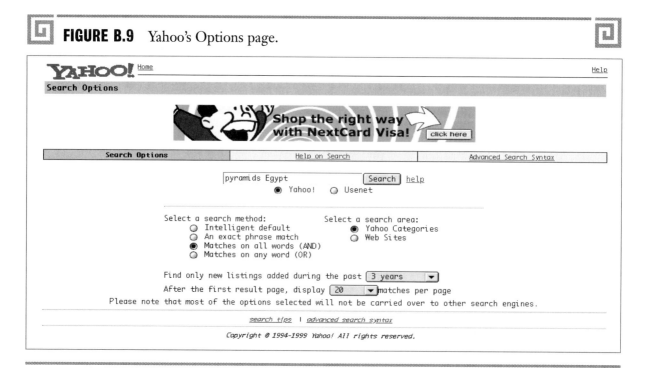

FIGURE B.10 Search results for keywords *pyramids AND Egypt.*

YAHOO! Personalize   Help - Check Email

Search Result Found **4** categories and **43** sites for **pyramids Egypt**

| Categories | Web Sites | Web Pages | Related News | Net Events |

Yahoo! Category Matches   (1 - 4 of 4)

Regional > Countries > **Egypt** > Social Science > Anthropology and Archaeology > Archaeology > **Egypt**ology > **Pyramids**

Regional > Countries > **Egypt** > Social Science > Anthropology and Archaeology > Archaeology > **Egypt**ology > **Pyramids** > Pyramids at Dashur

Regional > Countries > **Egypt** > Social Science > Anthropology and Archaeology > Archaeology > **Egypt**ology > **Pyramids** > Step Pyramid of Djoser

Regional > Countries > **Egypt** > Social Science > Anthropology and Archaeology > Archaeology > **Egypt**ology > **Pyramids** > Great Pyramid of Cheops (Khufu)

Yahoo! Site Matches   (1 - 16 of 43)

Regional > Countries > **Egypt** > Social Science > Anthropology and Archaeology > Archaeology > **Egypt**ology > **Pyramids**

- **Pyramids of Egypt** - CNN
- Wind, **Pyramids** and Obelisks - Maureen Clemmons explores the theory that wind was used to lift, transport and raise the **Egypt**ian monuments.
- **Pyramids: The Inside Story** - NOVA Online presents the current Giza excavation, a QuickTime VR tour of the Great Pyramid and clues to its builders.
- Comet Pyramid Project - offers proof that the three **Pyramids** of Kufu, Kafra, Menkaura and the Great Sphinx at Giza, **Egypt** were designed by one person.

NOTE:

A search provides a higher degree of accuracy in matching your keywords when you use Yahoo's Option for refining a search.

Other Search Directories

Explore the subject directories listed below. You will find that their subject categories vary; most have advanced search options for refining your search and as well as built-in search engines for finding keyword matches within their database and the World Wide Web.

- Magellan   http://magellan.mckinley.com
- Galaxy   http://galaxy.einet.net/galaxy.html
- Snap   http://ww.snap.com

NOTE:

Most search engines also have subject categories to assist with quickly finding information. Yahoo, Magellan, Galaxy, and Snap frequently have categories of information better suited to research.

Magellan
http://magellan.mckinley.com

Magellan is an excellent search directory for quickly finding quality information.

FIGURE B.11

Magellan's home page.

Magellan Internet Guide and the Magellan logo are trademarks of The McKinley Group, Inc., a subsidiary of Excite, Inc., and may be registered in various jurisdictions. Excite screen display copyright 1995-1998 Excite, Inc. Magellan screen display copyright 1998 of The McKinley Group, Inc., a subsidiary of Excite, Inc.

Notice that Magellan has an option that expands your keyword search to the

- entire World Wide Web
- green light sites containing no content intended for mature audiences, or
- reviewed sites that Magellan has chosen for high quality content

Galaxy

http://www.galaxy.com

Galaxy's home page displays a more detailed subject listing.

FIGURE B.12

Galaxy's home page directory.

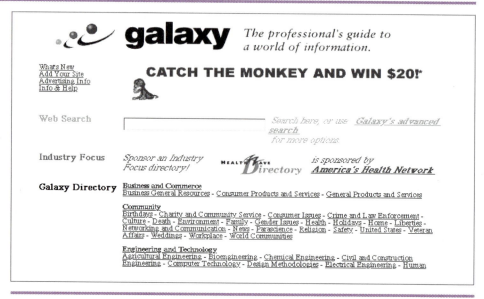

Click on Galaxy's advanced search option and be taken to a page for search options.

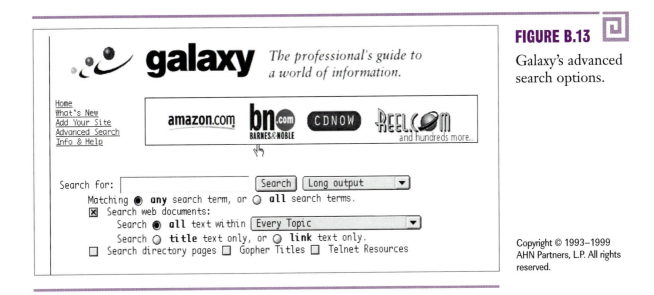

FIGURE B.13

Galaxy's advanced search options.

Snap.com

http://www.snap.com

Snap.com's search directory looks very much like Yahoo's. The comprehensive directory is helpful for quickly finding information.

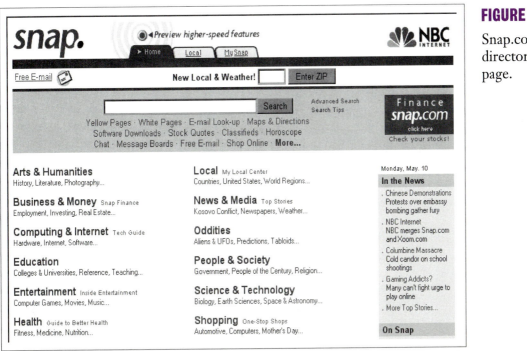

FIGURE B.14

Snap.com search directory home page.

SEARCH ENGINES

Search engines require a keyword(s) or phrase that is descriptive of the information you are looking for. Begin by listing keywords or phrases on your topic. When you connect to a search engine look for its Search Tips or Advanced Search Options to help you conduct a more efficient and effective search. Taking this step will save time and help to prevent information overload frustration.

Research Tips for Using Search Engines

Understanding advanced searching options is essential if you are going to quickly find information using search engines. When researching a topic with more than one keyword (i.e., multiple intelligence) use the search engines' advanced capabilities. Most search engines recognize the following conventions for increasing the precision of a search.

Boolean Operators (AND, OR, NOT)

Boolean operators limit and refine keyword searches.

Use **AND** to find documents with both keywords. A search with

> multiple AND intelligence

will return documents that contain the word *multiple* and *intelligence*.
Use **OR** to find documents that include any of the search words. A search with

> multiple OR intelligence

will return sites that include either the word multiple or intelligence.
Use **NOT** to indicate that a word must not appear in the document. A search with

> intelligence NOT multiple

will return results of sites with the word intelligence only.

Quotation Marks

Use quotation marks around a word or phrase to find occurrences of the phrase in quotes.

For example a search with

> "Howard Gardner multiple intelligence"

focuses the search on sites that have each of these four keywords.
Quotation marks can also be used with Boolean operators. For example this keyword search with quotes

> "multiple intelligence AND frames of mind"

will return documents with the phrase *multiple intelligence and frames of mind*. Internet sources and discussion of Howard Gardner's book *Frames of Mind* will be located using these search refining symbols.

Plus (+) and Minus (-) Signs

The use of the plus (+) sign indicates that the word **must** be present in the document. A minus (-) sign indicates that those words **must not** be present.

A search with

> + comet + Hale-Bopp

returns documents on the Hale-Bopp comet only.
A search with

> +comet - Hale-Bopp + Shoemaker-Levy

returns documents with information on Shoemaker Levy comet and **not** Hale-Bopp.

Wildcards

Many search engines support the use of wildcards or truncation symbols in a search. The asterisk (*) is the most commonly used symbol to replace multiple characters.

The search **psych*** produces matches to psychology, psychologist, psychiatrist.

NOTE:

Some search engines such as Hot Bot (see Figure B.17) have these operations built in. Selections are made from a pull-down menu for limiting and refining searches.

Using Search Engines' Advanced Search Options

There are many search engines to help you find information. You will need to use each of them at least several times before you can select the ones that best meet your needs. We will use two search engines, AltaVista and Hot Bot, to research the topic *multiple intelligence*.

AltaVista

http://altavista.digital.com

Digital's AltaVista is an excellent search engine with options for simple and advanced searching. AltaVista's Help states that the standard search tool found on the home page can be used for quickly finding what you are looking for with good results. The advanced search feature is for very specific searches and not for general searching. The advanced search feature is used to find documents within a range of dates or for complex searching using Boolean operators.

In this example we will search for information on *multiple intelligence* using AltaVista's standard search.

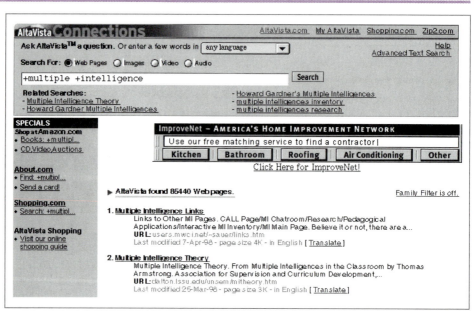

The AltaVista logo and Search Engine Content are copyright and trademarks of Compaq Corporation. Used with permission.

AltaVista suggests using a plus (+) sign in front of words that must be included in the search; a minus (-) is used to exclude words from a search.

FIGURE B.16

Search results from a standard AltaVista search on *multiple intelligence.*

The AltaVista logo and Search Engine Content are copyright and trademarks of Compaq Corporation. Used with permission.

Notice that AltaVista found over 96,710 Web pages matching these keywords as well as books that can be ordered online on the subject.

Hot Bot

http://www.hotbot.com

Hot Bot uses a pulldown menu to refine searches eliminating the need for Boolean operators, plus and minus signs, and parenthesis.

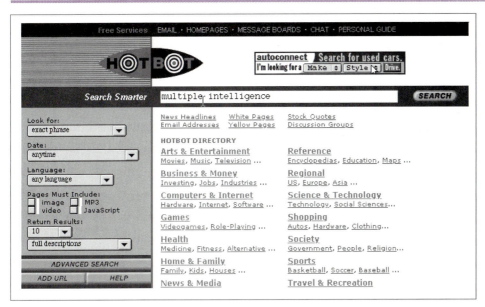

Hot Bot search engines showing the pulldown menu option (exact phrase) for refining search.

The search for *multiple intelligence* is conducted using Hot Bot. Notice in Figure B.18 that Hot Bot found 1,560 matches to the keyword phrase *multiple intelligence*. The results also display a link to the 10 most visited multiple intelligence Web sites. This would appear to be a very useful feature of this easy to use search engine.

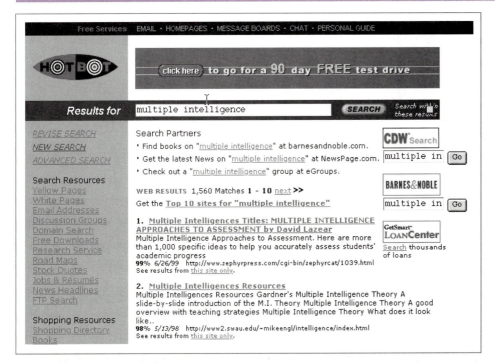

FIGURE B.18

Hot Bot search results using an exact phrase match to keyword *multiple intelligence.*

Northern Light

http://www.northernlight.com

Northern Light is a search service that saves time by providing quality information. Search results categorize Internet resources matching keywords in **Custom Search Folders.**

In addition to Internet resources, the Northern Light's **Special Collections** lists articles representing 4,500 journals, reviews, books, magazines, and newswires not readily found on the Web. When choosing a Special Collections item from the results list, a free summary of the article is displayed. If you like the summary and decide to purchase the article you can do so on line by initiating a secured online credit card transaction. Northern Light offers a unique service whereby articles usually only available with a subscription can now be ordered at an affordable price.

A search for *comet* resources will illustrate these two Northern Light search services.

NOTE:

Northern Light supports full Boolean capability, the use of plus and minus signs, and parenthesis.

FIGURE B.19

Home page for Northern Light showing a keyword search for *comet*.

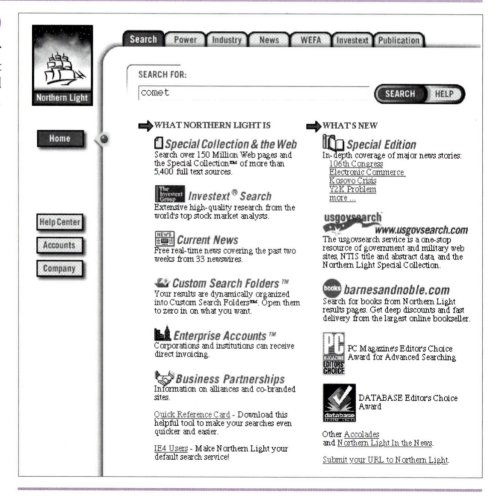

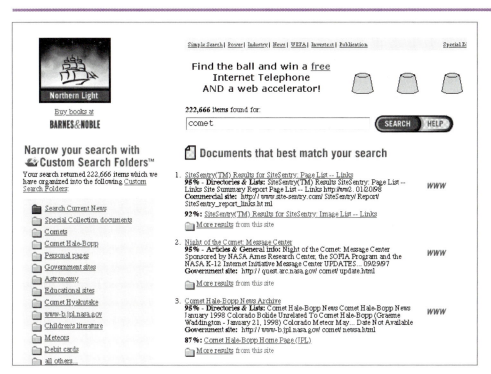

Northern Light's search results for the keyword *comet*.

Notice in the left column (Fig. B.20) the Custom Folders: Comets, Comet Hale-Bopp, **http://www.nao.ac.jp,** Comet Hyakutake, Government sites, Eclipses, Astronomy, and Haley's comet. The Special Collection documents folder is also displayed. Click on this folder for articles on comets from *Astronomy* magazine, *Colliers Encyclopedia*, and *Sky and Telescope* magazine. The full text article is available from Northern Light for a small fee usually ranging from $1.00 to $4.00.

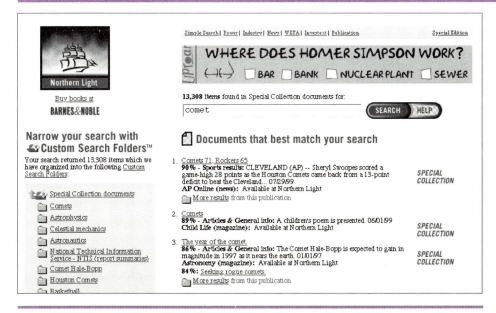

Northern Light Special Collection folder displaying articles on comets.

OTHER SEARCH ENGINES

Explore the subject engines listed below to find which best meets your research needs.

- Excite   http://www.excite.com
- Infoseek   http://www.infoseek.com
- Lycos   http://www.lycos.com
- Web Crawler   http://www.webcrawler.com
- LookSmart   http://www.looksmart.com

Image Surfers

A few search engines are offering services whereby they search for images. Some even search for video and sound. The two most widely used image surfers are Lycos and AltaVista.

Lycos

http://www.lycos.com

Lycos is one of the older search tools that became one of the first to expanded its services with new search capabilities for finding images and sounds. There are two places to select the pictures search feature (see Figure B.22): the home page in the left column of search features and by clicking on Search Options under the keyword search box.

 **FIGURE B.22**

Lycos home page.

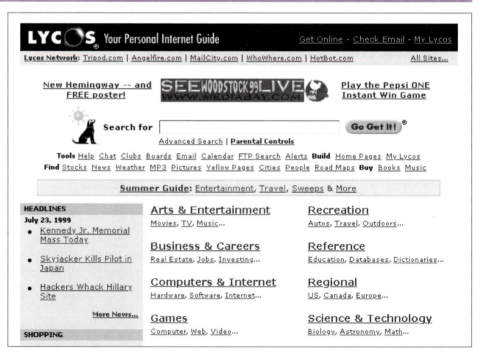

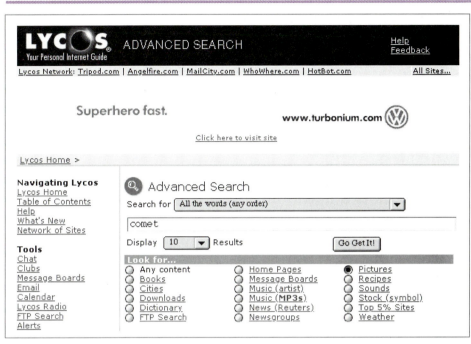

FIGURE B.23

Search options page for selecting pictures.

A keyword search is done in Lycos for comet pictures. The following returns are given.

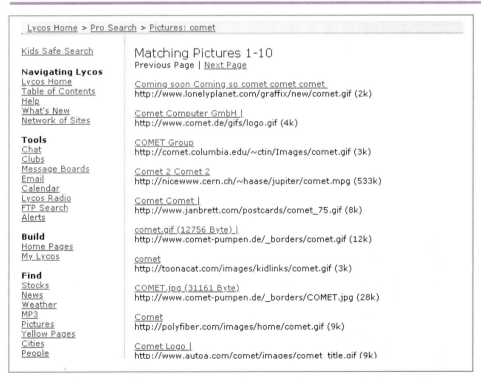

FIGURE B.24

Lycos search returns for comet pictures.

AltaVista Photo Finder

http://www.altavista.digital.com

AltaVista photo finder helps to find color and black and white photographs and art work that match keywords.

FIGURE B.25

AltaVista search options.

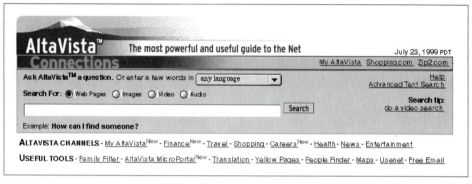

The AltaVista logo and Search Engine Content are copyright and trademarks of Compaq Corporation. Used with permission.

Click on AV Photo Finder.

FIGURE B.26

AV Photo Finder search box.

The AltaVista logo and Search Engine Content are copyright and trademarks of Compaq Corporation. Used with permission.

Click on Search and the following color photo resources are displayed. Notice that AltaVista found 4,524 pictures of comets.

FIGURE B.27

Search results for color photos of comets.

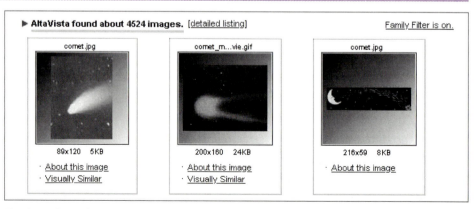

The AltaVista logo and Search Engine Content are copyright and trademarks of Compaq Corporation. Used with permission.

REFERENCE RESOURCES

The Internet is the newest and perhaps largest reference library. This rich source of information is available to Net users. Listed below are a few reference resources that you will find useful.

- **Britannica Online**
  http://www.eb.com
  For a minimal fee you can subscribe to the Britannica Online and Merriam-Webster's Collegiate Dictionary. Some of the encyclopedia text is linked to Internet sites.

- **CIA World Fact Book**
  http://elo.www.media.mit.edu/people/elo/cia
  Published by the Central Intelligence Agency (CIA), The World Fact Book has a subject index for researching facts about countries.

- **Encyberpedia**
  http://www.encyberpedia.com/ency.htm
  The HOTTEST encyclopedia from cyberspace designed to help you find good stuff in the jungle of over two million Web Sites.

- **Library of Congress**
  http://www.loc.gov
  A must visit site of government documents and resources.

- **Library Spot**
  http://www.libraryspot.com
  LibrarySpot is a goldmine of library and reference resources on the Web. Find to dictionaries, encyclopedias, newspapers, maps, geneology tools, and more.

- **megaConverter**
  http://www.megaconverter.com
  MegaConverter.com is an ever-growing set of weights, measures, and units conversion/calculation modules.

- **My Virtual Reference Desk**
  http://www.refdesk.com/main.html
  Links to many excellent reference resources including a link to a subject directory of resources—My Virtual Encyclopedia.

- **Noble Citizens of Planet Earth**
  http://www.s9.com/biography
  This dictionary contains biographical information on more than 18,000 people who have shaped our world from ancient times to the present day. Information contained in the dictionary includes birth and death years, professions, positions held, literary and artistic works, and other achievements.

- **OneLook Dictionaries**

  http://www.onelook.com

  Type in a word and this search tool will look for multiple definitions from a variety of online dictionaries: computer/Internet dictionaries, science, medical, technological, business, sports, religion, acronym, and general.

- **Reference Center—The Internet Public Library**

  http://www.ipl.org/ref

  This virtual library helps to make finding valuable information online easy. Click on a reference shelf and be linked to resources.

- **Reference Desk**

  http://www-sci.lib.uci.edu/~martindale/Ref.html

  This GOLDMINE site has won multiple awards for its SUPERB resource collection. A go to the top of the bookmark list site.

- **Reference Indexes**

  http://www.lib.lsu.edu/weblio.html

  Links to online references such as dictionaries, library catalogs, newsstand, and subject collections.

- **Reference Shelf**

  http://gort.ucsd.edu/ek/refshelf/refshelf.html

  The University of California, San Diego, sponsors this collection of online reference resources.

- **Researchpaper.com**

  http://www.researchpaper.com/directory.html

  This award-winning online research tool offers an archive of thousands of magazines, newspapers, books, and photographs.

- **The Virtual Reference Desk**

  http://thorplus.lib.purdue.edu/reference/index.html

  Purdue University's links to an AWESOME list of valuable online resources.

- **US Census Bureau**

  http://www.census.gov

  An AWESOME resource for data on social, demographic, and economic information.

 EVALUATING INTERNET INFORMATION

The Internet is analogous to a wilderness frontier that is wild and untamed. With an estimate of 20 to 50 million pages of data created from a variety of sources—individuals, businesses, corporations, nonprofit organizations, schools, special interest groups, or illicit if not illegal sources—it is inherent that not all the information is accurate, unbiased, reputable, scientifically valid, or up-to-date. Unlike scholarly publications, there is no editorial board for most Internet information. It is therefore essential that you understand how to evaluate information you research on the Net.

How strict you are with your evaluation will depend on your purpose. For example, if you are writing a factual report, dissertation, thesis, or paper that others will rely on for accurate content, it will be essential that you are judicious in choosing what information will be reported from the Net.

The first thing you must do when using the Internet for your studies is to determine which resources to use. The following guidelines will assist you with evaluation.

- **Information Source.** Where does the information come from—an individual, organization, educational institution, or other source? One way to quickly determine the source of the information is to look at the URL—Net site address. The first address protocol often will give you the source of the information—name of institution and domain. For example, an address such as http://gort.ucsd.edu tells the name of the institution—University of California, San Diego—and the edu ending indicates an educational institution. An educational institution has a good chance of being a reputable source. Other address endings that are highly likely to be reputable are gov for government or mil for military. Naturally, you will want to evaluate the information further. Just because the information is from an educational institution, government, or military source does not ensure that the content is factual and reliable.

  Check to see if the document resides in an individual's personal Internet account or is part of the organization's official Internet site. This information can often be determined by looking at the URL address pathway.

  Is the organization that publishes this document recognized in the field you are studying? Is the organization qualified to be an expert in this topic?

- **Authorship.** Closely related to the information source is the reputation of the data and the reliability of its source. Information on an educational institution Web site may be compiled by a student or graduate student who is not as yet an authority on the subject and may enter in written errors or present incorrect data without realizing it. The content may not have been reviewed for accuracy and reliability.

  Who is the author? Does the author have credentials to be an expert on the topic? Consider educational background, experience, and other published writings. Have you encountered the author's name in your reading or in bibliographies?

  Does the Internet document furnish information on the author such as institutional affiliation, position, experience and credentials? If none of this is provided, is there an email address or a mailing address from which you can request biographical information? Correspond with the author to obtain more information about the source of his or her content.

- **Accuracy.** Is the data accurate? Check to see if there is a reference for the information. Does the information come from a published research paper or report, historical document, news publication, or a personal viewpoint? Does the document include a bibliography? Does the author acknowledge related sources?

  Although information may be written from a personal view point, don't invalidate it. Bias is to be expected especially if one is a participant in an event. If the writing seems biased, look for inconsistencies or incorrect thinking. Does the author acknowledge that his treatment of the subject is controversial? Are there political or ideological biases? Can you separate fact from opinion? Do any statements seem exaggerated or overly simplified? Has the author omitted any important details? Is the writer qualified to be authoritative?

  One example of inaccuracy in Web writing is the use of the words endangered species when referring to animals that may in fact be only threatened or vulnerable. Many authors loosely use the words endangered species. To cross check this information, a reliable source such as the Convention on International Trade and Endangered Species (CITES) and the International Union for the Conservation of Nature (IUCN) must be used. These international organizations keep the working lists of which species are categorized as either extinct, endangered, threatened, vulnerable, indeterminate, or out of danger.

- **Verifiability.** Can the data be verified? Does it appear to be well-researched? Does the author make generalizations without proof or validation? Always be thinking "Show me why or how." In some instances you may need to ask if the data has statistical validity—supported by statistical testing. Watch for errors or omissions.

  When numbers or statistical information is reported, it is critical that the data be cross checked with a reliable publication source. For example, some Web factual data contain errors due to carelessness in copying and transposing numbers from a print version to a Web site. Reporting that 17,000 areas of rain forest are destroyed daily when the correct number is 700 acres is an inexcusable error in sloppy copy.

- **Consistency of data.** Is the data consistent or does it reflect contradictions with other information on the topic? Are definitions used consistently throughout?

  For example, search for reputable Web sites on the rain forest led to the discovery of Public Broadcasting System (PBS) and the Rain Forest Action Network as excellent online references to cross check the consistency of data.

- **Quality.** Is the text error free? Is it well organized and grammatically correct? Check for the misspelling of names or carelessness and lack of attention to details in other areas. Information that contains these types of careless errors probably should not be relied on.

  Is the tone scholarly, technical, factual, authoritative, or personal?

- **Currency.** Is the information current and up-to-date? Does the document include a publication date or a date of copyright? Does it appear to be appropriate and relevant for today? Information that was reported in 1985 is probably not valid today. Look for the most current information unless currency is not an issue.

Bonus Guidelines—Other Important Suggestions

- Whenever possible, check online information against other sources.
- Never use information that you cannot verify.
- Question everything that you read. Learn to be critical and skeptical.
- Information found on the Internet should complement information from traditional research resources. Never use Internet information as your sole source of knowledge.
- "When in doubt, leave it out."

TIP:

If you don't know where to find a reliable source to cross check your information go talk with a resource librarian, teacher, or professor. These individuals can be excellent resources for finding publications to verify your data. You can also call a reputable organization.

The information for "Researching Information and Resources on the Internet" was taken from Chapter IV of *Student Resource Guide to the Internet: Student Success Online* by Cynthia B. Leshin, and published by Prentice Hall. The chapter has additional research resources (subject-oriented collections and virtual libraries) and a comprehensive section on how to reference Internet resources.

Endnotes

Chapter 1

[1]Robert J. Marzano and Debra J. Pickering, *Dimensions of Learning*, 2d edition (Aurora, CO: McREL, 1997), p. 262.

[2]Marzano and Pickering, p. 139.

[3]Marzano and Pickering, p. 148.

[4]Marzano and Pickering, pp. 46–47.

Chapter 2

[1]John Chaffee, *The Thinker's Guide to College Success*, 2d edition (New York: Houghton Mifflin, 1999), p. 65.

[2]H. Scott Fogler and Steven E. LeBlanc, *Strategies for Creative Problem Solving* (Upper Saddle River, NJ: Prentice Hall, 1995), p. 29.

[3]Chaffee, p. 69.

[4]Fogler and LeBlanc, p. 41.

[5]Fogler and LeBlanc, p. 61.

[6]Roger von Oech, *A Kick in the Seat of the Pants* (New York: Harper & Row Publishers, 1986), pp. 5–21.

[7]T. Z. Tardif and R. J. Sternberg, "What Do We Know About Creativity?" *The Nature of Creativity*, ed. R. J. Sternberg (Cambridge, MA: Cambridge University Press, 1988).

[8]J. R. Hayes, *Cognitive Psychology: Thinking and Creating* (Homewood, IL: Dorsey, 1978).

[9]T. M. Amabile, *The Social Psychology of Creativity* (New York: Springer-Verlag, 1983).

[10]Roger von Oech, *A Whack on the Side of the Head* (New York: Warner Books, 1990), pp. 11–168.

[11]Dennis Coon, *Introduction to Psychology: Exploration and Application*, 6th edition (St. Paul: West Publishing Company, 1992), 295.

Chapter 3

[1]Ben E. Johnson, *Stirring Up Thinking* (New York: Houghton Mifflin, 1998), pp. 268–270.

[2]Johnson, p. 342.

[3]M. Neil Browne and Stuart M. Keeley, *Asking the Right Questions: A Guide to Critical Thinking*, 5th edition (Upper Saddle River, NJ: Prentice Hall, 1998), p. 52.

[4]Gary R. Kirby and Jeffery R. Goodpaster, *Thinking*, 2d edition (Upper Saddle River, NJ: Prentice Hall, 1999), p. 228.

[5]Elizabeth Chesla, *Critical Thinking and Logic Skills for College Students* (Upper Saddle River, NJ: Prentice Hall, 1999), p. 56.

[6]Chesla, p. 76.

Chapter 4

[1]Center for Media Literacy, 1998.

Chapter 5

[1]Paul R. Timm, *Successful Self-Management: A Psychologically Sound Approach to Personal Effectiveness* (Los Altos, CA: Crisp Publications, 1987), pp. 22–41.

[2]Stephen Covey, *The Seven Habits of Highly Effective People* (New York: Simon & Schuster, 1989), pp. 70–144, 309–318.

[3]Jane B. Burka and Lenora M. Yuen, *Procrastination* (Reading, MA: Perseus Books, 1983), pp. 21–22.

Chapter 6

[1]Howard Gardner, *Multiple Intelligences: The Theory in Practice* (New York: HarperCollins, 1993), pp. 5–49.

[2]Developed by Joyce Bishop, Psychology faculty, Golden West College, Huntington Beach, CA. Based on Howard Gardner, *Frames of Mind: The Theory of Multiple Intelligences* (New York: HarperCollins, 1993).

Chapter 7

[1]Francis P. Robinson, *Effective Behavior* (New York: Harper & Row, 1941).

[2]Walter Pauk, *How to Study in College*, 5th edition (Boston: Houghton Mifflin Company, 1993), pp. 110–114.

[3]John J. Macionis, *Sociology*, 6th edition (Upper Saddle River, NJ: Prentice Hall, 1997), p. 174.

[4]Teresa Audesirk and Gerald Audesirk, *Life on Earth* (Upper Saddle River, NJ: Prentice Hall, 1997), pp. 55–56.

Chapter 8

[1]Analysis based on Lynn Quitman Troyka, *Simon & Schuster Handbook for Writers* (Upper Saddle River, NJ: Prentice Hall, 1996), pp. 530–531.

Chapter 9

[1]Adapted from "Do You Believe?" by Ashley DuLac and Kathryn Brooks, as reprinted in *Overcoming Math Anxiety* by Sheila Tobias (New York: W.W. Norton & Co., 1993), p. 237.

[2]National Council of Teachers of Mathematics, *Curriculum and Evaluation Standards for School Mathematics*, 1989.

[3]George Polya, *How to Solve It* (London: Penguin, 1990).

[4]Rick Billstein, Shlomo Libeskind, and Johnny W. Lott, *A Problem Solving Approach to Mathematics for Elementary School Teachers* (Reading MA: Addison-Wesley Longman, 1993), pp. 5–36.

[5]Adapted from Kathy Acker (March 1997). *Math Anxiety Code of Responsibilities* [online]. Available: http://fc.whyy.org/CCC/alg1/code.htm (March 1998).

[6]Sheila Tobias, *Overcoming Math Anxiety* (New York: W. W. Norton & Co., 1993), pp. 226–227.

Chapter 10

[1]Tamera Trotter and Joycelyn Allen, *Talking Justice: 602 Ways to Building and Promoting Racial Harmony* (Saratoga, CA: R & E Publishers, 1993), p. 51.

[2]Sheryl McCarthy, *Why Are the Heroes Always White?* (Kansas City, MO: Andrews and McMeel, 1995), p. 137.

[3]Louis E. Boone, David L. Kurtz, and Judy R. Block, *Contemporary Business Communication* (Upper Saddle River, NJ: Prentice Hall, 1994), pp. 49–54.

[4]Isaac Asimov, "My Own View," in *The Encyclopedia of Science Fiction*, eds. John Clute and Peter Nicholls (New York: St. Martin's Press, 1995).

[5]Thomas Moore, *The Care of the Soul* (New York: Harper Perennial, 1992), pp. xi–xx.

[6]Sarah Delany and Elizabeth Delany with Amy Hill Hearth, *Book of Everyday Wisdom* (New York: Kodansha International, 1994), p. 123.

[7]Adapted by Richard Bucher, Professor of Sociology, Baltimore City Community College, from Paula Rothenberg, William Paterson College of New Jersey.

Appendix A

[1]Barbara Soloman, North Carolina State University.

Bibliography

There is certainly more to know about the subjects we've covered than we can possibly present in a book of reasonable size. Following are some additional resources you may want to consult, some of which have been mentioned in the text. The resources are listed in two sections: books and internet sites. The listing of books is in alphabetical order, by author, within the alphabetical listing of subject areas.

 ## BOOK RESOURCES

College Success

Baker, Sunny, and Kim Baker, *College After 30: It's Never Too Late to Get the Degree You Need!* Holbrook, MA: Bob Adams, Inc., 1992.

Jeffers, Susan, *Feel the Fear and Do It Anyway*. New York: Fawcett Columbine, 1992.

Shields, Charles J. *Back in School: A Guide for Adult Learners*. Hawthorne, NJ: Career Press, 1994.

Weinberg, Carol. *The Complete Handbook for College Women: Making the Most of Your College Experience*. New York: New York University Press, 1994.

Critical and Creative Thinking

Bianculli, David. *Teleliteracy: Taking Television Seriously*. New York: Simon & Schuster, 1994.

Cameron, Julia, with Mark Bryan. *The Artist's Way: A Spiritual Path to Higher Creativity*. New York: G. P. Putnam's Sons, 1995.

deBono, Edward. *Lateral Thinking: Creativity Step by Step*. New York: Perennial Library, 1990.

Kirby, Gary R, and Jeffrey R. Goodpaster. *Thinking*, 2nd ed. Upper Saddle River, NJ: Prentice Hall, 1999.

Noone, Donald J. *Creative Problem Solving*. New York: Barron's, 1998.

Postman, Neil, and Steve Powers. *How to Watch TV News*. New York: Penguin, 1992.

Sark. *Living Juicy: Daily Morsels for Your Creative Soul.* Berkeley, CA: Celestial Arts, 1994.

von Oech, Roger. *A Whack on the Side of the Head.* New York: Warner Books, 1998.

von Oech, Roger. *A Kick in the Seat of the Pants.* New York: Harper & Row Publishers, 1986.

Communication

Qubein, Nido R. *How to Be a Great Communicator: In Person, on Paper, and at the Podium.* New York: John Wiley & Sons, 1996.

Tannen, Deborah. *You Just Don't Understand: Women and Men in Conversation.* New York: Ballantine Books, 1991.

Tannen, Deborah. *Talking from 9 to 5: Women and Men in the Workplace: Language, Sex and Power.* New York: Avon Books, 1995.

Diversity

Belenky, Mary, Blythe Clinchy, Nancy Goldberger, and Jill Tarule. *Women's Ways of Knowing.* New York: Basic Books, 1997.

Blank, Renee, and Sandra Slipp. *Voices of Diversity: Real People Talk about Problems and Solutions in a Workplace Where Everyone Is Not Alike.* New York: American Management Association, 1994.

Edmunds, R. David, ed. *American Indian Leaders: Studies in Diversity.* Lincoln: University of Nebraska Press, 1980.

Gonzales, Juan L., Jr. *The Lives of Ethnic Americans,* 2d ed. Dubuque, IA: Kendall/Hunt, 1994.

Hockenberry, John. *Moving Violations.* New York: Hyperion, 1996.

McCarthy, Sheryl. *Why Are the Heroes Always White?* Kansas City: Andrews and McMeel, 1995.

Takaki, Ronald. *A Different Mirror: A History of Multicultural America.* Boston: Little, Brown, 1994.

Terkel, Studs. *Race: How Blacks and Whites Think and Feel About the American Obsession.* New York: Free Press, 1995.

Trotter, Tamera, and Joycelyn Allen. *Talking Justice: 602 Ways to Build and Promote Racial Harmony.* Saratoga, FL: R & E Publishers, 1993.

English as a Second Language

Blosser, Betsy J. *Living in English: Basic Skills for the Adult Learner.* Lincolnwood, IL: National Textbook, 1989.

Hornby, A. A., and C. A. Ruse. *Oxford ESL Dictionary for Students of American English.* New York: Oxford University Press, 1991.

Inspiration

Delany, Sarah, and Elizabeth Delany, with Amy Hill Hearth. *Book of Everyday Wisdom.* New York: Kodansha International, 1994.

Moore, Thomas. *The Care of the Soul.* New York: Harper Perennial, 1992.

Learning and Working Styles

Barger, Nancy J., Linda K. Kirby, and Jean M. Kummerow. *Work Types: Understand Your Work Personality—How It Helps You and Holds You Back, and What You Can Do to Understand It.* New York: Warner Books, 1997.

Gardner, Howard. *Multiple Intelligences: The Theory in Practice.* New York: HarperCollins, 1993.

Goleman, Daniel. *Emotional Intelligence.* New York: Bantam Books, 1997.

Goleman, Daniel. *Working With Emotional Intelligence.* New York: Bantam Books, 1998.

Listening

Robbins, Harvey A. *How to Speak and Listen Effectively.* New York: AMACOM, 1992.

Math

Hart, Lynn, and Deborah Najee-Ullich. *Studying for Mathematics.* New York: HarperCollins College Publishers, 1997.

Lerner, Marcia. *Math Smart: Essential Math for These Numeric Times.* New York: Villard Books, 1995.

Memory

Lorayne, Harry. *Super Memory—Super Student: How to Raise Your Grades in 30 Days.* Boston: Little, Brown, 1990.

Reading and Studying

Armstrong, William H., and M. Willard Lampe, II. *Barron's Pocket Guide to Study Tips: How to Study Effectively and Get Better Grades.* New York: Barron's Educational Series, 1990.

Frank, Steven. *The Everything Study Book.* Holbrook, MA: The Adams Media Corp., 1996.

Silver, Theodore. *The Princeton Review Study Smart: Hands-on, Nuts and Bolts Techniques for Earning Higher Grades.* New York: Villard Books, 1996.

Resumes, Interviews, Job Searches, and Careers

Adams, Bob. *The Complete Resume and Job Search Book for College Students.* Holbrook, MA: Adams Publishing, 1993.

Baldwin, Eleanor. *300 New Ways to Get a Better Job.* Holbrook, MA: Bob Adams Inc., 1991.

Beatty, Richard H. *The Resume Kit,* 3d ed. New York: John Wiley & Sons, 1995.

Beatty, Richard H. *The Interview Kit,* 3d ed. New York: John Wiley & Sons, 1995.

Boldt, Laurence G. *Zen and the Art of Making a Living: A Practical Guide to Creative Career Design.* New York: Arkana, 1993.

Bolles, Richard Nelson. *The 1998 What Color Is Your Parachute?* Berkeley, CA: Ten Speed Press, 1998.

Farr, J. Michael. *The Quick Resume and Cover Letter Book.* Indianapolis, IN: JIST Works, 1994.

Kleiman, Carol. *The 100 Best Jobs for the 1990's and Beyond.* New York: Berkeley Books, 1994.

Self-Improvement

Covey, Stephen. *The Seven Habits of Highly Effective People.* New York: Simon & Schuster, 1990.

Test Taking

Browning, William G. *Cliffs Memory Power for Exams.* Lincoln, NE: Cliffs Notes, 1990.

Fry, Ron. *"Ace" Any Test,* 3d ed. Franklin Lakes, NJ: Career Press, 1996.

Time Management

Burka, Jane B., and Lenora M. Yuen. *Procrastination.* Reading, MA: Perseus Books, 1983.

Fry, Ron. *Managing Your Time,* 2d ed. Hawthorne, NJ: Career Press, 1994.

Lakein, Alan. *How To Get Control of Your Time and Your Life.* New York: New American Library, 1996.

McGee-Cooper, Ann, with Duane Trammell. *Time Management for Unmanageable People.* New York: Bantam Books, 1994.

Timm, Paul R. *Successful Self-Management: A Psychologically Sound Approach to Personal Effectiveness.* Los Altos, CA: Crisp Publications, 1996.

Volunteering

Digeronimo, Theresa. *A Student's Guide to Volunteering.* Franklin Lakes, NJ: Career Press, 1995.

Writing

Andersen, Richard. *Powerful Writing Skills.* Hawthorne, NJ: Career Press, 1994.

Cameron, Julia. *The Right to Write: An Invitation into the Writing Life.* New York: Tarcher/Putnam, 1998.

Delton, Judy. *The 29 Most Common Writing Mistakes (And How to Avoid Them).* Cincinnati, OH: Writer's Digest Books, 1991.

Friedman, Bonnie. *Writing Past Dark: Envy, Fear, Distractions, and Other Dilemmas in the Writer's Life.* New York: HarperCollins, 1994.

Frueling, Rosemary, and N. B. Oldham. *Write to the Point! Letters, Memos, and Reports That Get Results.* New York: McGraw-Hill Book, 1992.

Gibaldi, Joseph. *MLA Handbook for Writers of Research Papers,* 4th ed. New York: Modern Language Association of America, 1995.

Goldberg, Natalie. *Writing Down the Bones: Freeing the Writer Within.* Boston: Shambhala, 1986.

Markman, Peter T., and Roberta H. Markman. *10 Steps in Writing the Research Paper,* 5th ed. New York: Barron's Educational Series, 1994.

Staff of the Research and Education Association. *REA's Handbook of English Grammar, Style, and Writing.* Piscataway, NJ: Research and Education Association, 1995.

Strunk, William, Jr., and E. B. White. *The Elements of Style*, 3d ed. New York: Macmillan, 1995.

Troyka, Lynn Quitman. *Simon & Schuster Handbook for Writers*, 5th ed. Upper Saddle River, NJ: Prentice Hall, 1999.

 ## INTERNET RESOURCES

The following list of Internet sites is just the tip of the iceberg. The World Wide Web contains thousands of sites, many of which may be of interest to you. The immensity of the web can make it hard to know where to look, and this list will help you get started. These sites can put you in touch with the latest information and with people who share your interests. In addition, they often contain links to related sites not listed here.

The Internet is changing every day, and sites are often renamed, relocated, or eliminated altogether. Therefore, some of these sites might have changed or might no longer exist when you visit. If you are interested in the subject, however, don't give up. Search for additional Internet locations through the search engines and directories described in the appendix.

College Survival and Student Life

Student Center

http://studentcenter.infomall.org.network.html

An online hub for student communication, this site includes discussion forums on music, sports, careers, and other topics. A student home page directory will lead you to students with similar interests.

Student.Com: College Life Online

http://www.student.com/

This online "hang-out" includes personal student pages and chat rooms, student writing, Net contests, movie reviews, health information, and more.

t@p Schools and Money

http://www.taponline.com/tap/higher.html

Click here for the Ultimate College Survival Guide. Included are articles on off-campus living, budgeting, goal setting, overcoming roommate problems, eating cheaply, and much more.

Critical and Creative Thinking

Creativity Web Page

http://www.ozemail.com.au/~caveman/Creative

Click on here for a creative boost, including methods to increase your creativity and techniques for personal growth and self-improvement.

Diversity

Asian-American Resources

http://www.mit.edu:8001/afs/athena.mit.edu/user/i/r/irie/www/aar.html

Here you will find links to clubs, events, and organizations that pertain to Asian-American life, as well as links to related personal home pages.

Britannica Guide to Black History

http://blackhistory.eb.com

Among the features of this site are a timeline of black history, sound clips from the speeches of Malcolm X and Martin Luther King, Jr., and biographies of Blacks who achieved greatness.

Diversity Web

http://www.inform.umd.edu:8080/DiversityWeb

Diversity Web has information about diversity initiatives in certain colleges and universities. It shows how those schools are engaging diversity in educational mission, campus climate, curriculum focus, and connections with the larger society.

Latino USA

http://www.latinousa.org

This site of Latino USA, a radio journal of Latino culture, seeks to inform varied audiences about the perspectives of Latinos and about the issues affecting their lives and to improve cross-cultural communication.

English as a Second Language

ELS Language Centers

http://www.els.com

Click on here for information about English as a second language (ESL) courses available nationwide.

George Washington University ESL Study Hall

http://gwis2.circ.gwu.edu/~gwvcusas/

Maintained by George Washington University, this site will help ESL students improve their reading, writing, vocabulary, grammar, and listening.

Inspiration

Wellspring

http://www.wellmedia.com

Here you'll find coverage of meditation, spirituality, and relationships, as well as links to other Web sites that cover personal development and spirituality.

Index

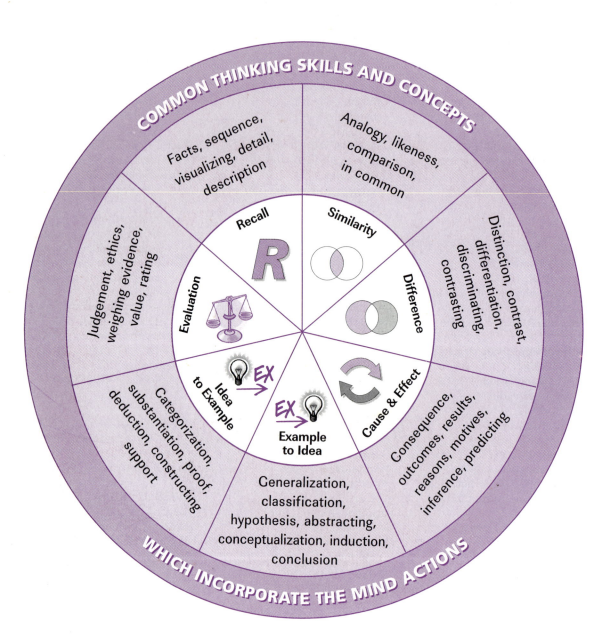

COMMON THINKING SKILLS AND CONCEPTS

Facts, sequence, visualizing, detail, description

Analogy, likeness, comparison, in common

Judgement, ethics, weighing evidence, value, rating

Distinction, contrast, differentiation, discriminating, contrasting

Recall

Similarity

R

Evaluation

Difference

Categorization, substantiation, proof, deduction, constructing support

Idea to Example

EX

EX

Example to Idea

Cause & Effect

Consequence, outcomes, results, reasons, motives, inference, predicting

Generalization, classification, hypothesis, abstracting, conceptualization, induction, conclusion

WHICH INCORPORATE THE MIND ACTIONS